To Thomas E. Davis,
With the hope that
you enjoy this history of
the USS Flasher and
her crew,
William R McCants
December 4, 1995

WAR PATROLS
OF THE
USS FLASHER

U.S.S. FLASHER

The True Story of One of America's Greatest
Submarines, Officially Credited With Sinking the
Most Japanese Shipping in World War II

Written and Illustrated by
William R. McCants

WAR PATROLS OF THE USS FLASHER

The author invites comments, corrections and suggestions.

ISBN Number 1-57087-054-3

Production Design by Robin Ober

William R. McCants
1015 Atlantic Blvd.
Suite 249
Atlantic Beach, FL 32233

Professional Press
P.O. Box 4371
Chapel Hill, North Carolina 27515-4371

Manufactured in the United States of America
96 95 94 93 92   10 9 8 7 6 5 4 3 2 1

DEDICATION

This book is dedicated to the U.S. Submarine Force of World War II—to the submariners who risked, and too often lost, their lives for their country; to the men and women who constructed, equipped and supported the submarines; and to the families of the submariners, who knew little or nothing of the very dangerous and successful submarine activities during the war.

The author also wished to especially honor the brave men of the *USS Flasher*, including his father, the late Captain Thomas R. McCants, U.S.N.

ACKNOWLEDGMENTS

Some years ago, I asked my father to sit down and tell me some of his Navy experiences. Like most children, I had been too young, too busy, or too ignorant to learn about the lives of my own parents. Not long thereafter, he was no longer able to communicate due to illness. I realized somebody should be actively researching the wartime exploits of the *USS Flasher*.

Little has been written of *Flasher's* accomplishments despite her truly superb war record. Her impressive story needed to be recorded with the help of her surviving officers and crew. It seemed better for me to make an attempt than let the story go untold. Any resulting shortcomings in this story reflect my inadequacies, rather than any deficiencies on the part of my sources or the valiant deeds of the men of *Flasher*.

Former officers and crew of *Flasher* who unselfishly contributed their time and efforts in relating anecdotes, supplying photographs or other materials, redirecting me, reviewing manuscript drafts, or proposing corrections and improvements, include Mr. J. Edwin Atkinson, Mr. William L. Beaman, Lt. Cmdr. Robert P. Briggs, USN, Ret., Mr. Ross Brown, Jr., Mr. Thomas A. Burke, Cmdr. G. F. Coffin, USN, Ret., Mr. John F. Cook, Mr. Joseph D. G. Corneau, Mr. Frank J. DeBois, R. Adm. Raymond F. DuBois, USN, Ret., Mr. Joseph M. Ferrell, Mr. Vincent J. Filippone, Capt. Philip T. Glennon, USN, Ret., Mr. Ralph B. Heilstedt, Mr. Joseph Holmes, Mr. Frank R. Kristl, Mr. Blaine M. Knop, Mr. George A. Markham, Capt. Thomas R. McCants, USN, Ret., and Mr. Ralph J. Van Horn. Mrs. Reuben T. Whitaker was also most helpful.

For their assistance in locating and furnishing copies of official records, as well as their preservation of these important documents, the author is indebted to personnel at the Operational Archives Branch and the Ships' History Section at the Naval Historical Center, Department of the Navy, Washington Navy Yard, and personnel at the National Archives and Records Administration, in Suitland, Maryland and Washington, D.C.

This book would never have been attempted if author Clay Blair, Jr., had not provided such an excellent list of available research materials on World War II submarine operations in his most authoritative work *Silent Victory - The U.S. Submarine War Against Japan.*[1] Blair also thoughtfully transferred his research materials and irreplaceable interviews of submarine veterans to the American Heritage Center of the University of Wyoming in Laramie, including a lengthy discussion with Admiral Whitaker. I am indebted to Mr. Blair for permission to use the interview, and to the Center for access to the materials. Valuable assistance on Ultra intercepts from another noted submarine veteran, author and researcher, Cmdr. John D. Alden, U.S.N., Ret., is also appreciated.

Mr. and Mrs. Hidetaro Wakahara and Mr. Carl Terry, veteran of *USS Catfish,* assisted me with Mr.

---

[1] Philadelphia: Lippincott Co., 1975.

Wakahara's experiences on the *Oi*. Jim and Yoko Clark helped me by translating Japanese materials on light cruisers of the *Kuma* class. Months of access to a microfilm reader was made possible thanks to the good offices of the Jacksonville, Florida, Public Library. Editing by Mrs. Ginny Turner through Professional Press, and by The Intelligent Eye of the Florida First Coast Writers' Festival, Inc., considerably improved the final product.

I received invaluable (free) help from my family members. Mrs. T. R. McCants, Mrs. Jean G. Crockett, and Mr. Thomas R. McCants, Jr., provided leads and support, literary advice, and encouragement. Most of all, however, I am indebted to my wife, Terry, for her typing and retyping innumerable drafts with our little computer's word processing program, and for putting up with the years of attention devoted to researching and writing about *USS Flasher* and her crew.

The most rewarding aspect of my research was the uniformly GRACIOUS manner in which everyone received my many questions, and assisted in this project. Part of this, I realize, was due to respect for my father, but the extent of support I received from everyone involved was still an incredible, once-in-a-lifetime experience.

To all of these people I am truly indebted.

William R. McCants

Contents

INTRODUCTION

JAPAN'S GREATEST MENACE

A merican submarines effectively immobilized and isolated the Empire of Japan during World War II.

Japanese authorities on the war acknowledge the importance of the American subs. According to Japanese military commentator Masanori Ito:

> U.S. submarines...proved to be the single most potent weapon against the Imperial Navy in the Pacific War.[2]

Zenji Orita, a Japanese submarine commander in World War II, stated it another way when he compared the largely ineffective Japanese submarine force with the American submarines, which he felt had won America's war against Japan.[3]

In his article "Why Japan's Antisubmarine Warfare Failed," Captain Atsushi Oi of the Imperial Naval General Staff concluded:

---

[2] Masanori Ito, *The End of the Imperial Japanese Navy* (New York: W.W. Norton & Co., 1962; Jove Publishing, Inc., 1984), pp. 16-17.

[3] Zenji Orita and Joseph D. Harrington, *I-Boat Captain* (Canoga Park, Cal.: Major Books, 1976), p. 88.

> At the end of the war, economic hardship was keenly felt. The effect of the sea blockade was visible everywhere. The government reported to the Diet, which was convened immediately following the surrender, that the greatest cause of defeat was the loss of shipping.[4]

Captain Oi also stressed that the Japanese Navy largely ignored the important shipping losses to submarines, while concentrating on major surface-fleet engagements, and that post-war publications on the war in the Pacific have made the same mistake.

Ex-Premier Tojo credited three factors for the defeat of Japan: America's island-hopping strategy, her fast-attack carrier task forces, and her submarines.[5] Admiral Tomiji Koyanagi said of American submarines, "[B]y late 1944 they were our greatest menace."[6] In contrasting the American successes with the failures of the Japanese submarine tactics, Admiral S. Fukutome, Chief of Staff for the Combined Fleet, Imperial Japanese Navy, concluded that Japan had received a mortal blow from the American subs.[7]

---

[4] Atsushi Oi, "Why Japan's Antisubmarine Warfare Failed," in *The Japanese Navy in World War II: In the Words of Former Japanese Naval Officers*, ed. David C. Evans, 2nd ed. (Annapolis: Naval Institute Press, 1986), p. 414.

[5] Samuel E. Morison, *The Two-Ocean War* (Boston: Little, Brown & Co., 1963), p. 493, and John Keegan, *The Price of Admiralty* (New York: Penguin Books, 1989), p. 318.

[6] Tomiji Koyanagi, "The Battle of Leyte Gulf" in Evans, p. 363.

[7] Mochitsura Hashimoto, *Sunk: The Story of the Japanese Submarine Fleet, 1941-1945* (New York: Henry Holt & Co., 1954), p. 240.

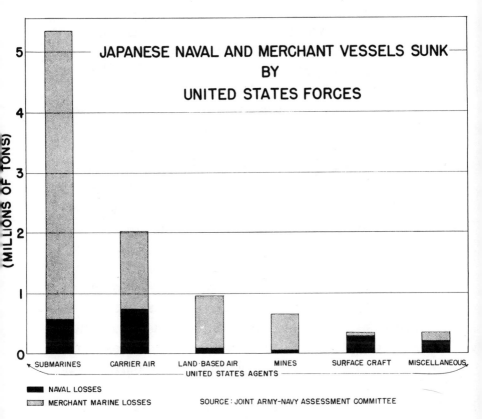

The American submarine force accomplished its mission with less than two percent of the U.S. Navy's World War II personnel, but at a high price. The submarine force experienced the worst losses of any branch of the United States military in World War II. Fifty-two submarines, and 22 percent of U.S. submariners, never returned from the war.

Most Americans are still unaware of the great role her submarines played in defeating the Japanese. This is partially due to the emphasis on surface fleet engagements that monopolized the attention of the Japanese Navy throughout the war, and dictated the United States Navy's pre-war submarine strategy.

Mostly, however, the public's ignorance is due to the wartime news "blackout" the submarine force imposed on its activities, earning it the nickname the "Silent Service."

Secrecy was warranted for at least two reasons. One was that immediately after Pearl Harbor the United States authorized "unrestricted submarine warfare," ignoring a convention outlawing such tactics. More importantly, the submarine force became the "Silent Service" to avoid dangerous breaches in security. One U.S. Congressman actually disclosed to newspaper reporters that the American subs were successfully evading the Japanese because the Japanese were not setting their depth charges deep enough, and the explosive charges were too small to sink our submarines. At least one newspaper published the story. According to a post-war statement by Admiral Charles A. Lockwood in a Navy film on the submarine war:

> You can imagine how joyfully the Japs received that news. They radically changed their tactics, and we lost, I should say, about ten submarines with all on board before we could improve our construction sufficiently to slow the Japs down.

He stated that "right then and there" the submarines became the "Silent Service."

One sailor aboard the submarine *USS Flasher*, Signalman Charles J. Moore, wrote about the submariners' anonymity:

THE SILENT SERVICE

Hark to the tale I wish to unfold,
A story that cries for the right to be told,
The saga of men who sail under the sea,
Of men who price nothing above liberty.

They bring death and destruction to Nippon's
  own shore,
They carry the war to the enemy's door.
They fight on in silence unsung and unseen,
The brave, hard-hitting crew of the lone
  submarine.

There's hardly a spot where they haven't gone,
From the Straits of Makassar to Tokyo Wan.
They've nosed into Subic and fought off Attu,
That terror of tyrant—the submarine crew.

Theirs not the glory of public acclaim,
The applause of the crowd or the spotlight
  of fame.
Others may bow to the nation's loud cheer,
But the roar of the multitude they seldom hear.

Some day there may come a man to relate,
The submariner's part in this drama of hate.
The odds that he faced to keep his country free,
And the times he faced death to insure victory.

When this war is over and the last battle's won,
You'll not hear them boast of the things they
   have done.
They'll still carry on with quiet dignity,
These nameless men who sail under the sea.

During the war the submarine force resisted government, press, and public pressure for news of their activities. The Navy finally published a pamphlet entitled "Facts About the Submarine Service" (NavPers 44205 9/12/44) wherein Secretary of the Navy James Forrestal, Chief of Naval Operations Ernest J. King and Admiral Chester W. Nimitz, Commander in Chief, Pacific Fleet, were quoted to the effect of "Trust us, the submarines are doing an important job." King stated "When the full story can be told, it will constitute one of the most stirring chapters in the annals of naval warfare."

At the end of the war, Lockwood appeared in a Navy film (narrated by Actor/Naval Officer Gene Kelly) to publicize the submarines' wartime accomplishments, with the following preamble:

Unheralded and unsung because of the
necessity for operating under a heavy
cloak of secrecy--the men who went
down to the sea in submarines carried
the battle to the enemy in his own waters
from Pearl Harbor to the surrender in
Tokyo Bay.

The film emphasized statistics crediting the submarine force with devastating Japanese shipping.

Nevertheless, the role of submarines in the defeat of Japan never recovered from the wartime press blackout. An American public, flooded with daily news and movies of the air war, bitter island fighting, and fleet engagements, remains largely unaware of the submarines' amazing record. The stunning news of the two atomic bombs, followed shortly by Japan's capitulation, also overshadowed the fact that Japan had already lost the war. Even now, after the true story has been repeatedly told of how submarines devastated the vital Japanese shipping, it is common for books on World War II to address the American submarine role with only a passing reference or a footnote, while emphasizing surface fleet confrontations, island fighting, and the air war.

Only a few American submarines received any measure of wartime or post-war publicity. The *USS Wahoo*, perhaps the most publicized submarine during and since the war, has been characterized by one source as "legendary," while the *USS Flasher* and other successful boats have been described as "great record boats," or "forgotten famous boats."[8] Unfortunately, these characterizations are probably accurate, as few submarines are well known. Most American subs would be "legendary," however, if only the public knew their incredible stories. Certainly the crews' exploits and sacrifices deserve more attention than they have received.

Any public knowledge of the submarine *Flasher* is due to the entertaining book by George Grider and

[8] Steve Ewing, *Memories and Memorials* (Missoula, Montana: Pictorial Histories Publishing Co., 1986), pp. 164-165.

Lydel Sims of Grider's wartime experiences. In *War Fish*[9] they relate Grider's war patrols on the submarines *Wahoo*, *Pollack*, and *Hawkbill*, prior to his command of *Flasher*. Only *Flasher's* fifth and sixth war patrols under Grider are covered to any extent in *War Fish*. This book covers events prior to the *Flasher's* construction through the end of the war.

Flasher's war record certainly merits attention. After World War II, a Joint Army-Navy Assessment Committee (JANAC) analyzed Japanese and Allied records to assess the true wartime destruction of Japanese shipping. JANAC's report was imperfect, but it remains the official post-war analysis of Japanese ship sinkings. Of the 193 American submarines listed in the JANAC report, the *USS Flasher* was credited with the highest tonnage sunk (100,231 tons, plus half credit for an 8,666-ton ship), and was ranked fourth in the number of ships over 500 tons sunk (21½), after *Tautog* (26), *Tang* (24) and *Silversides* (23).

JANAC's statistics also placed *Flasher's* first skipper, Reuben T. Whitaker, among the top ten submarine skippers of World War II, in terms of both ships sunk and tonnage sunk. *Flasher's* fifth war patrol under Grider was the third-best patrol recorded out of all 1,682 submarine war patrols. Only *Archerfish's* sinking of the immense Japanese aircraft carrier *Shinano*, and *Rasher's* unsurpassed sinking of five vessels for 52,600 tons on a single patrol, ranked higher. No submarine sank more of Japan's vital oil tankers on a single patrol than *Flasher*, and JANAC credited *Flasher* with the most tanker tonnage sunk during the war.

---

[9] Boston: Little, Brown & Co., 1958.

Like *Flasher*, most of America's submarines performed "legendary" exploits for this country in World War II—true stories that will never be told. This book chronicles the actual missions by *Flasher*, and hopefully, relates an accurate picture of the boat, her officers, and her crew. It should also convey the same dangers and daily activities experienced by the rest of America's brave, largely unheralded, and very deadly, "Silent Service."

CHAPTER 1

WAR BEGINS IN THE PACIFIC

I n December, 1941, the submarine *USS Flasher* existed only on paper. The man who would be her first commanding officer, 30-year-old Lt. Reuben Thornton Whitaker, was the executive officer (second in command) of the submarine *USS Sturgeon* (SS 197). Because of increasing tensions with Japan, *Sturgeon* was sent with other submarines to reinforce the meager U.S. Naval forces in Manila, Philippines.

Whitaker was a handsome man of medium height or less, with an erect posture that made him seem taller, and a high degree of self assurance and poise that helped give him a "presence." A man of few words, he spoke those with a Southern accent, derived from his Georgia birth and upbringing in eastern Arkansas, near Memphis, Tennessee.

On the night before the Japanese surprise attack on Pearl Harbor, Whitaker went ashore to see the new movie "Sergeant York" starring Gary Cooper. He returned to the submarine around 11 p.m., had a cup of coffee in the officer's wardroom, and went to bed. *Sturgeon's* skipper, Lt. Cmdr. William Leslie ("Bull") Wright was still ashore.

Around 2 a.m. Whitaker was suddenly awakened when the bright light just above his head in the tiny stateroom was turned on. Bull Wright had come in. In Whitaker's words, "he was obviously pretty well

Lt. Cmdr. Reuben T. Whitaker on *Flasher's* Bridge, by
TBT and Compass (by Author)

fixed for the evening—he'd had quite a few drinks."

"Hey Reuben! I've just been out and had a couple of drinks with the boys!"

Not moving, Whitaker replied, "Yessir, I can see that."

"I just figured it out," declared Bull.

"What do you mean?"

Wright said, "I've just figured it out. In a short time we're gonna be at war with Japan, and we're gonna have the toughest goddamned patrol station you ever thought of."

"Yes, captain, yes, captain," murmured Whitaker.

Wright must have noted Whitaker's lack of enthusiasm, "Hey, you don't want me bothering you, do you?"

"Oh no, captain, I'm enjoying it."

"The HELL you are!" With that Wright snapped off Whitaker's light, returned to his cabin, and went to sleep.

Two hours later, about 4 a.m., Whitaker was again awakened. This time it was by a messenger. "Mr. Whitaker, I've got a message here I think you ought to read." The radio message was from Chief, Naval Operations, to all ships and stations. It said simply:

THE JAPANESE HAVE COMMENCED
HOSTILITIES.
GOVERN YOURSELVES ACCORDINGLY.

Whitaker thought, "Now what in the hell does that mean? Commenced hostilities with whom? With the U.S.? With the British? Or what?" The message said nothing about the Pearl Harbor attack under way.

After thinking it over, Whitaker concluded, "Nobody in his right mind would send that message out unless it meant we're at war with Japan."

Whitaker took the message into the skipper's cabin, and this time he got to turn the cabin light on in Bull Wright's face. It didn't wake him. Wright slept on, undisturbed. Reuben spoke to him, called to him, nudged him and finally lightly slapped the captain on the side of the face. Wright simply rolled over.

Whitaker slapped him on the other side, and Wright rolled the other way.

Bull finally opened one eye, glaring at Whitaker, and said, "WHAT IN THE HELL DO YOU WANT?!"

Whitaker said, "Captain, we just got a message we're at war with Japan."

Wright took it in. "Oh, the sons-a-bitches want to FIGHT, do they? I'll whip HELL out of 'em."

"Aye-aye, sir," said Whitaker. "I'm going up on the bridge and get ready to get under way to move out in the harbor where we can dive, because they might bomb us as soon as daylight comes."

As Whitaker was leaving Wright said, "Hey Reuben! Take care of that for me, will you? I'm going back to sleep." He turned over and was immediately asleep.

Sturgeon made four war patrols with Whitaker as exec, sinking several enemy ships, most notably the 7,267-ton transport *Montevideo Maru* on July 1, 1942 off the northwest coast of Luzon, Philippines. An early attack generated the famous message (composed by Whitaker), "*Sturgeon* no longer virgin." Wright often deferred to his junior officers in the handling of attacks. In this way, Whitaker and shipmate Chester W. Nimitz, Jr., son of Admiral Nimitz, gained valuable experience in submarine command.

During these patrols *Sturgeon* underwent several severe and lengthy depth chargings, all the more harrowing since it was a new experience to the U.S. submariners. Before the war there was no way for the Americans to know how effective the Japanese attacks would be, nor how well the submarines would survive. *Sturgeon's* sound operator, right after a depth charge exploded close by, exclaimed: "I knew that was gonna happen!" He was sternly told to share such information with the rest of the boat *before* the explosion. During the first year of the war, the American submarine force had a lot to learn.

The United States Navy's recently improved submarines were named "fleet-types" since they were supposed to be sufficiently fast and seaworthy to accompany the fleet on maneuvers. The subs were designed to act as scouts for the battleships, carriers and cruisers, in an all-important showdown with the entire enemy surface fleet.

After the Pearl Harbor raid, however, there simply was no United States fleet with which the "fleet" submarines could operate. The remnants of the U.S. Pacific fleet were totally inadequate for the planned frontal attack on the Japanese. The submarines, with their ability to escape underwater, were the only forces that could routinely patrol deep into the vast, Japanese-dominated seas. Since the American submarine force was largely intact, it immediately began unrestricted warfare against all enemy shipping.

These early submarine war patrols were disappointing for the Americans. The existing sub force contained numerous antiquated "S-boats," which were unfit for warfare in the tropics and off Alaska, and their crews deserved special recognition just for surviving the initial, dangerous patrols.

Peacetime training was also a problem. Only one month prior to the attack on Pearl Harbor, *Sturgeon* had participated in fleet exercises. The Commander, Submarines Pacific, held a meeting aboard *USS Holland* (AS 3) following the exercises, and criticized the submarine commanders who had made attacks by periscope observations instead of by sound. As Bull Wright and Reuben Whitaker listened, the Admiral told the audience, "Gentlemen, I notice that some of you submarine commanders have made periscope attacks on fleet ships, and this has to stop. You cannot afford to do such things. You must make sonar attacks because we cannot afford to take the risk of losing our submarines by making attacks with periscopes." So America's front-line submarine commanders were expressly instructed to make inaccurate sound attacks. Had this advice been followed throughout the war, U.S. submarines would have sunk very few targets.

The standards that guaranteed promotions for submarine officers in a poorly funded peacetime Navy also favored many older, conservative skippers who lacked the daring and initiative needed for war. As more submarines were built, and many cautious senior officers were replaced, a large number of aggressive, younger skippers such as Whitaker, aided by better torpedoes, would finally exploit the submarine's full potential.

The Navy awarded Whitaker the Silver Star for gallantry on *Sturgeon's* second war patrol. In September, 1942, he transferred from *Sturgeon* to his first command, the obsolete but effective *S-44.* The *S-44,* an "S-boat" designed and built shortly after World War I, had already overcome severe design limitations and equipment failures to sink at least three enemy vessels, including the formidable heavy cruiser *Kako.* In September, 1942, Whitaker took the 20-year-old boat out on her fourth war patrol, headed for the Solomon Islands, then the hottest battle area of the Pacific and site

of Guadalcanal. Patrolling off the island of New Georgia, constantly harassed by enemy aircraft and surface forces, and fighting frequent, dangerous equipment failures, *S-44* aggressively attacked three destroyers and suffered severe depth chargings for her efforts.

When *S-44* returned to Brisbane, Australia, Whitaker was again commended, receiving a Gold Star in lieu of a second Silver Star. Whitaker's boss, Captain Ralph W. Christie, advised him the *S-44* had to go back to the United States for a much-needed overhaul.

"Reuben," Christie said, "I'd like to give you a couple of choices. I personally would like to take you off the *S-44* and have you relieved, with the understanding that you will get command of the first fleet-type submarine that comes through here that needs a new commanding officer. I'll give you some other job in the meantime, but I promise you, you'll get command of the first fleet boat that comes through. Or, you can take the *S-44* back to the States and put it through overhaul. Which would you rather do?"

Should he wait for command of a prestigious new fleet boat in the war zone, or take his chances with an obsolete S-boat headed stateside for overhaul? There was no issue for Whitaker. He said "Captain, I'll stay here." With Christie on his side, Whitaker's chance to command a modern fleet boat appeared to have just taken a dramatic upturn. (*S-44*, after her overhaul, would be sunk by a Japanese destroyer on the next patrol, with the loss of all but two of her crew.)

Whitaker's command of a fleet boat became less certain when Christie was suddenly summoned stateside to help resolve the torpedo production problem. However, Christie was not a man to forget a promise,

so, before he left Brisbane, he summoned Whitaker. In front of Captain James Fife, his replacement, Christie said to Whitaker, "Reuben, I wanted to recall to you our conversation when I took you off the *S-44*, that I'd give you command of the first submarine coming through here that needed a commanding officer."

Christie then asked Fife if he would honor the arrangement, to which Fife said, "Ralph, that's perfectly fine. I know Whitaker. I know his reputation and I'd be delighted to have him as a commanding officer."

Not two weeks after Christie departed Brisbane, however, a surprised Whitaker received orders to report as executive officer, not commanding officer, of the *USS Flying Fish* (SS 229). There must have been reasons why Fife needed Whitaker in *Flying Fish* as exec and ignored the promises of command, but if so, Fife never communicated them to Whitaker, or apologized. It was a treatment Whitaker would always resent, and a blow to his morale.

Flying Fish had her own morale problems. Whitaker found her skipper, the aggressive Lt. Cmdr. "Donc" Donaho, difficult to get along with and the officers and crew "the most unhappy people I ever saw." Whitaker believed he had been ordered aboard to help ease relations between Donaho and the crew. He spent a single patrol serving as a buffer between the fiery captain and the crew on the *Flying Fish*, which daringly entered Apra Harbor, Guam, for one attack, and Tinian's Sunharon Roadstead for another.

After *Flying Fish's* third patrol, Whitaker was ordered stateside, as experienced officers were needed to man the numerous new submarines nearing comple-

tion. His orders allowed him a short liberty with his wife Peg in Memphis before reporting to Cmdr. William S. Stovall, Jr., to become executive officer of the *USS Darter* (SS 227), then under construction at Electric Boat Company (EB). Whitaker's fleet-boat command seemed to have escaped him again.

Then, while on leave in Memphis, Whitaker suddenly received new orders. Instead of executive officer on *Darter*, he was to be skipper of the new *USS Flasher* (SS 249), also being built at EB. Lt. Cmdr. Reuben T. Whitaker was finally to command a brand-new, fleet submarine.

CHAPTER 2

COMMISSIONING THE WEAPON

Assignment to "new construction" meant the supervision of the final stages of building, the commissioning, and the command, of the new submarine. Whitaker was no stranger to new construction, having participated in *Sturgeon's* manufacture and commissioning in California in 1938. *Flasher* was being built by EB in Groton, Connecticut, near the New London Submarine Base and the Navy's Submarine School. Her construction was part of the massive U.S. military build-up then in full swing.

America was militarily unprepared for World War II, but she had drastically increased military construction prior to Pearl Harbor. In the summer of 1940, the growing hostilities in Europe led Congress to authorize an 11 percent increase in the naval forces, followed in September with an unprecedented "70 Percent Expansion Act." Included in the latter authorization were the funds to pay for *Flasher*. To some extent the expansion was misleading, since the 1940 authorization did not envision *Flasher's* completion until the spring or summer of 1945. The Pearl Harbor attack shortened the protracted building schedule.

Still, it was two years before *Flasher's* construction even began. Facilities were entirely inadequate to build the new submarines authorized in 1940. For years the Navy had produced only two or three sub-

20

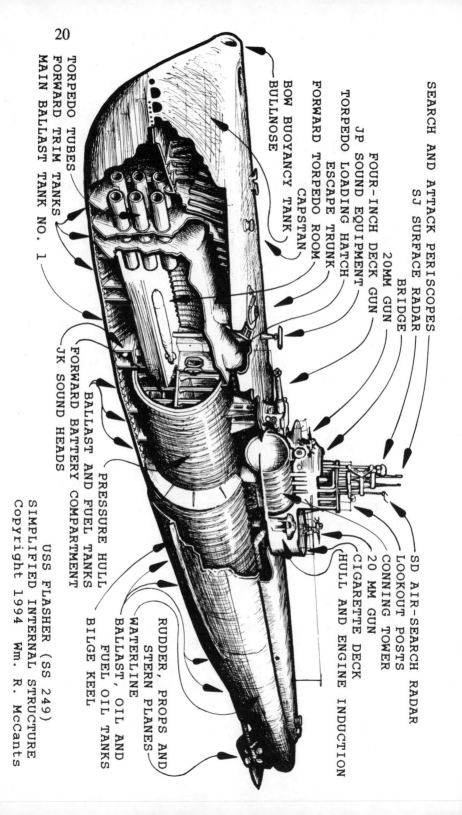

SEARCH AND ATTACK PERISCOPES
SJ SURFACE RADAR
BRIDGE
20MM GUN
FOUR-INCH DECK GUN
JP SOUND EQUIPMENT
TORPEDO LOADING HATCH
ESCAPE TRUNK
FORWARD TORPEDO ROOM
CAPSTAN
BOW BUOYANCY TANK
BULLNOSE

TORPEDO TUBES
FORWARD TRIM TANKS
MAIN BALLAST TANK NO. 1

FORWARD BATTERY COMPARTMENT
JK SOUND HEADS
BALLAST AND FUEL TANKS
FORWARD

PRESSURE HULL
BALLAST AND FUEL TANKS

SD AIR-SEARCH RADAR
LOOKOUT POSTS
CONNING TOWER
20 MM GUN
CIGARETTE DECK
HULL AND ENGINE INDUCTION

RUDDER, PROPS AND
STERN PLANES
WATERLINE
BALLAST, OIL AND
FUEL OIL TANKS
BILGE KEEL

USS FLASHER (SS 249)
SIMPLIFIED INTERNAL STRUCTURE
Copyright 1994 Wm. R. McCants

marines a year, with a prewar burst of around six submarines per annum. Between 1921 and the end of 1940, only 40 U.S. submarines had been commissioned. The U.S. Navy's submarine shipyards at Portsmouth, New Hampshire, and Mare Island, California, increased production, and some new private companies (most notably Manitowoc Shipbuilding Company in Wisconsin) began building submarines.

Electric Boat expanded its shipyard by adding three shipbuilding "ways" to its existing four ways, and building an adjacent yard with four more ways. This tripling of facilities was not enough for EB, and a new shipbuilding yard optimistically named the "Victory Yard" was built with ten ways on the Thames River a half mile downstream. With quintupled facilities, EB would complete 82 submarines during the war, virtually matched by production at Portsmouth (81), and followed by Manitowoc (28), and Mare Island (17). (Also, ten submarines were built at the Cramp Shipyard, and three at the Boston Navy Yard). With so many of the skilled workers already employed in the older facilities or serving with the armed forces, the Victory Yard tapped a large female work force to help build submarines. According to some, women outnumbered men at the new yard.

The Victory Yard was not ready to start construction until July, 1942, when first the USS Dace (SS 247), followed by the USS Dorado (SS 248) in August, and then the USS Flasher (SS 249) in September, were begun. Flasher's keel was laid September 30, 1942, while Whitaker was patrolling the Solomons in S-44. When he arrived in Connecticut in May, 1943, Flasher was well on her way toward completion.

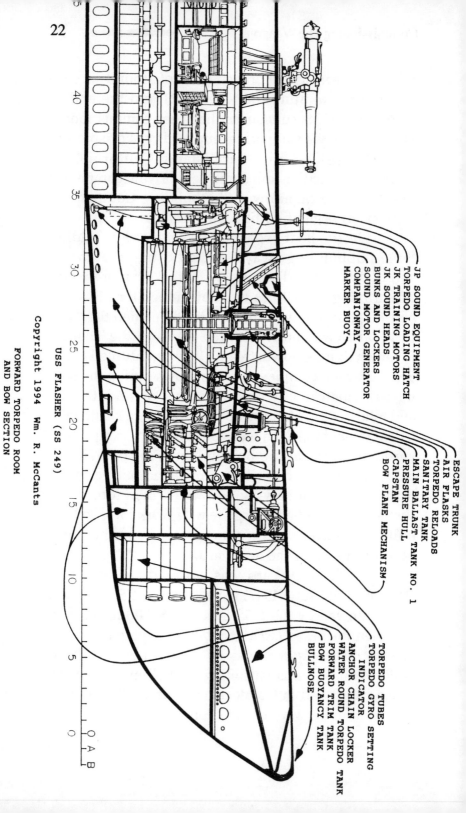

22

USS FLASHER (SS 249)

Copyright 1994 Wm. R. McCants

FORWARD TORPEDO ROOM
AND BOW SECTION

JP SOUND EQUIPMENT
TORPEDO LOADING HATCH
JK TRAINING MOTORS
JK SOUND HEADS
BUNKS AND LOCKERS
SOUND MOTOR GENERATOR
COMPANIONWAY
MARKER BUOY

ESCAPE TRUNK
AIR FLASKS
TORPEDO RELOADS
SANITARY TANK
MAIN BALLAST TANK NO. 1
PRESSURE HULL
CAPSTAN
BOW PLANE MECHANISM

TORPEDO TUBES
TORPEDO GYRO SETTING
INDICATOR
ANCHOR CHAIN LOCKER
WATER ROUND TORPEDO TANK
FORWARD TRIM TANK
BOW BUOYANCY TANK
BULLNOSE

Building a fleet-type submarine was a lengthy process. The boats were among the most sophisticated and expensive weapons of the period. Pound for pound, submarines cost more to build than any other naval vessel. More than seven million items were used in building each fleet-type submarine, and the cost was over seven million dollars, a lot of money in 1943.

Prewar submarines evolved over the years, but with the wartime need for a vast increase in production, the Navy wisely decided to "freeze" the current basic submarine pattern. This design was eventually known as the *Gato* class, after the *USS Gato* (SS 212), the first submarine built under the 1940 authorizations. Constant improvements in equipment and a thicker hull would be implemented during the war (such boats being in the *Balao* class), but the basic specifications and configuration of American submarines would not change. The *Gato* class and the thicker-hulled *Balao* class would constitute the bulk of the combatant submarine force by war's end.

American *Gato*-class submarines were relatively large. Flasher would be longer than a football field at 311 feet, 9 inches in length, but a mere 27 feet, 3 inches wide. On the surface she displaced 1,526 tons of water, and submerged, over 2,000 tons. By contrast, the standard German Type VII-C U-boat then in the Atlantic was a third shorter, with half the displacement and half the crew of the American boats. For the war in the Pacific and the tropics, the large, air-conditioned *Gato/Balao* boats were the best-designed submarines of the era.

Despite their large size, the American fleet subs were still cramped. With interior floor space of around

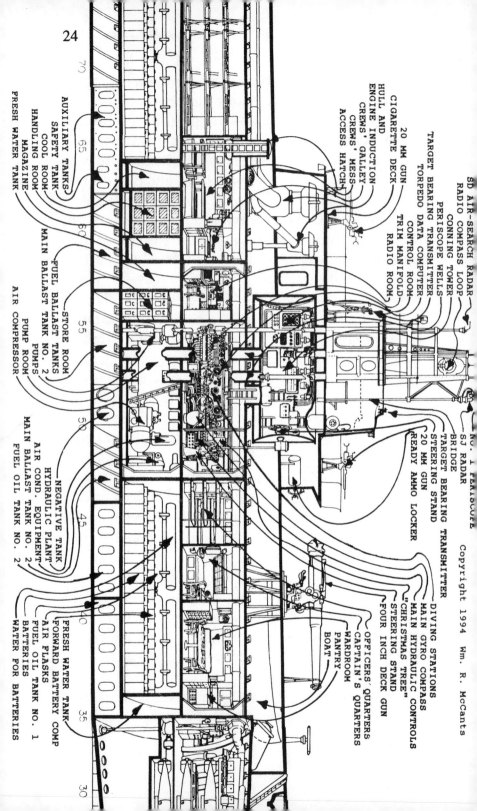

24

SD AIR-SEARCH RADAR
RADIO COMPASS LOOP
CONNING TOWER
PERISCOPE WELLS
TARGET BEARING TRANSMITTER
TORPEDO DATA COMPUTER
CONTROL ROOM
TRIM MANIFOLD
RADIO ROOM

CIGARETTE DECK
HULL AND
ENGINE INDUCTION
CREWS' GALLEY
CREWS' MESS
ACCESS HATCH
20 MM GUN

AUXILIARY TANKS
SAFETY TANK
COOL ROOM
HANDLING ROOM
MAGAZINE
FRESH WATER TANK

FUEL BALLAST TANKS
MAIN BALLAST TANK NO. 2
STORE ROOM
PUMP ROOM
PUMPS
AIR COMPRESSOR

NEGATIVE TANK
HYDRAULIC PLANT
AIR COND. EQUIPMENT
MAIN BALLAST TANK NO. 2
FUEL OIL TANK NO. 2

FRESH WATER TANK
FORWARD BATTERY COMP
AIR FLASKS
FUEL OIL TANK NO. 1
BATTERIES
WATER FOR BATTERIES

NO. 1 PERISCOPE
SJ RADAR
BRIDGE
TARGET BEARING TRANSMITTER
STEERING STAND
20 MM GUN
READY AMMO LOCKER

Copyright 1994   Wm. R. McCants

DIVING STATIONS
MAIN GYRO COMPASS
MAIN HYDRAULIC CONTROLS
STEERING STAND
"CHRISTMAS TREE"
FOUR INCH DECK GUN

OFFICERS' QUARTERS
CAPTAIN'S QUARTERS
WARDROOM
PANTRY
BOAT

2,600 square feet (the size of a large, four-bedroom house), the compartments were placed end to end and the side walls (bulkheads) curved inward to meet overhead. The limited living space was then crammed full of electrical and mechanical gear, intricate wiring, myriad water pipes, high pressure air pipes, hydraulic lines, air ducting, and the boat's crew, who would be stuck there, with enough food, water and supplies for the two months it took to complete a war patrol. Designed for a crew of 60 (six officers, 54 enlisted men) *Flasher* would routinely carry more than 80 men within her "pressure hull," the reinforced, cigar-shaped capsule substantially shorter and narrower than the exterior dimensions. Consuming additional space were the six loaded torpedo tubes forward and four tubes aft, with another 14 of the 22-foot torpedoes carried among the crews' bunks in the two torpedo rooms.

General Motors Corporation supplied *Flasher* with four massive, 1,535-horsepower, 16-cylinder diesel engines, designed to power submarines and train locomotives. The engines would propel *Flasher* through four 1,375-horsepower General Electric motors on the surface to a top speed of around 21 knots, and charge the 252 massive Exide storage batteries that powered the electric motors when submerged, for a maximum of eight knots. These limited speeds did not allow the subs to catch the much-faster enemy warships, but did allow them to overtake the slower merchant ships, and, with stealth and luck, to trap approaching warships.

All submarines produced during World War II were named for fish. The name *"Flasher"* came from the large, edible, salt-water fish of the same name (bet-

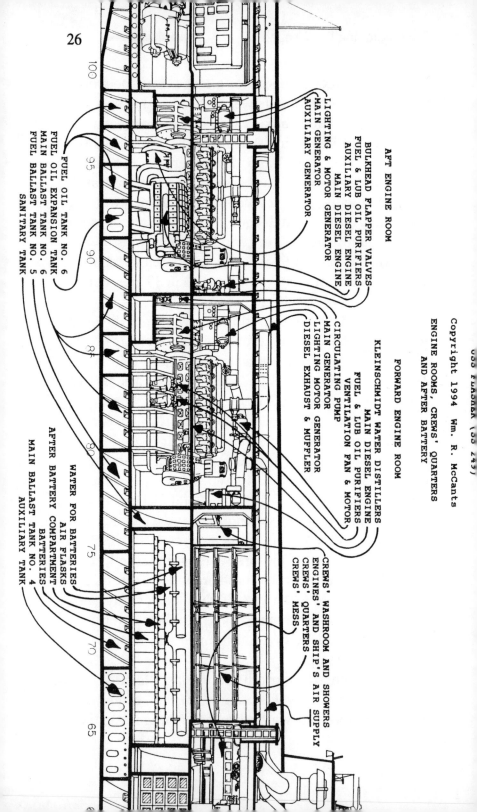

USS FLASHER (SS 249)

Copyright 1994 Wm. R. McCants

ENGINE ROOMS, CREWS' QUARTERS
AND AFTER BATTERY

ter known as "Tripletail") found mostly between Florida and Uruguay in the western Atlantic.

From May, 1943, when Whitaker arrived in New London, he became increasingly involved in the submarine's final stages of construction. As *Flasher's* prospective skipper, he was responsible for monitoring the boat's progress. He also had some input into minor design details. During this period he was required to form and train a crew. Whitaker later said that he "never had a finer time in his life" than in commissioning the *Flasher*.

Another May arrival in New London was Lt. Raymond F. DuBois, *Flasher's* prospective executive officer. (The name is pronounced DOO'-boys.) DuBois, like Whitaker, was a Navy career officer and graduate of the U.S. Naval Academy at Annapolis, Maryland. (Whitaker was Class of 1934; DuBois was Class of 1938). An unmarried 27-year-old Connecticut native, DuBois had been a captain of Navy's football team at Annapolis, an All-Eastern football player, an All-American lacrosse player and a member of the varsity wrestling team. Before the Pearl Harbor attack, DuBois had served with Whitaker as a gunnery officer in *Sturgeon*. When war broke out, he was with *USS Snapper* (SS 185) in Manila as her communications officer. DuBois made six war patrols in *Snapper*, evacuating personnel from the Philippines and Java, rescuing the disabled submarine *USS Searaven* (SS 196), and experiencing the same frustrating lack of success with torpedoes that most submarines had in the early years of the war.

Third officer on *Flasher* was to be Lt. Philip T. Glennon, Annapolis class of 1940. Glennon had served

USS FLASHER (SS 249)

Copyright 1994 Wm. R. McCants

AFTER TORPEDO & MANEUVERING ROOMS

STERN PLANE & CAPSTAN MOTOR
STEERING GEAR MOTOR
TORPEDO GYRO SETTING INDICATOR
TORPEDO TUBES
AFTER TRIM TANK

PROPELLER
STERN PLANES
RUDDER
WATER ROUND TORPEDO TANK
MAIN BALLAST TANK NO. 7
LUB OIL TANK

AFTER TORPEDO ROOM

ENGINEER'S OFFICE
TORPEDO LOADING HATCH
ESCAPE TRUNK
TORPEDO RELOADS

MOTOR ROOM

WATER PUMP
REDUCTION GEAR
OIL SUMP
MAIN MOTORS
FUEL OIL TANK NO. 7

MANEUVERING ROOM

HEAD
MAIN PROPULSION CONTROLS
MAIN PROPULSION CUBICAL

130   125   120   115   110   105   100   95

as Assistant Gunnery Officer in three hot, very successful war patrols on *USS Greenling* (SS 213) prior to his
transfer to *Flasher*. In a major sinking of the war, *Greenling* sank the 12,752-ton *Brazil Maru* on August 5, 1942,
two days before the U.S. landings on Guadalcanal.
Brazil Maru was transporting 400 Japanese soldiers sent
to reinforce the Solomons. *Greenling* won the coveted
Presidential Unit Citation and Glennon was awarded
a Silver Star medal for these patrols. Glennon's experience in gunnery and torpedoes led Whitaker to utilize
him as *Flasher's* Gunnery and Torpedo Officer.

   Flasher's Chief of the Boat (COB) was to be Felix
Perkowsky, Chief Torpedoman's Mate. As the highest-
ranking enlisted man, Perkowsky bore authority
and responsibility similar in many ways to that of
Whitaker, but with much more directness. Perkowsky
operated without threatening or bullying. He was
never boastful, and he never ran roughshod over his
sailors. As Chief of the Boat, he would listen to his
men and was willing to talk with them, but no one
wanted to argue with him. He expected an order to be
carried out without explaining it, and he did not repeat
himself. Whitaker rarely interacted with *Flasher's* crew,
but he always had time to listen to Perkowsky. Like
DuBois, Perkowsky had previously served with
Whitaker.

   Together with Whitaker and DuBois, Perkowsky forged standards of performance on *Flasher* that
would survive long after all three had moved on to
other duties. Veteran submariners could come and go
on *Flasher*, but they all had to adjust to fit the boat, not
vice versa.

   Another arrival in New London that May was

Electrician's Mate Robert Peasley Briggs. Briggs' middle name wasn't Peasley--that was a chief petty officer's typing error, but once recorded, it became too hard to correct in the official Navy records, so Peasley it became. Like Whitaker and DuBois, Briggs was in a sub in Manila when Japan started the war, but in *S-37*, one of the older S-boats. *S-37* made three patrols before she, and Briggs, were ordered stateside. From there he went to *Flasher*. (He was earlier ordered to the submarine *USS Shark* (SS 174), but another electrician who really wanted to be in a fleet-type sub asked if he could take Briggs' place. Since it made no difference to Briggs, the other electrician was the one transferred. *Shark* was sunk shortly thereafter, only two months into the war, with the loss of the electrician and all others aboard.)

Briggs, a Massachusetts native, would be one of the "controllers" responsible for operating the large electric motors that propelled *Flasher* both on the surface and submerged. He would also continually service and inspect her 252 batteries, contained in the cramped forward and aft battery compartments underneath the interior deck plates. Crawling on hands and knees over the large batteries, he would measure the batteries' gravity and check for grounds. As the acid ate holes in cotton clothing, Briggs and his fellow electricians wore wool and special aprons in the claustrophobic, hot spaces.

Another electrician aboard *Flasher* was Ross Brown, Jr., known as "Brownie." From Champaign, Illinois, Brownie was young and conscientious, often working through the night crawling over the batteries, checking for grounds. Upright and religious, he

abstained from much of the drinking, smoking and colorful profanity practiced by many of his young ship-mates.

A late arrival aboard *Flasher* was Chief Electrician's Mate Victor Murphy Cypherd, nicknamed "Pappy" for his advanced age. (He was probably still in his mid-30's.) The boat's head electrician, he replaced another man who had "not worked out." There would never be any questions raised as to Cypherd's performance aboard *Flasher*. While Navy motor machinists used to say "MOKEFU" ("Mechanically O.K., Electrically F____-Up"), Cypherd and his electricians were able to minimize electrical problems in *Flasher's* powerful and complex electrical system.

A few of *Flasher's* prospective crew members arrived for duty in May. Two who appeared early were Signalman Joe Corneau and Quartermaster Sydney Herbert Pool. Corneau was a French Canadian, fluent in French but still learning to speak in English. On *Flasher* he became known as "Frenchy." He astonished his friends when he gave up both military deferment and good pay at EB to join the Navy, because he wanted "to do something more" to help with the war effort.

Pool acted as a spokesman presenting himself and other sailors reporting to Whitaker for duty. Whitaker and Pool did not get along from the start, as Whitaker apparently felt Pool was too cocky. Pool's run-in with the Shore Patrol probably did not help his relations with Whitaker.

If anyone had justification to be self-assured, it was Pool. A large, powerful man, he had survived the sinking of the old submarine *R-12* off Key West,

Florida, less than a year earlier. Only a few officers and enlisted men on the bridge escaped when the boat suddenly and unaccountably plunged to the bottom, taking 42 crewmen to their deaths. A powerful swimmer, Pool was credited with single-handedly saving two of the survivors, including *R-12's* commanding officer. Pool received a well-deserved medal for his feat—the U.S. Treasury Department's Lifesaving Medal. He was only the fifth person to receive that commendation. Because he received the Treasury medal, however, Navy regulations required that he give up the Navy Special Commendation ribbon he had previously received for the same feat.

With only a handful of her crew assigned, a sleek new *Flasher* slid stern first down Way Number 4 into the Thames River, on June 20, 1943, decorated with ribbons and banners and amid much fanfare. In EB's official photograph of her launching, Whitaker is dressed in "blues" with Glennon, standing on *Flasher's* starboard bow looking aft, while DuBois, dressed in khaki uniform, watches over her port bow. Shipyard workers proudly lined the sub's narrow deck, alongside the U.S. Navy personnel aboard. Though launched, *Flasher* was still largely an Electric Boat Company responsibility.

In peacetime a submarine was almost fully completed when launched, but this was not the case with frantic wartime production. The shipbuilding ways were needed for starting more hulls, so major work continued after the subs were in the water. Launched Victory Yard submarines were maneuvered to a "fitting-out" pier for the substantial outfitting still to be done. There, much of the submarine's electrical and

SUBMARINE FLASHER
N THE WAYS
20, 1943
TRIC BOAT CO. GROTON, CONN.

Launching of *USS Flasher*, June 20, 1943
(Electric Boat Company - Author's Collection)

mechanical equipment (such as periscopes) was installed, adjusted and tested.

The crew found that a pound of coffee given to the right person could sometimes obtain more than the most authoritative requisition form. Such bribes got them added amenities, like padding for the steel flooring in the engine rooms, to ease the strain of standing four-hour watches.

Flasher's plans called for 50-caliber machine guns and a three-inch deck gun, but wartime demands showed more firepower was needed, so she received instead two 20mm Oerlikon machine guns (roughly 80 caliber) on the raised fairwater decks fore and aft of the bridge, and a four-inch deck gun forward of the conning tower fairwater.

Under Navy procedures, Whitaker had to verify that all specified equipment, manuals, spare parts, and personnel were aboard and operating efficiently by *Flasher's* estimated completion and delivery date of September 16, 1943. Written progress reports were due on July 16, and every week thereafter as to the number of personnel received, the estimated completion date, and progress in the acquisition of equipment, stores and spare parts. Copies of Whitaker's weekly reports went to everybody, including the Bureau of Ships; the Bureau of Personnel; the Bureau of Ordnance; the Inspection and Survey Board; the Commanders in Chief, Atlantic and Pacific Fleets; the Commanders, Submarine Forces Atlantic and Pacific; the Commander, Submarine Division 13; the Newport Torpedo Station; the Supervisor of Shipbuilding at Electric Boat Company; and every Prospective Commanding Officer in New London. Through receipt of these lists of missing parts and equipment, personnel in BuShips and other departments verified the availability of the missing items and ordered their supply to *Flasher*. A vast number of personnel in the Navy and private industry contributed to every submarine's construction.

While the boat was fitted out, *Flasher's* new crew was quartered ashore. Whitaker and his men operated from a large room in the Victory Yard close to the submarine, as did the officers and crew of the submarine *Dorado* (SS 248), one month ahead of *Flasher's* (SS 249) building schedule, and the officers and crew of the *Flier* (SS 250), about one month behind the *Flasher*. Much of the crews' time was devoted to classes and exercises at the nearby submarine base on the numerous training simulators.

From 18 officers and men on July 16, *Flasher's* complement grew to 27 by July 30, to 68 by August 13, and to 75 by September 3. During this period the new crew devoted massive efforts to obtaining all parts specified in the Navy contracts and regulations. In the six weeks prior to commissioning, the missing parts and supplies shrank from over 4,200 items listed on 15 legal-size pages, to fewer than 300 items (excluding charts) listed on only four pages. There would be no spare parts available in the middle of enemy territory, except for those aboard. Even at the time of trials and commissioning, *Flasher* lacked two armored compasses, an octant, 500 charts, complete plan books for the submarine, most spare parts for the four-inch gun, tools and spare parts for Mark 18 electric torpedoes, and a Mark 18 demolition outfit to scuttle the submarine and prevent her salvage by the Japanese. Other missing equipment included the SD and SJ radar equipment, to be installed by the New London submarine base after commissioning, due to the top-secret nature of radar technology.

Because of delays in fitting out, *Flasher's* river trials and Board of Inspection results were postponed a week, to September 23, 1943. Chief Board of Inspection and Survey member was Rear Admiral W.S. Anderson. BuShips was represented by Captain E. H. ("Swede") Bryant, a submariner and one of the officers behind the prewar push for a successful fleet-type submarine design. Of 22 tests required for the dock trials and inspection, *Flasher* completed only ten. Most major trials involving maneuvers under way were not conducted. She was also drydocked because the hull of the brand-new submarine, launched only 12 weeks earlier, was not good:

> The condition of the underwater body was poor. Fouling was great and paint was missing from 100% of the underwater portion of the hull. No anti-fouling paint had been applied.

The hull was power-brushed clean, and three coats of different-formula paints were applied. *Flasher* was off to an inauspicious start.

The Board of Inspection and Survey report was also a mixed review. It began by commending the materials and workmanship as excellent, and the boat's preparations for the dock trials as "well made." There followed, however, three single-spaced pages of major and minor defects, and 16 pages listing repairs, installations and tests that still needed to be done. *Flasher* also received bad marks for cleanliness "below the usual high standard of the previous boats inspected at Groton." This was criticism of Electric Boat and not the crew. Thereafter *Flasher* always received especially high marks for cleanliness.

The crucial watertight hatches at bulkheads 35 (between the officers' quarters and forward torpedo room) and 99 (between the aft engine and maneuvering rooms) failed to seal. The bulkhead 35 hatch was easily fixed, but the maneuvering room hatch would require more work. The bow planes' electric clutch also failed to function properly, due to a poor design that was probably corrected on later boats.

As a positive note, the Board of Inspection was impressed with *Flasher's* periscope optics, which lacked certain fringe aberrations noted on other recent submarines.

One alteration that was requested by Whitaker but not recommended by the Board was lowering the lookout stations from atop the fairwater to inside the fairwater. This was to be accomplished by mounting four raised platforms in the fairwater deck for the lookouts to stand on, and by cutting four holes in the lookout platform so only their heads and shoulders would be exposed. This change would have lowered the lookouts by five feet, and lessened their viewing range considerably.

Despite all the proposed work and defects noted, the Board of Inspection and Survey authorized acceptance by the Navy of the *USS Flasher* on September 25, 1943.

In a ceremony on that Saturday afternoon, the Navy accepted the new submarine from the Electric

Flasher's Commissioning Party, September, 1943

(Back Row, L to R: Markham, Bartl, Butts, Bryant, Ezerosky, Gadbois, Avery, Pool, Farmer, Van Horn, Steinkamp, Sherman, Brown, Bergen.
Third Row, L to R: Williams, Spencer, Briggs, Corneau, Furgeson, Calloway, Paczkowski, Baker, Van De Veere, Webb, Barbour, Tracy, Crilly, McDonald, Beeson.
Second Row, L to R: Dolese, DeBois, Doty, Precup, Brokovich, Enders, Filippone, Kowalski, McLaren, Buck, (Marshall?), Tillman, Pearce, Schlee, Elliott, Reichert.
Front Row, L to R: Turcotte, Liggett, Johnson, Cypherd, Holbrook, Coffin, DuBois, Whitaker, Glennon, Burke, Kristl, Wilson, Perkowsky, Carey, Newton, Wieder. Courtesy of Tom Burke)

Boat Company, represented by Lawrence Y. Spear. Spear had left the Navy more than 40 years earlier, and designed EB's first fleet-type submarine in 1913 with double hull construction and a combination diesel-electric propulsion. These were features the brand-new *Flasher* still employed three decades later. Mrs. W. A. Saunders, wife of submarine skipper Willard A. Saunders, was the boat's sponsor. *Flasher* was officially declared a unit of the United States Navy, after which Whitaker read his orders and assumed command.

Three Naval Reserve officers added by this time to *Flasher* were Lieutenant G. F. "Snap" Coffin, and Lieutenant Junior Grades (jg's) Thomas A. Burke, Jr., and Frank R. Kristl. Coffin had enlisted in 1929, but was denied entry to Annapolis for lack of two wisdom teeth. Why the Naval Academy required a full set of molars is unknown. After serving a decade as an enlisted man, Coffin obtained an officer's commission in 1941, only to be rejected from the hazardous submarine service in a letter signed by Admiral Chester Nimitz, as "too old." He persisted, however, and became Communications Officer of *USS Shad* (SS 235). He made three war patrols in *Shad* in the Atlantic Ocean before the Navy discontinued submarine war patrols there. He joined *Flasher* at the fitting-out pier. Coffin would be *Flasher's* Engineering Officer, and act as her Diving Officer during attacks.

Burke, an engineer, joined the naval reserves a month prior to Pearl Harbor, and was initially assigned as a "Sound Silencing Officer," to check submarines for noises and help silence them. He volunteered for submarine duty and served in the old submarine *O-6* (SS 67) for a few months, as there were no openings at the

Electric Boat Employees (in Suits) Celebrating after Commissioning Party with (L to R) Chief Cypherd, Bob Briggs and Frank DeBois (in Uniforms) (Courtesy of Bob Briggs)

submarine schools. Less than a third the displacement of fleet boats like *Flasher* and extremely out of date, "O-boats" served mainly as training vessels during World War II. When a student billet opened in April, 1943, Burke started submarine school. He graduated in June, while *Flasher* was still at the fitting-out piers in Groton. Burke served as *Flasher's* Communications Officer. During attacks he would handle the "plot" as Plotting Officer, calculating the target's position and course.

Kristl, also an engineer, had been a civilian employee of the Navy Department prior to the war, had volunteered for service, and had attended Officers' Training School at Northwestern University in Chicago. He applied for submarines but was transferred by mistake to sub*chasers* in San Francisco. He spent eight months in California and saw his first child born (a son) while waiting for the Navy to straighten things out, before he was finally sent to submarine school in Portsmouth, New Hampshire. From sub school he reported to *Flasher* at the fitting-out pier. Kristl would serve as her Assistant Torpedo Data Computer Officer at battle stations, setting torpedo spreads, as officer in charge of the auxiliaries (air compressors, pumps, etc.), and as *Flasher's* Commissary Officer.

On the following Tuesday, Lt.(jg) Thomas R. McCants reported to *Flasher* after a year as Gunnery Officer of the *USS Marlin* (SS 205), a smaller, submarine-school training submarine. McCants was to replace a warrant officer who had been transferred from *Flasher* to help with the conversion of the submarine tender *Euryale* (AS 22). Whitaker had specified that his last officer be a "regular" Navy officer already qualified in submarines (like McCants), as he wanted a balance between reservists and career officers who had graduated from the Naval Academy.

Since there was already a "Tom" aboard, McCants would be called "Mac." He and two other submarine-qualified Navy lieutenants in New London had drawn straws, with McCants winning the single opening on *Flasher*. Whitaker and McCants were the only two officers from the South. Ray DuBois and Tom

Burke were both from Connecticut, Phil Glennon was from New York, Snap Coffin was from Washington, D.C., and Frank Kristl was from Omaha, Nebraska. Whitaker announced that all decisions aboard the *Flasher* would be decided by vote, but that votes by Southerners Whitaker and McCants would outweigh all others combined. McCants never got to vote, of course. The Yankee/Southern mix provided a source of constant give and take among the officers. On returning from one war patrol, one of the northerners remarked he would signal the waiting Navy band to strike up "Marching Through Georgia." This brought a rejoinder, "Tell them if they do we'll man the 20-millimeter guns."

On October 5, 1943, *Flasher's* four-inch, 50-caliber deck gun and her two 20mm machine guns were fired and performed satisfactorily, with no signs of hull deformation or weakness.

Torpedo trials were conducted on October 8, 9 and 11 off the nearby Newport, Rhode Island, Torpedo Station. On the first day Mark 14-3A steam torpedoes with dummy warheads were fired from each of *Flasher's* six forward and four stern tubes, while she proceeded at flank speed (17-18 knots) on the surface. Two torpedoes broached on firing, five dove 30 to 40 feet before leveling out, and three experienced regulator kicks, but all ten eventually ran "HSN" (hot, straight and normal). The second day of torpedo-firing trials was conducted from periscope depth. The first submerged shot circled right 70° and then sank, the third torpedo would not fire, and another three ran strangely. Only one of the ten shots clearly ran hot, straight and normal. The number-three tube had not

fired because of a mangled spindle (used to set the torpedo's course) that wedged in the tube and would not retract.

The third day of exercises consisted of "deep shots" fired from 84 to 86 feet below the surface. The third day's shots were similar to the misadventures of the second day. The first torpedo went fine for 1,600 yards, then "rolled over and ran cold." The second shot broached, then dove to 70 feet, broached through the surface again, then "rolled over, ran erratic and cold." The torpedo from the third tube, which had failed to fire at periscope depth the day before, made the only HSN launch of the day. The other torpedoes all ran with some irregularities, and the eighth shot, "Circled left out of tube - 90° hit coal dock on Gould Island."

The last test of the day was to refire the third tube at periscope depth, to make up for its failure to fire during the second day's testing. Again, there were spindle problems in the third tube, as it automatically returned into the tube after firing. Now the spindle was too loose instead of too tight. This spindle problem was the only failure clearly attributable to *Flasher*. The poor torpedo runs were due to exercise torpedoes supplied to the sub. Although four of *Flasher's* tubes had lower differential pressures than the minimum prescribed, the ejection velocities were excellent and there was a war on, so the test results were deemed "satisfactory."

After *Flasher* arrived back at the New London Submarine Base on October 12, Rear Admiral F.A. Daubin, Commander, Submarines Atlantic, and his Chief of Staff, Cmdr. George C. Crawford, came aboard for a half hour, then left. Daubin had commanded a Pearl Harbor submarine squadron until March of 1942. Crawford had been one of the early, brave submariners who were outspoken against the faulty magnetic torpedo detonator, but his criticisms had been rejected, then stifled. It is unknown why they had visited *Flasher*, but the boat had ruined its starboard propeller, and was to go into the busy dry dock for replacement. A bent prop would have been a major disaster in the peacetime Navy, but it was a relatively minor incident in wartime. Another prop was borrowed from Electric Boat, and Daubin wrote BuShips requesting they replace the propeller taken from EB.

As noted in *Flasher's* survey, her diesel engines lacked chrome-plated cylinder liners. The chromed liners were more durable, but were not specified in her contracts. In June, the Navy had ordered some of the submarines to have the chrome liners installed at the Navy's expense, and *Flasher* was on the list. On October 23, 26 sailors under Chief Machinist Mate H.D. Stultz reported aboard for the laborious, week-long job of replacing the engine liners on *Flasher's* four, 16-cylinder General Motors diesel engines.

New permanent personnel continued to trickle in to fill out the boat's complement, temporarily offset by an occasional incident where a crew member would overstay his leave, resulting in loss of future liberties ashore. While in Newport, DuBois had had to retrieve ten of *Flasher's* sailors from jail, after they had gotten into a fight. More serious infractions, such as "refusing to obey the orders of the Shore Patrol and destruction of property," resulted in Captain's Mast (a disci-

plinary hearing) and three days solitary confinement on bread and water. That's right: bread and water.

Other crewmen had less boisterous plans for their leave. One of *Flasher's* lookouts, Signalman John Precup, had a special reason for looking his best prior to liberty ashore one day, as he was due to be married that afternoon. He carefully shaved, showered and dressed, only to look up through the deck hatch to see the underside of the Thames River Bridge pass by. The submarine was proceeding down river for exercises at sea! He had heard the massive diesel engines start up, of course, but that happened every day alongside the pier to charge *Flasher's* electrical storage batteries. Precup raced to the officers to explain his need to get ashore, but it was no use. He would have to wait to get married.

A few of the officers and crew were temporarily detached to the Naval Hospital in Newport, due to an appendicitis and other ailments. There would be no doctors available once the boat put to sea. The submarines did carry pharmacist's mates, who coped well under the circumstances.

On November 1, a steward's mate failed to show for morning muster. Since he failed to appear prior to *Flasher's* sailing date of November 4, he was transferred by order of ComSubLant (Commander Submarines, Atlantic Fleet) to duty and disciplinary action "upon reporting or apprehension" by the shore patrol.

On the sailing date "Gunner" Schwartz fell through the forward torpedo room hatch, sustaining multiple lacerations. Despite this he was able to stay aboard. Gunners Mate Schwartz was a large, powerful sailor, with the looks of a Hollywood movie star. Lifting one of the sub's heavy Oerlikon 20mm machine guns through the hatches was a difficult task for anyone, yet Gunner could manhandle TWO of the guns in a single trip. Once, when a shipmate grabbed a meat cleaver and threatened Gunner with it, Schwartz easily picked the man up and carried him to an officer with the comment, "This guy could get himself hurt that way."

Other personnel temporarily assigned to the Naval Hospital were recalled if fit, and two sailors were expropriated from submarines *S-14* and *Flier* to fill out *Flasher's* roster.

While in New London, Whitaker made a short talk to his assembled crew. He had watched Donaho tell his crew on *Flying Fish*: "We're going to go out there and sink ships or we're not coming back." Whitaker had a different approach. He told the men on *Flasher* they were going into the Pacific and they would sink a lot of Japanese ships, but, he said "Mrs. Reuben T. Whitaker's boy is going to get you back." He told them, "I guarantee you one thing. If I don't think on any individual attack that we have AT LEAST a 50-50 chance of surviving the attack, I won't make it. I wouldn't attack the biggest damn carrier in the Jap fleet if I thought that to sink it, it was going to sink my ship or lose my crew." This statement, and Whitaker's comments that he wanted to survive the war to get home to his wife Peg, guaranteed him the strong support of *Flasher's* crew.

CHAPTER 3

TRANSIT TO THE WAR ZONE

*F*lasher left New London on November 6, 1943. Because of secrecy, wives were not supposed to be informed of her departure until after the boat had left. Many knew anyway. Alyce W. Kristl, wife of Lt.(jg) Frank Kristl, photographed *Flasher* as she passed New London headed to sea.

From New London the boat sailed easterly to the 70th meridian, then proceeded south along the meridian to a point about 500 nautical miles east of Jacksonville, Florida. She veered to the southwest across the northern end of the Bahamas, and headed down around the southern tip of Florida toward Key West.

Although it would be a month before *Flasher* reached Japanese-controlled waters in the Pacific Ocean, the transit south off the east coast of the United States was still dangerous, as attested by the many Allied merchant ships sunk off the coast by German U-boats. Oil and debris from sunken Allied shipping could be found on many east coast beaches. The patrol craft (PC) escort provided to *Flasher* helped, but the escort was only available for part of the trip.

Men of the *Flasher* had a heightened awareness of these dangers. Their sister ship, the *USS Dorado*, which had been constructed in the adjacent way at EB's Victory Yard, had been lost with all hands from unknown causes on her maiden trip south from New

Flasher **Heading Down Thames River, Photographed by Alyce Kristl (Courtesy of Frank and Alyce Kristl)**

London only three weeks earlier.

Many of *Flasher's* crew had close friends on the *Dorado* and were shocked at her loss. Whitaker's good friend, Lt. Cmdr. E. C. "Penrod" Schneider, had been her skipper. Frenchy Corneau lost his buddy, fellow Signalman C.E. Fackrell. Frenchy and Fackrell were the only two of five classmates from the University of Chicago Signal School who also made it successfully through sub school. Fackrell had even received clearance for Frenchy to transfer over to *Dorado* from *Flasher*, warning Frenchy that it was widely known in Groton that *Flasher* was a boat headed for certain disaster, because of a truly inexperienced crew, a mere Lt. Commander assuming his first fleet boat command, and a

Overhead View of *USS Flasher* Taken November 6, 1943
(National Archives)

boat built mostly by women! Corneau declined to leave his new shipmates, and so survived *Dorado's* loss.

Aboard *Flasher* it was thought *Dorado* had been torpedoed by a U-boat. It was later determined she had probably been sunk by "friendly" aircraft on October 12, 1943, near Cuba. Attack by American aircraft and surface ships was a continual hazard for U.S. subs during World War II. The distinguished veteran *USS Seawolf* (SS 197) and its entire crew were lost after attacks by the destroyer escort *USS Rowell* (DE 403). Numerous other submarines were targeted for attacks by U.S. planes and ships but survived. Throughout the war *Flasher* was to be plagued by sightings of friendly aircraft that she was unable to reach on radio, and that therefore constituted real threats. She would also be approached by, and would initiate approaches on, unidentified subs that later proved to be "friendly" allied submarines. Her lookouts had reason to be alert on the voyage south, both for the German submarines, and for the "friendly" antisubmarine forces that were such a danger.

Flasher was also under a strict timetable on her trip down the coast, to stay at the center of a moving square 20 miles on a side. If she strayed from the square, she was fair game for the American as well as the enemy forces. Both *Dorado* and *Seawolf* occupied such supposed "safety zones," however, and they were still destroyed by their own forces.

Dorado's sinking occurred on her trip to Key West, where she was to have assisted in training at the new underwater sound and sonar school. After Whitaker learned of her loss in October, he immediately went to Adm. Daubin and Cmdr. Crawford to find out what submarine would replace her in the sound-school training. This was so soon after *Dorado's* loss they had not chosen a replacement. Whitaker told them, "Well, I'm going to be the next submarine going down that way. Why not the *Flasher*?"

So it was that on November 13, *Flasher* arrived

in Key West. Minor repairs were made at the yard for decking damaged in the Atlantic transit, and electrical gear was adjusted, including the sub's sound gear, radar, and torpedo data computer. Nine pairs of her binoculars were also repaired, and radio speakers were installed in the crew's mess, the officers' mess, and both torpedo rooms.

Whitaker had held Captain's Mast before arriving at Key West, probably as a warning to those about to go on liberty ashore. For one radioman there was no liberty, due to his AOL (absent over leave) offense in New London. He had been sentenced to ten days confinement as well as a $10 per month decrease in pay for two months. Ten dollars was more important to a sailor in 1943. Base pay ran from $50 per month for an apprentice seaman to $138 per month for a chief. Hazardous duty pay for submariners and clothing allowances substantially raised these pay amounts.

In Key West, *Flasher* took on fuel, lost one man to the Key West Naval Hospital, and took aboard Motor Machinist Mate First Class Roland E. Noel from the old submarine *R-20* in his place.

Flasher was one of the first new fleet submarines to arrive in Key West. Base personnel and *Flasher's* crew were to train at the sound school for a week and a half before the sub would head on to the Canal Zone. The training helped the antisubmarine forces learn to detect and track a submarine, and the sub's crew learn to evade detection.

Training was essential to efficient operation of any machine as complex as a World War II submarine, and doubly so for a new boat with an inexperienced crew headed straight for the war zone. Whitaker and his handful of veterans were constantly training *Flasher's* crew. Little time had been allotted new submarines for training in New London. This was the reason Whitaker quickly volunteered to replace *Dorado* at Key West—to get another precious week or ten days of training. Phil Glennon estimated that only a quarter of *Flasher's* crew had submarine experience, and many of these men had never been in combat. In Connecticut, two of *Flasher's* chiefs were overheard complaining about the crew's inexperience, with one vowing there was no way he would "stay aboard this S.O.B." Both chiefs were able to transfer off *Flasher* before her first patrol.

Reuben Whitaker was later to attribute *Flasher's* wartime success to intensive training. He described the problem of taking a new submarine into combat:

> When you put a new submarine in commission, when we did in the war, you know, they were short of people, short of submarines—so it was a pretty high-pressure job. From the day you put that submarine into commission until the time you had it ready to fight, they allowed you one month....
>
> So what you must do then is, you must get your Goddamned crew trained and you must train them well. And you've got to do it in a hell of a hurry. So this is about the single, most important facet, I think, in getting a submarine ready to fight.
>
> But I worked them like hell. And

I'm a son of a bitch at sea myself! I talk about [Donc] Donaho, I hope I'm not unreasonable, but when you're fighting a war there's only one way to do something if you're commanding officer, and that's to get it done YOUR way.

And if somebody made a mistake, I didn't hesitate to tell them so. And this was the way I did business, and pretty soon we had a reasonably trained crew. I tried to be as kind to them and as little horseshit as the situation would permit, and this is very important too.

During *Flasher's* first three months in commission, her intensive training included almost 180 dives, and numerous collision, fire, casualty, torpedo attack, and battle surface drills. All of this training was to be tested during the trip south. After losing her escort, *Flasher* detected distant sonar pinging and decided to slip by unnoticed. The submarine dove and rigged for silent running. The pinging U.S. Coast Guard vessel detected *Flasher* anyway, and quickly closed so that the submarine had to surface and be identified, or be depth charged. She surfaced "with our hands up," and with less of the self-confidence nurtured by intensive training.

After leaving Key West on November 21, 1943, the submarine followed an S-curved course west and south around Cuba, southeast to avoid the shallow waters off Yucatan, and then southwest toward Panama. *Flasher* was photographed by Fleet Air Wing 12 off Cuba on the 23rd, spent Thanksgiving Day

***Flasher* Photographed November 23, 1943 off Cuba by Naval Reconnaissance Aircraft (National Archives)**

passing southwest of Jamaica, and arrived at Colon, Panama, shortly before noon on November 27.

Flasher was required to unload all of her torpedoes prior to entering the Panama Canal to avoid any accidental damage to the vital canal locks. It was bad enough that her torpedomen had to first unload torpedoes and then reload on the far side of the canal, because the heavy, sensitive torpedoes had to be snaked carefully out and back into the cramped torpedo rooms. What really infuriated the men was that they received different torpedoes from the ones unloaded. This meant the new torpedoes were of an un-known quality that had to be thoroughly checked and "routined" to bring them to the same status as the ones unloaded on the Atlantic side of the canal. *Flasher* tran-sited the Panama Canal on November 30, arriving in Balboa, Canal Zone, and departing the following day for Pearl Harbor, training intensively along the way.

The new submarine arrived at Pearl Harbor on December 15, to conduct four days of refit, followed by two weeks of training. In Honolulu, Exec Ray DuBois borrowed a car from a Naval Academy friend and took fellow officers around for a tour of Oahu. Another officer had friends in Honolulu where they could visit and be entertained. The rest of the crew made the best of a short liberty in Hawaii.

Flasher had arrived at Pearl wearing overall black paint, which was fine for the North Atlantic, but too dark in the mid-Pacific latitudes. Several lighter paint schemes would provide better camouflage, and could be applied to the boat while at Pearl Harbor.

DuBois had a fellow Naval Academy lacrosse teammate at Pearl Harbor, Lt. John L. ("Whitey") Mehlig, a Navy pilot. Mehlig took DuBois up in a Navy plane to impress Ray with some scary flying, but mainly to view subs arriving and departing Pearl, so Ray could judge how different camouflage versions looked at dawn and dusk, when camouflage made the most difference. DuBois picked out what he felt was the best paint technique and informed Whitaker of his selection. *Flasher* was painted with Measure 32/3SS-B, one of the best paint schemes of the war. Her result-ant "haze-gray" camouflage would prove to be a good choice, enabling her to spot other subs before they sighted her, and to operate in surface attacks without being sighted by the enemy. (DuBois' friend, fellow alumnus and pilot, Whitey Mehlig, would be killed in enemy action February 21, 1945. Submarine assignments were not the only hazardous duty.)

Early in her service, *Flasher* also had her bridge fairwater cut down to lower her silhouette. This probably occurred at Pearl Harbor, and involved removing over a foot of the steel bulkhead from around the top of the conning tower fairwater, exposing the periscope support framing, and making less-obstructed observations possible for men standing on the decking above the conning tower. This "covered wagon" modification did not occur before Pearl Harbor, since the photo taken of *Flasher* in the Caribbean shows the unmodified bridge fairwater.

While in Pearl, Whitaker ran into his friend, Cmdr. Johnny Moore, at the officers' club. Moore was skipper of the *USS Grayback* (SS 208), back in Pearl after two very aggressive, very successful patrols. In their conversations Moore told of his daring torpedo attacks and surface gun actions. Whitaker was alarmed by Moore's talk and warned him, "Look, I think you've lost respect for the enemy, and unless you learn better, you're not going to come back from one of these patrols." Moore dismissed the danger, saying, "They can't lay a glove on me."

Grayback would leave Pearl less than a month after *Flasher* to conduct her third, very hot patrol under Moore. She would sink another three cargo vessels and a tanker, before she herself was sunk with her crew of 80 men off Okinawa by Japanese antisubmarine attacks. In just five fiery months Moore and his

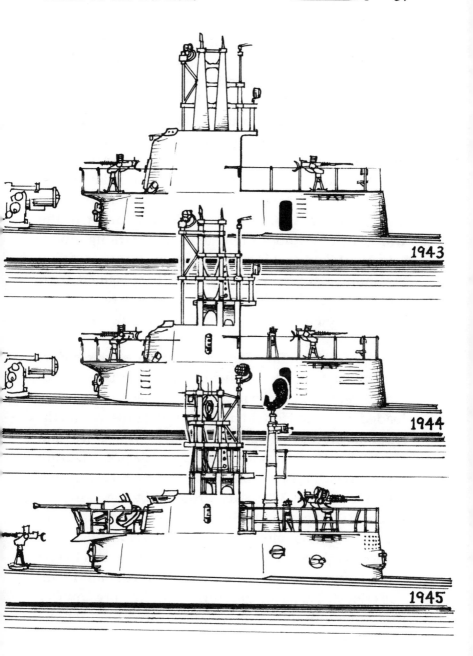

Flasher Bridge Fairwater and Armament Modifications,
1943 - 1945 (by Author)

crew had sunk at least ten enemy vessels over 500 tons, including a destroyer, for a total of over 50,000 tons.

Flasher participated in several days of torpedo attack approaches on the submarine rescue vessel USS Florikan (ASR 9) in the vicinity of Pearl Harbor, making frequent alterations in course and numerous dives, and conducting surface training. After the training Whitaker approached Commander Mike Fenno, Flasher's "training officer" at Pearl, and veteran skipper of Trout (SS 202) and Runner (SS 275) earlier in the war. "I think I ought to extend this training a bit," said Whitaker, seeking an extension. Fenno replied, "Dammit, Reuben, you've got the best-trained crew I've seen yet! Why do you want to stay here and train more?" No amount of training was enough to satisfy Whitaker.

Also attending Flasher's torpedo exercises during Christmas week in Hawaii was Commander Spike Hottel, an expert in the new Mark 18 electric torpedoes loaded aboard. Hottel had been one of the vocal critics of the defective magnetic exploders when it was still politically dangerous to question the devices. During the exercises on December 21, Flasher received two depth charges at 300 yards, dropped by the destroyer escort USS Wyman (DE 38). On December 23, Flasher returned to moor alongside the USS Scorpion (SS-278), veteran of three hazardous war patrols. In less than a week Scorpion would depart on her fourth patrol with her crew of 77, never to return. She was presumably lost to enemy mines as she attempted to enter the Yellow Sea.

After the new year, more torpedoes were fired and sound tests were conducted in Pearl Harbor's west loch. The submarine also "depermed" or "degaussed," by going through an underwater demagnetizing field at Pearl Harbor that would hopefully make the boat less likely to detonate magnetic mines. Even now, almost a half century later, ships still "run the ranges" to make them less likely to detonate the mines left at sea from World War II, and other mines more recently deposited.

Flasher returned to the submarine base and moored alongside another new sub, the *USS Angler* (SS 240). Angler had also been built by Electric Boat and was commissioned the week after *Flasher*. She would be rerouted on her first patrol by General Douglas MacArthur to rescue an incredible 58 men, women, and children from a Japanese-held Philippine island. It was to be very cramped aboard *Angler* on her first patrol.

After *Angler* departed for her exercises the next morning, *Flasher* moved in next to the dock to take on stores, torpedoes and ammunition for the four-inch gun and the two 20mm guns. Divers also came alongside in their diving boat to work on *Flasher's* sea valves. The last payday for a while was held shortly before noon. On January 5, she took on fuel oil and lubricating oil as well as stores and fresh water for the upcoming patrol. The following day sailing preparations continued and a noon muster showed the boat's full complement prepared for departure, along with a passenger, Lt.(jg) Raymond Knight, to be transported by *Flasher* for duty at Midway.

Chart of First Patrol (Jan. 6, 1944 to Feb. 29, 1944), excluding Hawaii
to Western Pacific (by Author)

CHAPTER 4

ENGAGING THE ENEMY
FLASHER'S FIRST WAR PATROL

S hortly after noon on January 6, 1944, *Flasher* eased from the pier to begin her first war patrol, proceeding on two main engines southward through Pearl Harbor's antisubmarine net entrance, thereafter zigzagging on a base course of 322°, headed for the Midway Atoll. The stunning defeat of the superior Japanese carrier fleet at Midway 19 months earlier left the American submarine force with a valuable forward base for refit and refueling, allowing subs from Pearl Harbor to patrol an additional 2,600 miles on station.

The five-day trip to Midway found *Flasher* alternating main engines, practicing dives, and occasionally sighting friendly vessels and aircraft. Because of westward progress, ship's clocks were set back to conform with the Midway time zone and on the morning of January 10, *Flasher* took aboard a pilot to steer the boat through the treacherous, coral-flanked channel to the submarine piers at Midway. Just one week after *Flasher* came through this channel her sister submarine *Flier* (SS 250), built at EB next to *Flasher*, would smash against this reef, delaying her first war patrol another four months while she returned stateside for repairs.

Mooring alongside the sub *USS Herring* (SS 233) at the submarine piers in Midway, *Flasher* began taking on fuel, and detached Lt. Knight for his duty assignment there. During an aggressive patrol five months later, *Herring* would be lost with all hands in the icy waters north of Japan to Japanese shore artillery.

On the trip from New London to the war zone, the brand new *Flasher* had leaked excessively through a "soft patch" in the hull, right over the crews' quarters and the aft battery compartment. It was discovered in Connecticut that one of *Flasher's* 252 electrical batteries was defective, and a hole in the pressure hull had been cut to extract and replace the 1,660-pound electric battery. The area was resealed, but the seal leaked. Seaman Brokovich was the unfortunate sailor who bunked directly under the leak, and had to sleep wearing a raincoat.

Because the leak was over the aft battery compartment, and because water mixed with the battery acid would emit toxic chlorine gas, another sailor was assigned to catch the runoff from the bunk in buckets. Attempts to tighten the seal at Key West, the Canal Zone, and Pearl Harbor proved unsuccessful, so the area was finally unsealed and taken apart at Midway. Workmen found that Electric Boat workers had failed to remove raised welding beads from the hull, which prevented the patch from mating with the hull. The EB workmen had also omitted a canvas gasket and grommets necessary to seal the patch. This generated proper repairs, a memo from Commander, Submarine Base 128 to ComSubPac (Commander Submarine Pacific), and ultimately, from ComSubLant (Commander, Submarines Atlantic – Admiral Daubin) to BuShips (Chief, Bureau of Ships) complaining of the "poor workmanship" on *Flasher's* soft patch in Groton.

While at Midway she also had temporary repairs made to the forward deck that had been damaged by rough seas on the trip from Pearl. Lookout John Precup had also been knocked around by the pounding waves, injuring his right arm on the periscope shears. The boat, repaired and fueled to capacity, departed the harbor the same afternoon. She adopted a zigzag course to frustrate any lurking Japanese submarines.

Prior to departure from Midway the crew had been mustered, revealing no unauthorized absentees, as if someone would desert at the desolate atoll. Nevertheless, the log reflects a strange entry made three hours out of Midway, when at 7:30 p.m.:

> Discovered that we had a TM3 from Division 44 Relief Crew aboard as stowaway. Put him to work.

Unknown to the officers of the *Flasher*, Torpedoman Joe Holmes came aboard when she arrived at Midway, and sailed off with her. For an 18-year-old who had enlisted shortly after Pearl Harbor, Holmes had already compiled an impressive service record, having served in *Growler's* (SS 215) first three war patrols, followed by two in *Grayback*, Cmdr. Johnny Moore's submarine that would soon be lost.

After *Flasher* had docked at Midway, Holmes saw his friend and former *Growler* shipmate, Bill Pearce. Pearce invited Holmes aboard, into *Flasher's* forward torpedo room. (Whereas Holmes left *Growler* after her third war patrol, Pearce stayed on for the deadly fourth patrol where she clashed with an armed

Japanese vessel, leaving *Growler's* skipper, Howard W. Gilmore, and two others dead, and the sub with severe bow damage. Gilmore was posthumously awarded the Congressional Medal of Honor for ordering *Growler* to submerge while he remained topside. Pearce had gone into the water after the incident to help with *Growler's* repairs or to free one of the exposed torpedoes. Now Pearce was a Torpedoman First Class on *Flasher*.)

When *Flasher's* crew was mustered topside prior to departure, Holmes was left alone in the torpedo room. Wanting to get back into the shooting war, he saw his chance. Holmes lifted the deck plates and slid into *Flasher's* torpedo room bilges. A few hours out he heard from the torpedo room conversation that *Flasher's* escort had been released to return to Midway, so he pushed up the deck plates and came out. Pearce took him to DuBois, who informed the captain. (Anyone who went straight to the skipper instead of through DuBois would have been in BIG TROUBLE with *Flasher's* no-nonsense exec.)

Whitaker asked Holmes why he stowed away. Holmes answered, "I just wanted to go with *Flasher* on her first war patrol." Whitaker told Holmes he might be sorry as he might not make it back alive. Holmes received several tough work assignments the first day or two, and then settled down to routine as a regular member of the crew. Because of his valuable experience as a torpedoman, he was a welcome addition to a sub manned mostly by men making their first war patrol.

Whitaker must have found it difficult to be stern with a sailor who deserted relatively safe shore duty for a hazardous submarine war patrol. Holmes would remain with *Flasher* for four patrols, and would be known to his shipmates as "Stowaway," or a shortened version: "Stoway."

The week following the departure from Midway was predictably occupied with even more training, including quick submergences, depth-charge drills, steering-casualty drills, and battle-surface practices using targets obtained at Midway. The crew fired six rounds from the four-inch forward gun and 60 rounds from the two 20mm guns located on the fairwater decks. Flasher lost a day crossing the International Date Line January 11-12, 1944.

Whitaker became worried that the fuel consumption of 13½ gallons per mile consumed while trying to average 13½ knots was excessive in heavy seas. He cut *Flasher's* speed to 12 knots until better weather would allow calmer seas and less fuel consumption.

On January 15, Whitaker decided their current "great-circle" track due west would take the sub within 30 miles of Japanese-held Marcus Island, and the unattractive prospect of being constantly chased under by planes from the island. Besides the obvious danger from aircraft, submergences would mean a loss of speed and flexibility, and substantial delays. Little Marcus Island (consisting of only 740 acres and now known as Minami-Tori-Shima), was Japanese-held prior to World War II.

Whitaker obtained a new plot to pass 80 miles north of Marcus in the hope of remaining on the surface and avoiding planes. The new course also meant *Flasher* would pass no closer than 120 miles to Marcus during the dangerous daylight hours. Seas increased the night of January 16 while *Flasher* was still about 150 miles away from the island. The next day Whitaker "changed to one-engine speed as seas became pretty rough and we started taking considerable water down conning tower hatch." Water down the hatch was more than a discomfort. It could damage delicate electrical equipment, and a really big wave could swamp the boat.

Proceeding westerly on the surface, *Flasher's* lookouts intensely scanned the horizon in all directions. Standard naval procedure required at least one officer and three sailors scanning three 140°, overlapping segments to port, starboard and aft. On *Flasher*, Whitaker had six men (two officers, four lookouts) scanning four 110°, overlapping sectors of the air, horizon and sea, plus a seventh man as "sun lookout," looking directly into the sun through special glasses. According to Whitaker, "Any pilot with a good brain would approach you from the sun."

Standing watch as a lookout on a World War II submarine was a demanding assignment. It allowed for absolutely no "small talk." Speaking was allowed only when a target was sighted or the watch was relieved by the next group of lookouts, contrary to the conversational image sometimes portrayed in Hollywood movies. To keep the lookouts fresh aboard *Flasher*, their watches were limited to two hours.

Each lookout methodically scanned his assigned segment over and over again. Visual sweeps began by searching the water from the sub to the horizon for one half of the sector through the binoculars, then lowering the binoculars to sweep the entire sector of sky, horizon and water with the naked eyes. Then the other half of the water to the horizon area was searched with binoculars, followed by a search of the horizon and lower sky, before dropping the binoculars for another unaided visual sweep of the entire segment. Then the lookout used the binoculars for a search of the remaining half of the horizon and lower sky. After dropping the binoculars for an unaided sweep, half segments of the upper sky were viewed through the binoculars before repeating the entire process.

Two of *Flasher's* best lookouts proved to be Seaman First Class John Precup and Boatswain's Mate Louis P. Reichert. A score sheet tacked on the bulkhead of the crews' quarters recorded the sightings and showed Reichert and Precup were always the big winners in the contest to be the first to spot enemy vessels. The winner received a coveted bottle of whiskey from the States or five Australian pounds, plus the respect of his captain and shipmates. Motor Machinist Frank DeBois received a bottle of Schenley's for spotting a plane once, and a lot of kidding for sighting "a man swimming in the water." DeBois saw the man through the periscope while visiting Signalman Doty in the conning tower. The skipper was summoned, and identified the "man" as a turtle.

Every dive *Flasher* made was made at full speed, and the lookouts had to scramble down fast, whether or not the boat was under attack. Getting below from the lookout posts was no easy task. Men on the upper decking around the periscope shears had to swing down eight feet to the bridge deck, clamber another nine feet through the narrow hatchway on a metal ladder to the conning tower steel deck, and descend through another hatch nine or ten feet to the control room deck below, all at breakneck speed. Most of the unyielding, slick metal surfaces provided sharp edges and poor traction, compounded by the ever-present wetness from ocean spray. Rough seas made the process all the more hazardous. Even the most coordinated, athletic personnel sooner or later sported major body bruises.

On January 18, the wind associated with the rough seas completely stopped, and the seas calmed to a slight swell. At 7 a.m., Precup sighted smoke to the south at about 15 miles. *Flasher* changed course to close on the smoke and increased speed to standard. Normal procedure called for heading directly at a sighting. Then the relative movement of the smoke to port or starboard would reveal which way the target was going, and the sub could alter course to intercept. Closing on the smoke revealed the target ship was headed easterly, back in the direction *Flasher* had just travelled. Also, an escorting Kawanishi H6K ("Mavis") patrol bomber was sighted above the ship, conducting a submarine search from seven miles in front of the target, to three miles astern. Whitaker altered course to the east to avoid being sighted and to parallel the target, with the hope the plane would return to base after verifying an absence of enemy submarines. Whitaker believed that *Flasher's* new "gray paint prevented him from sighting us."

As Whitaker anticipated, the escorting Mavis departed an hour later without seeing the surfaced submarine. *Flasher* proceeded with an "end-around" maneuver, where the sub parallelled the target's course at a faster speed to arrive in front of the target undetected, submerge, and wait for the target's approach. This was a tactic well practiced by American submariners by this stage of the war. As the target was zigzagging and making no more than 11 knots, *Flasher* readily outran it and three hours later submerged 15 miles ahead of the target. After 30 minutes *Flasher* sighted the mast of the ship, now identified as a freighter, "zigging radically with about 40° to 50° zigs every five minutes." There was also a patrol boat (SC type) escort off the freighter's starboard bow, so Whitaker decided to attack from the port side.

Shortly after noon *Flasher* was ready to fire from her four stern tubes when Whitaker raised the periscope for a final bearing. He saw the freighter had zigged towards *Flasher* so that it now had a 10° starboard angle on bow (AOB). This meant that the sub was located 10° off the freighter's starboard bow, and the freighter would soon be crossing in front of *Flasher's* unprepared bow tubes, not the stern tubes.

Whitaker ordered flank submerged speed to cross the target's new track so the stern tubes could still be used, but the "ship apparently saw wake and turned away." *Flasher* then slowed for Whitaker to steal another glimpse through the periscope, but just as it broke the surface, the target's escort dropped its first depth charge 500 yards away. Whitaker, who remained at periscope depth despite the depth charge, "took look at target but saw no hope of firing as freighter had pulled clear."

Flasher's approach on its first target had not gone at all well. She then went deep (to 300 feet), but could find no "temperature gradient," where a difference in water temperature or density caused sonar waves to bounce back to the surface. Radioman Vince Filippone maintained *Flasher's* delicate and important bathyther-mograph (BT), that traced seawater temperature changes on a candle-smoked card. Even without the gradient, the sub avoided the escort, because at 12:43 p.m. the second (and last) depth charge was dropped far away.

Twenty minutes later Whitaker brought *Flasher* back to periscope depth to watch the escort rejoin the target six miles to the southeast. She surfaced when the target was 15 miles away to perform another end around. The freighter was easily tracked by the heavy smoke she emitted from burning less refined fuel. At the same time the enemy ship was unable to see or detect the low profile of the sub as she made her end around on the surface at high speed.

Amid darkening skies, *Flasher* began closing on the target on the surface. Whitaker guessed from added smoke that the freighter now had a second escort. The crew was called to battle stations (where they probably were already), and *Flasher* commenced the "approach" phase of the attack, with a radar-generated range to the target of seven and a half miles.

During surface attacks Whitaker chose to be on the bridge as Safety Officer. With him was Tom McCants operating the Target Bearing Transmitter (TBT), a pair of bridge-mounted binoculars connected to the Torpedo Data Computer (TDC) located in the conning tower. DuBois, as Exec, would command the fire-control party in the conning tower, consisting of Glennon on the TDC, with Kristl assisting Glennon on the torpedo spreads. Burke (with Signalman Corneau or another assisting) was stationed at the plotting table, manually analyzing the position of the target and the torpedo-firing solution, while the TDC computed the same data. As Diving Officer, Coffin would be stationed with the men at the diving controls whether *Flasher* was at submerged or surfaced battle stations.

The surface battle stations arrangement presented one problem. The Target Bearing Transmitter (TBT) binoculars were permanently mounted at normal eye level, but McCants was too short to reach them without stretching. (To pass the Naval Academy minimum 5'4" height requirement, he had been carried to the doctor's office on a stretcher by his friends, under the theory the human spine settles during the day, and a person is tallest in the morning. Even then McCants passed the physical only because of his then-thick hair, liberally fortified with the doctor's vaseline.) One of the crew salvaged a crate for McCants to stand on to reach the TBT. During one attack the crate was left below, and McCants had to operate the TBT by standing on his toes. As *Flasher* closed on the target, Whitaker stood very close to ask details and hear responses. After one extended period of standing on his toes, McCants came down hard, his heels crushing the Captain's toes. Whitaker, as Safety Officer on surface attacks, was the only one aboard injured in the attack.

In submerged approaches, Whitaker was the Attack Officer, and manned the periscope. His executive officer then became detached from any single responsibility. Instead, DuBois was to perform "quality control" functions. Whitaker's idea was that the exec, freed from any single responsibility, could look over everyone's shoulder, checking to make sure no mistakes were made. "He even caught me in a mistake once or twice," said Whitaker, "Goddamn, that's al-

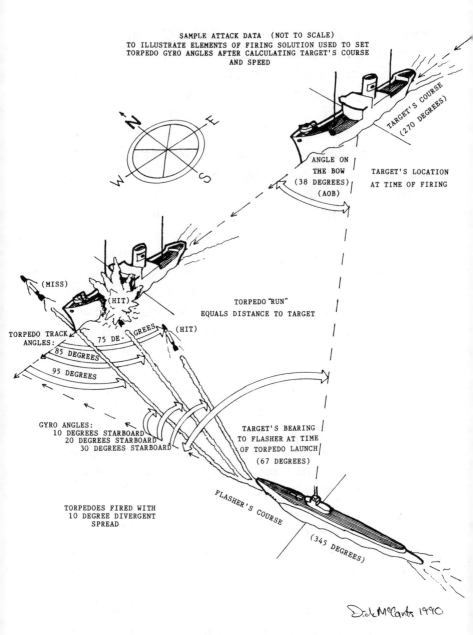

SAMPLE ATTACK DATA (NOT TO SCALE)
TO ILLUSTRATE ELEMENTS OF FIRING SOLUTION USED TO SET
TORPEDO GYRO ANGLES AFTER CALCULATING TARGET'S COURSE
AND SPEED

TARGET'S COURSE (270 DEGREES)

ANGLE ON THE BOW (38 DEGREES) (AOB)

TARGET'S LOCATION AT TIME OF FIRING

(MISS)

(HIT)

TORPEDO "RUN" EQUALS DISTANCE TO TARGET

TORPEDO TRACK ANGLES:
75 DE-GREES
85 DEGREES
95 DEGREES

(HIT)

GYRO ANGLES:
10 DEGREES STARBOARD
20 DEGREES STARBOARD
30 DEGREES STARBOARD

TARGET'S BEARING TO FLASHER AT TIME OF TORPEDO LAUNCH (67 DEGREES)

TORPEDOES FIRED WITH 10 DEGREE DIVERGENT SPREAD

FLASHER'S COURSE

(345 DEGREES)

Dick McCants 1990

Sample Attack Data (by Author)

most unforgivable!"

In this approach *Flasher* was making her attack at night, on the surface:

1815   Commenced closing target at 19 knots. It now appears that he has changed base course to about 130° T. and is still using a radical zig plan.

1842   Battle stations, commenced approach radar range 14,850 yards. Radar picked up two escorts at 8,000 yards, one on each bow of target and about 1500 yards from track. Took station 6,000 yards from target on his port bow and waited for favorable opportunity to attack.

1930   Port escort had dropped well aft and target zigged toward. Headed in for seventy port track at 10 knots.

1936   Fired 4 torpedoes from bow tubes with torpedo run about 2,450 yards, track about 70° port, target speed 10.5 knots. At this time we were about 20° on the port bow of the port escort at a range of about 2300 yards. Commenced turning left with full rudder after firing; went ahead flank (18 knots).

1937-30 Observed hit about midway between stack and stern. Sparks flew about 200 feet into the air and target began to settle rapidly by the stern. Fifteen seconds after first torpedo hit, another hit was heard but not observed as we were busy with escorts.

1938   Port escort astern, range 2200 yards.

1941   Escorts dropped first of about ten depth

charges. This was nice as it showed that they thought we were submerged. We opened out to 5500 yards and circled toward other side of target to be sure he sank.

2022   Observed target sink, and at same time he disappeared from radar screen. Commenced clearing area at four engine speed. Escorts still dropping depth charges.

2115   Went to course 270° T. at two engine speed, heading for area.

The ship *Flasher* sank on January 18, 1944, was the 2,980-ton *Yoshida Maru*, requisitioned in 1941 by the Japanese and converted to a gunboat, and then converted again to an oil carrier in 1943. The sub's pursuit and attack had taken over 12 hours. It was the first damage inflicted by the new submarine, other than to the torpedoed coal dock at Newport. After the sinking, *Flasher* headed due north for 45 minutes to clear the area, before resuming her prior course due west. A lookout sighted a searchlight astern, and Whitaker was called to the bridge. Post-attack jitters had mistaken the rising moon for an enemy searchlight.

Whitaker had told DuBois that while he was on *Sturgeon* he felt the sub claimed credit for too many sinkings, since some of the ships were not actually seen to sink. For *Flasher*, Whitaker wanted to witness each sinking if at all possible before making any claim the ship had sunk. Unless the sub was actually being chased by escorts, Whitaker would not break away until the sinking had been visually confirmed. During the war *Flasher* claimed credit for few sinkings where the targets were not seen disappearing beneath the

waves.

On January 20, *Flasher* made her morning dive for two reasons. The first was to check the boat's "trim," that affects the ability to keep the boat balanced, maneuverable and level underwater. Trim was maintained by complex movements of fluids from one area of the submarine to another. This was the responsibility of the Diving Officer, planesmen, and men manning the trim manifold and pumps. Controlling a World War II submarine in the three-dimensional underwater world was a demanding task, requiring both technical expertise and skill. Even the shift in balance caused by one man walking from the forward to aft torpedo rooms could change the boat's trim. For this reason movement through the boat was discouraged. Trim dives were made regularly to check the boat's balance, as supplies were consumed and torpedoes were expended.

The second reason for the morning dive was to remove a flooded torpedo from the number-seven stern tube, where it malfunctioned during the freighter attack. It was determined on inspection that this torpedo, obtained from Pearl Harbor, lacked an essential watertight gasket. Had the torpedo been fired it would have run erratically or well below its set depth because of the additional weight. The torpedo tubes were always loaded with live torpedoes during war patrols, but not flooded until shortly before firing. When torpedo tube number seven was flooded in preparation for the attack on the freighter, the torpedo in it had leaked.

Pulling the torpedo in the rear torpedo room was difficult since no stern torpedoes had been fired

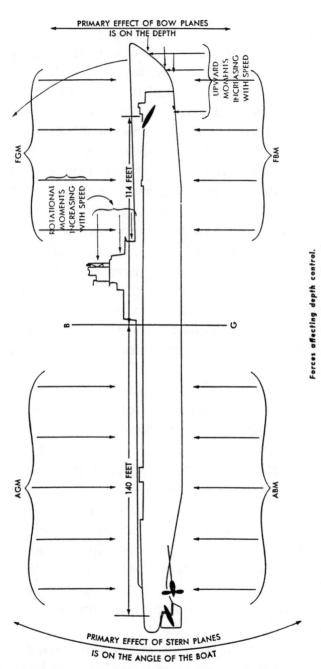

Forces Affecting Depth Control (Navpers 16160)

and there was no room to maneuver. Further complicating matters was the submarine's continued rolls about five degrees to each side, even though she dove to 100 feet seeking better stability than on the surface.

Lt. Phil Glennon, as Gunnery Officer, was responsible for torpedo performance. During his last patrol on the successful *USS Greenling* prior to joining *Flasher*, Glennon had been Assistant Approach Officer during a torpedo's "circular run." A jam or malfunction of the torpedo's steering mechanism caused it to travel in a wide, circular path. At least two American submarines lost in the war were sunk by their own, circling torpedoes. *Greenling's* erratic torpedo passed by just aft of the stern section. The close call on *Greenling*, in Glennon's words, "made a Christian out of me."

To eliminate future torpedo leaks and erratic runs, a mandatory procedure was initiated by Glennon that was to continue on *Flasher* throughout the war. Every one of her 24 torpedoes would be loaded into a torpedo tube and flooded while the boat was submerged at 100 feet, where water pressure exceeded the depth where the torpedo was expected to be launched. Then the tube was blown dry and the torpedo pulled and checked to see if the gaskets leaked. If not, and no other defects were found, the torpedo was cleared for firing.

Many torpedoes leaked during this test. Some were found to be lacking a gasket altogether. Torpedoes that could not be waterproofed were not fired. Although *Flasher* did encounter some torpedoes that suffered depth-mechanism malfunctions and ran too deeply, she never had a circular run that jeopardized the boat. Almost all of her war shots ran "hot, straight and normal." *Flasher's* intensive crew training, her effective leadership from officers and experienced enlisted personnel, and well thought-out procedures like this torpedo testing all contributed to her exemplary wartime record.

The following week *Flasher* headed west, conducting training exercises the whole way, and changing course from due west to a more west-southwesterly course (253°). On January 22, one of the lookouts spotted a periscope at less than a mile and *Flasher* began drastically zigzagging. Whitaker indicated in his patrol report that he did not radio the incident to Pearl Harbor as the periscope sighting may have been a false alarm.

The submarine continued on her westerly course on the surface and zigzagging. On January 24, *Flasher* came to a complete stop northeast of the Philippines, when it appeared the boat was about to run aground. After a sounding by the fathometer showed 3,000 fathoms (more than three miles) of water below the boat, she resumed her course at ten knots.

On January 25, lookouts sighted Balintang Island 17 miles to the southwest. The island lay in the channel between Formosa (Taiwan) and the Philippine island of Luzon. Since it had been two days since DuBois had been able to get a navigational fix (on the sun, stars or land), he had been forced to rely on less accurate "dead reckoning" navigation. Dead reckoning allowed him to calculate the boat's position from her estimated speed and course since the last fix, but this had incorrectly projected *Flasher's* position as 20 miles southeast of her actual location. Whitaker decided to pass around the north end of Balintang

Island because of the navigational error, and to proceed through on the surface, safely hidden by the continued bad weather. This would also allow *Flasher* to arrive at the expected enemy shipping lanes during darkness. Later in the morning the visibility suddenly improved, two sailboats were sighted, and she submerged to avoid being spotted.

Whitaker ordered *Flasher* to run submerged during daylight from this point on. She surfaced after dusk to proceed at two-engine speed toward the probable traffic lanes of shipping between Manila and Japan. *Flasher* was now in "convoy college," very desirable hunting grounds and much in demand by submarine captains because of the numerous enemy targets.

Still, the next day proved uneventful as *Flasher* conducted her patrol submerged. She surfaced after sunset to begin recharging her depleted electrical storage batteries. Soon the soundman picked up a contact to the south, and she headed toward the contact on the surface to investigate. Despite two-engine speed, she was unable to close on the target, which appeared to be intentionally avoiding *Flasher*. After initially deciding the small contact was probably an enemy patrol boat, Whitaker began to worry that it was a friendly submarine that was evading because it thought *Flasher* was a Japanese patrol boat. Since *Flasher's* assigned area was farther south and this area off Northern Luzon was assigned to another sub, Whitaker discontinued the chase and secured his tracking party.

About 1:30 the following morning (January 27), *Flasher* entered her assigned patrol area off the west coast of Japanese-occupied Luzon. She stayed within ten to 15 miles of land during most of this time, watching for traffic close to the coast by submerged periscope watches during the day, and with radar and lookouts on the surfaced submarine at night, as she gradually continued down the coastline toward the Bataan Peninsula, Corregidor and Manila Bay.

On January 28, a crewman developed a serious subperiosteal abscess in his right leg, that caused high fever and swelling. *Flasher's* pharmacist could only treat the man with sulpha drugs and dressings. The patient was unable to perform his duties for the remainder of the war patrol.

Just before dawn on the 29th, lookouts sighted lights ten miles to the northeast. *Flasher* closed on the surface at ten knots, only to discover the target was a large Japanese hospital ship, estimated at 9,000 to 10,000 tons, making 14 knots towards Manila and displaying all the proper hospital ship identification lights. Whitaker was chagrined: "Sure hated to let this one go as I don't believe in hospital ships and at any rate, unescorted ships are rare these days." McCants facetiously offered to take over the attack, claiming he was "color blind" and that would be the excuse for the sinking.

By this stage of the war many believed the Japanese were using hospital ships improperly to carry troops and war supplies, and there had been little indication to the Americans that any humane treatment was reciprocated by the Japanese. Japanese author Ienaga points out the hospital ship *Awa Maru*, mistakenly attacked by the submarine *Queenfish* (SS 393), was secretly transporting prohibited rubber, tin and other war materials when sunk.

Most Americans had developed an intense

hatred of the Japanese war machine that had ravaged China, launched the devastating sneak attack on Pearl Harbor amid diplomatic negotiations, brutally conquered the poorly defended populations of Southeast Asia and the South Pacific, and gained a reputation for unsurpassed bestiality after the Bataan Death March and similar incidents. Some of the Japanese atrocities, like those of the Nazis, were the product of government-promoted beliefs of superiority over other races and nationalities.

Flasher's poet, Signalman Charles J. Moore, reflected the growing American resentment of the Japanese in a poem he composed and distributed on the boat:

RETRIBUTION

Call down the wrath and the horrors of hell,
On the plundering Nip, and his family as well,
His all the fury and the blasting complete,
That comes when a ship and a torpedo meet.

He knows but one law, "Japan Rules Supreme,"
Until he meets up with a Yank submarine,
For ours is the vengeance that rides in the night,
He knows he's a dead man, if his ship we
    should sight.

His is a life with fear in each breath,
For he knows that we're lurking to tender him
    death.
While ours is a war of silent attrition,
As we fight for the loved ones, killed, captured
    or missing.

His is a future I envy him not,
As he roars into hell on a crashing war shot.
And although he talks big or blusters with vim,
He knows that out here, we're waiting for him.

So he curses us roundly, he vents all his spleen,
While his heart quakes in terror and his skin
　　turns to green,
For revenge is an ointment that soothes a sore
　　hurt,
And will not rest until he's ground in the dirt.

So come all you Japanese, you peons of hades,
Sail in your ships to your watery graves.
For waiting out here unsuspected, unseen,
Are the men you can't conquer in a Yank
　　submarine.

Moore knew firsthand about missing loved ones. His younger brother had been captured in the Philippines by the Japanese.

Flasher made a course change to the northwest and dove as dawn was breaking. After an uneventful day submerged, she surfaced after sunset to begin her patrol and a battery charge. Radar picked up a nearby contact, so the sub began an end around by heading westward to open out, and then northerly to parallel the target's course. Since the target was between *Flasher* and the land, it was invisible in the darkness except to radar. Whitaker decided from the target's behavior (patrolling back and forth along the same course), and its image on the radar screen, that it was probably a small patrol boat. *Flasher* therefore abandoned the chase, returning to a southerly course at midnight, to patrol off Luzon at a point 13 miles northwest of Capones Island for the next several days. Although Whitaker had decided against attacking the patrol boat, he continued to follow "with him as guide" southward. While still tailing the patrol boat, a fire developed after midnight in the maneuvering room, just after the battery charge was secured. The sub began circling to starboard and switched to battery propulsion before extinguishing the fire. The fire's cause was never determined.

At dawn *Flasher* submerged for another periscope patrol. A periscope was sighted a half mile away, but it turned out to be a stick attached to a float. Other sightings during the day included sailboats and a small two-masted vessel of approximately 150 tons, that was probably a native Philippine vessel that Whitaker did not want to attack, or a small Japanese patrol boat that was not worth torpedoes, even if they could hit the shallow-draft vessel.

Later in the afternoon, a ship was sighted nine miles to the southeast, bringing *Flasher* to battle stations once more. When the distance to the target closed to five and a half miles, the target turned out to be another 8,000- to 9,000-ton hospital ship, causing *Flasher* to secure from battle stations. Whitaker commented the target was:

> ...probably the same ship as we sighted before on his way to Manila. This one was hard to pass up as we were in beautiful position for attack. Took pictures of hospital ship at 4,000-yard range and resumed patrol.

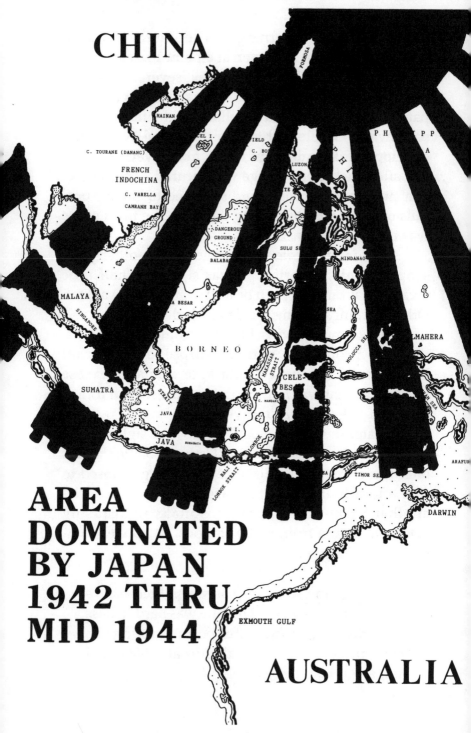

Area Dominated by Japan 1942 thru Mid-1944 (by Author)

That night was uneventful except for a patrol boat *Flasher* avoided. The following day was also uneventful with Whitaker conducting a periscope patrol in seas too calm for his liking. He commented that "the water has been like a mill pond ever since we have been here. Sure would like a few whitecaps." In addition to the ease of spotting a periscope in calm water, there was the danger the entire submarine was visible to patrol planes as the sub lay just underneath the calm surface. Prewar drills had repeatedly demonstrated aircraft's ease in spotting submarines in such waters.

On February 1, *Flasher* surfaced after patrolling submerged all day to find her vital SJ surface radar out of commission. The SJ radar was used to spot land and ships, while the non-directional SD radar was primarily for aircraft. Fortunately, the SJ problem lay with a burned-out rectifier tube that was located, removed, and replaced within 45 minutes. Other problems arose concerning the loss of sensitivity, represented by a diminution in "grass" on the radar screen, that *Flasher's* trained personnel were able to correct with spare tubes.

In the days before miniaturization and transistors, the bulky electronic equipment depended on vacuum tubes that were prone to overheat or malfunction, necessitating the numerous spares carried aboard, and skill in locating and remedying malfunctions. Because of the relatively cramped quarters on submarines and the heat generated by the vacuum tubes, trouble with the electronic equipment was commonplace. The vacuum tubes were also easily damaged by shocks received during depth charge attacks. Throughout the war, *Flasher* was lucky in having an exceptionally skilled radar technician in San Francisco native

Francis O. Sherman. He was able to repair her radars after even the worst damage or malfunctions.

Compounding electrical problems on a submarine was moisture that caused failures, shorts and dangerous electrical fires if the boat's air conditioning unit failed or was turned off for any length of time, as it was during silent running to evade enemy destroyers. Some prewar Naval officials complained submarines were too "luxurious" with their air conditioning, but World War II proved that air conditioning on subs was a necessity, without which men and equipment in the tropics were unable to function as effectively.

Flasher patrolled just north of Subic Bay, at a point where Whitaker figured ships leaving Manila would pass around midnight. Nothing of consequence was sighted, so *Flasher* began a "modified retiring search curve" towards Cape Calavite to the south. At dawn she dove to find herself unable to secure all high pressure air. By going to 125 feet, the crewmen were able to secure the air and "grind in" the safety tank blow valve so that it would seat and seal properly. Whitaker felt this problem was a major defect, placing the boat in a dangerous situation during repair, since the boat was unable to blow its main ballast tanks in an emergency. He recommended in his war patrol report that this design defect be corrected on all submarines.

At Cape Calavite *Flasher* was now patrolling the mouth of the Verde Island Passage, an important Japanese shipping lane separating the major Philippine island of Luzon to the north from the smaller Mindoro Island to the south. This position also allowed the sub to intercept vessels passing through the adjacent Mindoro Strait running down the west coast of

Mindoro. These two passages were principal routes for essential enemy shipping between the home islands of Japan, Manila, and Southeast Asia on the one hand, with bases in the southern Philippines, such as Davao Gulf, Tawi Tawi, and points south, on the other.

Enemy air coverage and the proximity to enemy-held land required the sub to patrol by periscope, submerged during the daylight. If *Flasher* were sighted, enemy antisubmarine forces would arrive, and shipping would be routed around her location. She routinely surfaced to patrol approximately ten miles off the cape at night, before submerging for periscope patrols about five miles off the cape during daylight. Whitaker noted numerous sampans and sailboats during this period. On February 2, for instance, he noted:

> Sighted sampan bearing 283° T distance about 6,000 yards (Ship Contact No. 12). I would sink this one with gunfire except that he is probably a native boat and not Japanese.

After the unproductive patrolling in what should have been a good hunting area off Manila Bay, Whitaker tried to assure himself the hunting would now be better at the Verde Island Passage and Cape Calavite:

> 1847 Surfaced and resumed patrol about 10 miles southwest of Cape Calavite light. With us in this position I don't see how shipping headed from Calavite Pass to either Palawan Passage or Mindoro Strait could get by without being picked up.

Late the afternoon of February 5, the periscope watch sighted smoke five miles to the east-northeast, about a mile off the Cape Calavite light. The sub changed course to the east-southeast to intercept the contact as it proceeded down the west coast of Mindoro in Mindoro Strait. Within a half hour *Flasher* went to battle stations submerged, approximately two miles off the mountainous Mindoro Island. The island became totally black as the evening progressed and the target's silhouette merged into the dark, tropical mountain backdrop. With the target now lost, *Flasher* reversed course to open from the land and secured from battle stations. She then surfaced, bathed in a bright moonlight, but was unable to locate the target. Ten minutes later lookouts sighted the enemy ship six miles to the east:

1915　Sighted ship as he came out from land south of Cape Calavite bearing 105° T. distance 12,000 yards. We were about 120° on his starboard bow so commenced end around at three engine speed using the other engine on charge. At this point we had about 40 miles of good water before reaching Apo Island Reef so commenced making full power on the three engines (18 knots).

2017　Almost ran over small sampan. Passed him at 1,000 yards to starboard. We didn't change course or speed and neither did he.

2057　Arrived ahead of target (his base course 145° T. range 12,000 yards). Submerged, went to battle stations and commenced approach.

Decided to fire stern tubes if possible (Ship Contact No. 14).

2122 Sighted three large sampans with target and to his starboard. Had already committed myself to a starboard track by turning off in this direction so did not change my plans.

2136 With torpedo run about 1500 yards fired four torpedoes from stern tubes using periscope spread of 1/2 target length between torpedoes. After one minute and five seconds torpedo run the first torpedo hit target about 3/4 way aft. Twenty-five seconds later another hit amidship. Both were observed. Target's stern seemed to blow up when hit, and he began to sink immediately. Second hit broke him in two, and three minutes later he was out of sight, his bow disappearing in a vertical dive. Usual breaking up noises were heard.

When the second torpedo exploded, Whitaker, the only one with a periscope view, exclaimed "What devastation!" His comment soon passed through the boat, as a two-word synopsis of the attack.

2141 Two loud explosions separated by about 15 seconds. These were probably our other two torpedoes exploding at end of run but could possibly have been depth charges.

2151 The three sampans didn't seem to be chasing us so decided to chase them and went to stations for battle surface.

2159 Battle surfaced, and headed for sampans

who were now 4,000 yards away and headed for beach under forced draft.

2212   Opened fire with 4" gun at range of about 1500 yards. Fired 15 rounds of four inch and sank one sampan and damaged another with a hit which did not explode, when at:

2220   Found we were getting dangerously near shoal water so reluctantly abandoned chase and secured guns. Both 20 MM failed me in this attack. Had they worked, we could have sunk all three during this time. Target was a maru of about 4,000 similar to *Mitakesan Maru*. The sampans were steam sampans and appeared large. They were probably of about 40 tons each. Headed back to patrol traffic lanes between Cape Calavite and Palawan Passage.

In the moonlit attack, *Flasher's* large deck gun fired 15 high-capacity, four-inch-diameter rounds with point-detonating fuses at the two sampans. Whitaker rated the radar and TDC (torpedo data computer) -directed gunfire as "only fair" in spite of the fact it succeeded in sinking one of the sampans and damaging the second.

Flasher had fired only 20 shots from the two 20mm Oerlikon machine guns fore and aft of the bridge. Whitaker was upset with the miserable performances of these two guns:

The forward 20 M/M gun failed to fire after 19 rounds and the after 20 M/M gun, after the first round. Both failures

were due to sluggish trigger mechanisms.

Whitaker complained of this in his gun action report
and repairs were to be performed on the guns during
refit. Nevertheless, *Flasher's* 20mm guns never lived up
to expectations. Other boats must have had similar
experiences or the war proved the 20mm's were inadequate, since most major overhauls of submarines
stateside by the end of the war replaced the Oerlikons
with the larger 40mm Bofors guns.

Based on Whitaker's identification, *Flasher* was
given credit for a 4,442-ton freighter of the *Mitakesan
Maru* class, but postwar analysis disclosed she sank a
smaller cargo vessel, the *Taishin Maru* (1,723 tons) on
the night of February 5, 1944. Although there were
some exceptions, estimates of enemy shipping sunk by
American submarines were overstated during the war.
It was only after the surrender of Japan and the investigation by the Joint Army Navy Assessment Committee (JANAC) that more accurate (but still imperfect)
figures of enemy sinkings were obtained. Compared
to some submarines, *Flasher's* estimates were extremely
conservative, and it was only after the postwar assessment that she turned out to be the top American
submarine in officially confirmed sinkings of enemy
tonnage. Consistent overestimation of damage was a
trait shared by most of the warring forces. The
Japanese claimed they sank 468 American submarines
during the war, or about ten times U.S. losses to all
Japanese antisubmarine actions. The Royal Air Force
claimed three times the number of German planes
actually destroyed in the Battle of Britain. By compari-

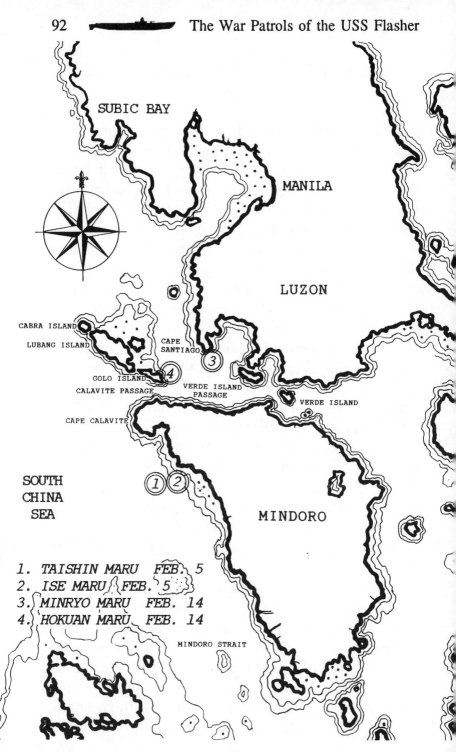

SUBIC BAY

MANILA

LUZON

CABRA ISLAND

LUBANG ISLAND

CAPE SANTIAGO

③

GOLO ISLAND ④

CALAVITE PASSAGE

VERDE ISLAND PASSAGE

VERDE ISLAND

CAPE CALAVITE

SOUTH CHINA SEA

① ②

MINDORO

1. *TAISHIN MARU FEB. 5*
2. *ISE MARU FEB. 5*
3. *MINRYO MARU FEB. 14*
4. *HOKUAN MARU FEB. 14*

MINDORO STRAIT

Chart of Mindoro, Verde Island Passage and Southern Luzon
(by Author)

son to these claims, American overestimations of ship sinkings were modest.

The sampans sunk and damaged were not counted in JANAC's postwar analysis, which only counted vessels over 500 tons. Cmdr. John D. Alden's research of "ULTRA" intercepts (the decoding of Japanese radio traffic by U.S. Naval Intelligence), indicates the sampans may have been the *Ise Maru* and the *Kamhoku Maru*.

Whitaker recorded in his patrol report that the attack on the sampans was broken off as he "found we were getting dangerously near shoal water." Burke had read the fathometer and called out that *Flasher* was in extremely shallow water. The gauge generated a multiple signal that spread over a large segment of the dial, and so could give a misleading reading. The charts showed deeper water in that location, but American charts were notoriously inaccurate. *Flasher* may still have been in deep water, but because of the alarm the screws were reversed, sending a shudder through the boat and mystifying Gunner's Mate George Markham and the rest of the gun crews blasting away topside.

Radioman Vince Filippone, told to double-check Burke's reading on the fathometer, yelled topside that *Flasher* had over 200 fathoms below her, but *Flasher* had begun backing and the attack had already broken off. Burke's action did not escape the crew's notice, and poet Moore created the following merciless commentary:

CONUNDRUM
(Riddle)

I take up the pen like a diligent clerk
To write of a man called "Four Fathoms Burke"
A man quite courageous, upright and true
Yet he carried the curse of a size 14 shoe.

They had just battle surfaced, all was going quite
    well
While the crew slammed the Japs with shot and
    with shell
Full speed ahead while the Nips blew apart
When up came the word that chilled every man's
    heart

The words put an end to that merry fight
And half the crew near dropped dead of fright
"Sir, the fathometer reading is only Four!
It shouldn't be much longer before we're ashore"

"Ye Gods," cried the Captain, "can I believe my
    ears"
Will someone tell me what we're doing here?
Cut in all engines, Full back astern
Cause to eat rice and sake I never did yearn."

"Now, how many fathoms?" he inquired once more
And back came the answer, "The reading is Four."
They finally managed to maneuver about
Then started to sea, when they heard someone
    shout

"Belay that word sir!" Came the bellow resounding
"There has been a mistake in the fathometer
   sounding
Instead of reading in fathoms just four
We found it reads two hundred or more."

Now here is the question, it is quite profound
How close were they really to running aground?
Were they in danger or was it the work
Of the man they had nicknamed "Four
   Fathoms Burke."

When you did ANYTHING on a submarine, every-body soon knew about it.

Even though *Flasher's* attacks announced her presence in the area, Whitaker decided to remain and patrol as before. Submerged five miles off Cape Calavite the next day, *Flasher* sighted through the periscope a Mitsubishi A6M2-N ("Rufe") airplane at five miles. The Rufe, a Japanese Zero with a large pontoon float and two small outriggers attached, was searching for the sub. Instead of deep submergence, Whitaker kept the boat at periscope depth to watch the plane until it disappeared.

Flasher sighted various sailboats but no worth-while targets for two days, then proceeded north on the surface early on the morning of February 8, to patrol the area west of Manila. She spent the day at periscope depth about 20 miles northwest of Cabra Island, which lies at the western mouth of Verde Island Passage. This would be a likely point for shipping headed in or out of Manila. *Flasher* travelled farther north the following night to patrol northwest of Manila Bay for a day, but this netted only a Mitsubishi A6M Zero fighter and another Rufe float plane patrolling nearby.

After surfacing the night of February 9, *Flasher* chased a surface contact to the north-northwest. Whitaker started an end around but was barred by shoal water, so he slowed and trailed the target. In the bright moonlight it appeared to be a patrolling destroyer, which suddenly reversed course toward *Flasher*. Whitaker reported as follows:

2340　Target came about and headed on course about 230° T. with range 12,000 yards we turned 180° and put our tail to him. He sighted us and gave us a zero angle on bow and started closing the range.

February 10, 1944
　　　　We ran with him until range closed to 10,000 yards when, thinking him to be a destroyer, and desiring to make an attack at:

0018　Submerged, and headed toward. He kept coming until range decreased to about 3,000 yards. By this time it was evident that he was a patrol boat too small to shoot at. He appeared to be something like a converted yacht.

0031　He dropped two depth charges. We remained at periscope depth in order to be in better position to avoid.

0032　Three more depth charges.

0057　He gave up and left area.

0141　Surfaced and resumed patrol.

0323   Radar contact 14,000 yards (Ship Contact No. 16). Identified to be same patrol vessel. He sighted us again at 12,000 yards and headed our way at about 14 knots. Not wishing to dive again we avoided at 18 knots.

0403   Lost contact, resumed patrol, moving south about 20 miles.

Veterans from other submarines had already experienced depth charges, but it was a new experience to most of *Flasher's* crew. The charges dropped from this hybrid patrol vessel were a good distance off, but when an experienced man like Bob Briggs was asked by novices if the explosions were nearby, he would adopt a worried look and say "Oh yes, very close, very close..." It must have been a shock to the newer men when *Flasher* was later blasted in severe depth charge attacks.

The day brought five separate enemy patrol plane sightings (four Rufes and one Zero) as *Flasher* remained submerged 12 to 18 miles off Corregidor at the mouth of Manila Bay. She moved northwest to patrol for a day, and then back off Manila for a day, sighting patrol boats each night that she avoided on the surface at high speed. Because of the difficulty in patrolling close to Manila with all the patrol boats around at night and patrol planes during the day, *Flasher* headed south on February 12, back toward Cape Calavite and the entrance to Verde Island Passage.

Verde Island Passage is in a 45-mile long east-west channel, varying from three to 17 miles wide. The channel is bounded on the north by Luzon, on the south by Mindoro, on the west by the South China Sea and the Lubang Islands, and on the east by Tayabas Bay and access to the Sibuyan Sea. At the center of the channel are two small islands, Maricaban and Verde, and the channel bottlenecks at Verde Island, where the navigable passages around the island narrow to about three miles. The only good thing about the passage is that it is all deep water except near shore.

Early in the war submarines had daringly entered the passage but had not sunk any ships there. Headquarters in Australia strongly hinted to *Flasher* in radio messages that perhaps it was time for an Allied sub (*Flasher*) to enter the passage again. This prompted an observation from Ray DuBois that the people at Fremantle headquarters "were the bravest bunch of bastards in the war." Whitaker decided that if there were no targets off Mindoro, they would enter the Verde Island Passage. No ships appeared, so *Flasher* was destined for virgin hunting grounds.

On February 13 she arrived at the western entrance to Verde Island Passage, submerged before dawn, and proceeded eastwardly through Calavite Passage into the Verde Island Passage. DuBois began charting the currents in the passage, as no information on currents was available from *Flasher's* charts. This data would be important for any escape from the area.

The submerged daytime transit was uneventful except for numerous sailboats that *Flasher* avoided without much difficulty. It was too bad no targets were seen, as Whitaker found conditions ideal for a sub: "It appears nice and peaceful in here and there are nice whitecaps. Nice weather for a periscope attack."

Shortly after dark the boat surfaced and headed into the center of the channel, about five miles north of the dark Mindoro Coast. *Flasher* charged her electrical storage batteries while remaining out of the traffic lanes, and prior to moonrise at 9:15 p.m. Soon after moonrise, an SJ radar contact appeared at seven miles, identified as a probable patrol vessel. The patrol craft soon reversed course and headed towards Manila to the northwest. At 2:45 the morning of February 14, *Flasher* got a radar contact to the east-northeast at ten miles:

0245   Radar contact bearing 070° T. range 19,350 yards (Ship Contact No. 21). It was apparent immediately that this was a rather large ship just rounding Maricaban Island, coming out of Verde Island Passage. We are now caught out of position as the target already has about 85°port angle on bow, and we only have about ten miles in which to get ahead. Got ready on four engines and commenced approach at maximum speed heading up toward Cape Santiago.

0318   We are still churning along with target now at range of about 14,500 yards with about 7,500 yards to track and Cape Santiago getting awfully large. We were trying to make up our minds to dive at this point as the moon is very bright when we sighted a patrol boat bearing 340° relative at 8,000 yards (Ship Contact No. 22). This decided things, and we submerged and commenced closing track at high speed. This patrol boat had small angle on bow, and we just hoped we hadn't been sighted and kept going. Our

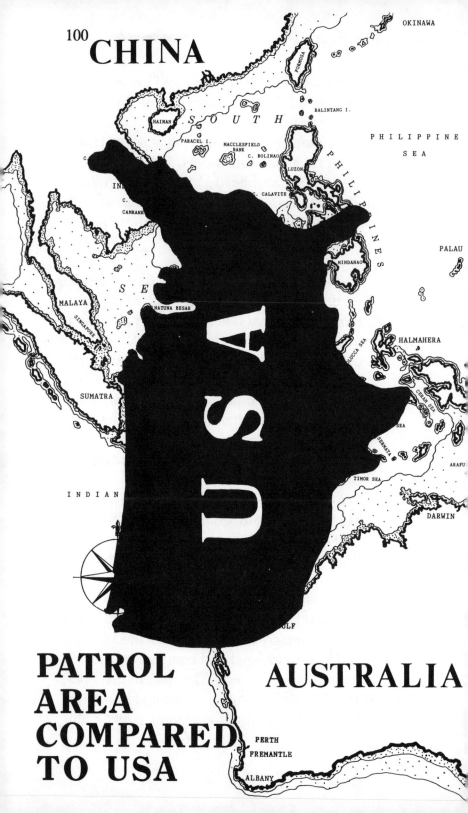

course now heads us for Cape Santiago and the navigator is worried plenty about running aground.

0335 Sighted target through periscope. He is a fairly large freighter of about 7,000 tons and has a PC boat escort on his port bow. Angle on bow about zero, range about 7,000 yards. Headed toward target.

0349 Commenced pulling off track for stern shot when target zigged 30° to left. Reversed course and headed in for a bow shot. We are now within about 2,000 yards of Cape Santiago.

0358 Fired four torpedoes from bow tubes, spread by periscope, at about 8 second intervals. One minute and fourteen seconds later one torpedo hit target between bridge and stack. This hit appeared to break his back as both ends raised and his middle began to settle. We began to watch target sink with one eye and the escort with the other. Our depth control wasn't the best at this point, the periscope was ducked, and we couldn't get back up without speed. As escort when last seen, had a small angle on bow and was making high speed, we were forced to go deep.

0405 Three depth charges, fairly close.

0412 Target screws stopped just after torpedo hit. At this point we could hear the loudest breaking up noises I have ever heard. It sounded as if he were right alongside, and I was a little worried as to whether we were too close. We feel that target sank at this time. Commenced avoiding heading in general direction of Calavite Pass. Two more depth charges, not very close.

0554   Could hear screws of two patrol boats astern, but they didn't appear close. Came up for look and saw two patrol craft at about 4,000 yards on starboard quarter. No signs of ship.

0604   One patrol craft bearing about 20° T. with zero angle on bow at about 3,000 yards. Observed him send our numeral eight with yard arm blinker. Wonder what this means to a Jap. Went down to 150 feet.

0630   Patrol boat having passed astern, came up to periscope depth for a fix so we could get through Calavite Pass. Got the fix and at the same time sighted three patrol craft astern at about 4,000-6,000 yards. Also sighted convoy of three large merchantmen with mine sweeper escort heading in from Calavite Pass (Ship Contact No. 23). This appeared a bit ironical as we had waited for days outside and seen nothing, and now we are rigged for silent running and trying to sneak out when here they come in. It was apparent that the first two ships were beyond range, but the last one was behind position with about a 60° starboard angle on bow at about 9,000 yards.

A 60° angle on the bow at 9,000 yards meant that the submarine was far out of position, and the convoy was moving away too fast. Whitaker handed the periscope to DuBois and said: "They've gotten by—Ray, you take a look." DuBois studied the three targets through the eyepiece, and then told the captain: "If we go deep, pull full power for 20 minutes, we might be able to get that last one." Whitaker agreed to try:

> Abandoned all idea of silent running and commenced approach at high speed. We only had two torpedoes loaded forward due to previous attack, so ordered forward room to reload two tubes as fast as possible. We never slowed below 4 1/2 knots during this approach and only took one look. We finally reached a point with generated torpedo run 4,000 yards with about a 97° starboard track. I was watching the torpedo run dial and it stopped decreasing at this point, so felt it was now time to fire. The forward room had done an excellent job of reloading, and four tubes were ready.

> 0648 Fired four torpedoes forward, spread by periscope with about three-fourth's ship's length between torpedoes. Two minutes and twenty-five seconds later one hit just abaft bridge. Fifteen seconds later another hit well aft. This target is estimated, I believe, conservatively at 9,000 tons.

> 0653 Still at periscope depth watching target as escort is still far away and the water is choppy. He appeared well on the way to sinking. He is well down with a good list and his whole upper works including the

bridge are blazing merrily. He apparently had gasoline on deck as these flames could hardly come from a normal ship's fire. We were enjoying the sight immensely with a play-by-play description when two aircraft bombs or depth charges landed pretty close and shook us up a bit. They did no damage except open valves and break a few light bulbs, knock cork around, and force us to go down to 275 feet, thus preventing us from seeing target sink. Commenced avoiding on a southerly course headed for Calavite Pass.

0706 The escort commenced dropping depth charges and was soon joined by one or more other patrol boats. During the next forty minutes a total of thirty-nine charges were dropped none of which were extremely close.

0711 Heard crackling noises which were probably caused by target sinking. At no time after second torpedo hit were screws of the target heard.

0815 Can no longer hear screws of patrol boats.

0824 Changed course to 260° T. heading for Calavite Pass on D.R. (dead reckoning), having obtained a fix just after firing.

0902 Water in forward bilges flooded out both sound training motors. JP still giving good results though and we shifted to hand training on JK.

0930 Came to periscope depth and got fix with Golo Island Light abeam to starboard and in the center of the Pass headed out. The

navigator had done an excellent job. Went down to 150 feet to avoid being picked up by planes.

0943 Fast screws. This fellow went right on by passing almost overhead, and then when he got about 1,000-2,000 yards ahead he reversed course and steamed by again without pausing, his screws soon fading out.

1300 Cleared western entrance of Calavite Pass. Headed out to patrol traffic lane from Calavite to Palawan Passage.

1416 Sighted land plane (Plane Contact No. 10) bearing 350° T. distant about four miles. He was apparently covering Calavite Pass waiting for us to come out.

1809 Heard two distant explosions, apparently aircraft bombs.

1848 Surfaced. Patrolling traffic lanes from Calavite to Palawan Passage. Remainder of day uneventful.

As navigator, DuBois had directed *Flasher* in a submerged escape out of Verde Island Passage and through Calavite Pass using the sound gear. He relied on the noise levels to the north from the Lubang Islands, and to the south from the Mindoro reefs. When Whitaker finally came to periscope depth for a navigational fix, *Flasher* was right where DuBois said she would be. The sound navigation had succeeded despite the JK equipment breakdown. DuBois' stock rose with the crew after this skilled navigation.

The loss of the JK sound-training motors after the second attack was due to their flooding by salt water from the forward torpedo room bilges "when the ship took a decided up angle." The loss of electrical motor-powered sound heads was partially compensated by the ability to direct the sound heads manually, but this was a poor substitute, as Whitaker remarked:

> This casualty was a major blow to our efforts of evading after the attack, as it was necessary to resort to hand training and the consequent inefficiency of operation of the equipment. It was on this occasion that the JP equipment became in its own right an integral part of our sound gear.

The JP sound gear received sonic signals, whereas the JK received supersonic signals. *Flasher* had not relied on the JP gear until it became necessary due to the loss of the JK training motors.

Radioman Paul Van De Veere operated *Flasher's* JP sound gear. He stayed with *Flasher* for six war patrols, operating the equipment calmly and confidently.

Although the training motors were submerged less than three minutes, they could not be fixed. After trying repairs for two days, the crew "jury-rigged" a small motor from a portable bilge pump along with a portable blower for cooling. This substituted for the ruined JK training motors for the remainder of the patrol. Whitaker recommended in his patrol report that the training motors in all submarines either be made waterproof or be relocated higher in the torpedo room to avoid water damage.

Whitaker also observed that the strange behavior of the last patrol boat indicated the Japanese might possess some form of "magnetic indicator" since "he never slowed to listen but made a very radical search at high speeds." Comments on enemy antisubmarine activities and evasion techniques were required in every patrol report. The Japanese did develop a "magnetic anomaly detector" (MAD) that they used in antisubmarine activities, but U.S. Naval Intelligence did not learn of this until later.

Flasher radioed Headquarters in Fremantle about the sinkings. All messages had to include extra wording (or "padding") to make code breaking more difficult for the Japanese. The padding in *Flasher's* February 14, 1944, message to Australia said "A VALENTINE PRESENT * * * * * FOR THE BOSS."

Fremantle gave *Flasher* credit for 7,000 tons and 9,000 tons for the two unidentified freighters sunk in Verde Island Passage. These two ships were identified after the war as the *Minryo Maru* at 2,193 tons and the *Hokuan Maru* at 3,712 tons, so instead of 16,000 tons, *Flasher* had sunk about 6,000 tons. As with other overestimations, the lack of good intelligence manuals on freighter identification and the fact that observations were quick glimpses through a periscope at night contributed to the over-optimistic claims.

Hokuan Maru's fatal meeting with *Flasher* was not her first contact with an American sub. Five months earlier, the same freighter-transport may have caused the sinking of the *USS Grayling* (SS 209). After the Pearl Harbor battleships were all damaged or sunk, Admiral Chester A. Nimitz assumed command of the Pacific Fleet in a ceremony conducted on *Grayling's* tiny deck. In July, 1943, *Grayling* left Australia on her

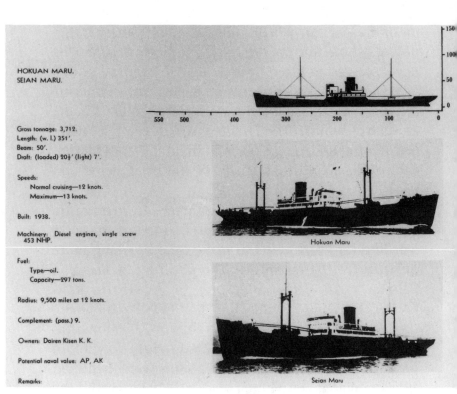

HOKUAN MARU.
SEIAN MARU.

Gross tonnage: 3,712.
Length: (w. l.) 351'.
Beam: 50'.
Draft: (loaded) 20½' (light) 7'.

Speeds:
  Normal cruising—12 knots.
  Maximum—13 knots.

Built: 1938.

Machinery: Diesel engines, single screw
  453 NHP.

Fuel:
  Type—oil.
  Capacity—297 tons.

Radius: 9,500 miles at 12 knots.

Complement: (pass.) 9.

Owners: Dairen Kisen K. K.

Potential naval value: AP, AK

Remarks:

Hokuan Maru
Seian Maru

Hokuan Maru (ONI 208-J)

eighth war patrol to deliver supplies to Philippine guerrillas on Panay. She then sank at least two Japanese vessels. *Hokuan Maru* reported sighting a submarine and then striking a submerged object at the location of the sighting, during the same period when *Grayling* disappeared with the loss of all hands.

Flasher spent the next day patrolling as before off Cape Calavite, sighting only a single patrol craft. While she still had eight torpedoes, she had been on patrol for 40 days and was very low on fuel. At midnight, February 15, she turned south toward Fremantle, Western Australia. The next two days she

proceeded surfaced at night and submerged during daylight, through Mindoro Strait into the Sulu Sea.

Flasher submerged off Calusa Island because of "reported ship movement through this area," but nothing showed until the morning of February 18. Then a vessel was sighted through the periscope and the sub began an approach on her new target. Fifteen minutes into the approach phase of the attack, the "target" was identified as another American submarine, the *USS Cod* (SS 224). Whitaker moved off *Cod's* track and let her pass by at one mile. *Cod* (now preserved as a museum and memorial in Cleveland, Ohio) was oblivious to the submerged *Flasher's* presence or approach, and sailed on to sink two enemy ships off Halmahera.

After watching *Cod* pass by, Whitaker decided *Flasher* would also conduct a surface patrol that afternoon. The faster surface speed would put her in a good position the following morning north of Pearl Bank in the southern part of the Sulu Sea. The sub proceeded on the surface the rest of the afternoon, except for one plane sighting (a "Pete"), that drove her down. Late in the afternoon *Flasher* experienced SJ radar interference. This was attributed to another friendly vessel equipped with SJ radar, probably *USS Cod* again. Whitaker continued to avoid any contact with *Cod*, however, as it was safer to evade.

It appeared *Flasher* had suffered her first loss of life when Signalman Corneau was missing after one of the dives. A check of all compartments failed to locate him. Corneau was ultimately found safe, sound, and asleep in his bunk, where he had been all the time. His bunk was the "Penthouse" on *Flasher*, so named because it was located high in the forward torpedo room under the torpedo loading hatch. The earlier search had missed the small Corneau, curled up under covers in the almost inaccessible bunk.

During *Flasher's* transit of the Sulu Sea, southward to Australia and a new base assignment, Officer of the Deck (OOD) watches continued from the bridge while surfaced, and through the periscope when submerged. The OOD's conned the boat on courses and speeds directed by the Navigator, zigzagging on the surface, and reporting all significant contacts to the captain. They also oversaw the boat's two logs—one kept by the quartermaster in rough form, and a second in "smooth" form by the OOD, digesting the watch events to their most succinct form. The following are typical smooth-log entries:

> 0-2 Underway in accordance with Comsubpac's Operation Order 10-44 dated 5 January 1944, on course 198° pgc, all ahead 2/3 150 RPM charging batteries. 0045 completed the battery charge.
>
> > G.F. Coffin, Lieut., U.S.N.R.

> 2-4 Underway as before.
>
> > T.A. Burke, Lieut., U.S.N.R.

> 4-6 Underway as before. 0415 c/c to 220° pgc. 0528. Made running dive on course 220° pgc.
>
> > T.R. McCants, Lieut.(jg) U.S.N.

> 6-9 Underway as before. 0615 Changed course to 259° pgc to investigate possible masts. 0618 Possible contact found to be

false. Changed course to 220° pgc. 0623
Changed course to 182° pgc.

>P.T. Glennon, Lieut., U.S.N.

The term "pgc" means "per gyro compass," and
"c/c" means "changed course." Two-hour assignments of OOD duty occurred during the night on the
surface, while three-hour watches were assigned during the daylight, when *Flasher* was often submerged.
Either Whitaker or DuBois reviewed the smooth log
and approved it each day.

Relief following watch duty did not mean lei-
sure time. Men on the *Flasher* were busy most of their
waking hours. Officers and crew put in long work
hours on and off their duty stations. They had only
limited recreation time, during which they might read,
watch the boat's movie, play cards, or try to catch up
on missed sleep. Other time was spent studying the
boat's many complicated systems in order to "qualify"
in submarines, studying for promotion to the next rating, or servicing all the complex, demanding equipment on which their lives depended.

Other than radar interference with the *USS Cod*
and some small boat sightings, *Flasher's* transit south
through the Sulu Sea, past Laparan Island and Pearl
Bank, and through Sibutu Passage between Sibutu Island and Tawi Tawi, all proved uneventful. She then
entered the long Makassar Strait between Borneo and
Celebes, headed straight for Lombok Strait.

At the northern entrance to Makassar Strait,
Flasher crossed the equator for the first time. Such a
crossing was normally the time for initiation of all
"polliwogs" into "The Solemn Mysteries of the Ancient

Top: Submarine Dolphins Awarded to "Qualified" Submariners (Enlisted and Officers), After Rigorous Training and Testing on Complex Submarine Operating Systems, and Bottom: Submarine Combat Insignia, Awarded to Boats and Personnel for a Successful Submarine War Patrol (Much Enlarged Here — Ones Shown Awarded Author's Father During the War)

Order of the Deep." The ceremony would be conducted by someone dressed as King Neptune. All officers and crew who could not prove they had previously crossed the equator and been inducted as "shellbacks," would be forced through an initiation, drinking foul liquids, having their hair shaved, or the like. On *Flasher's* first patrol deep in enemy-controlled waters and on constant vigilance for the Japanese, no such ceremony was held. Polliwogs were warned their initiation day was simply delayed, but it never happened on *Flasher*, despite numerous equatorial crossings and two transits of the International Date Line.

Several planes and small boats forced the sub to avoid and submerge intermittently during the Makassar Strait passage. Poor weather during this journey also made navigational fixes difficult except for prominent points of land located on the radars. The SD radar picked up a mountain peak at 55 miles on February 24, and the SJ picked one up at 35 miles the same day. These were the high mountains on the islands of Bali and Lombok, on either side of the dangerous, enemy-held Lombok Strait. That morning *Flasher* submerged before dawn at the north entrance of Lombok Strait, to transit the narrow passage between the islands undetected.

Only a single sailboat was sighted during the transit of the strait. Lombok was one of the few passages through the "Malay Barrier" that ran between Australia and the Japanese-controlled waters to the north. Despite the ideal gateway that it provided for Australian-based submarines to pass into Japanese-controlled waters, the Japanese never effectively sealed the strait with the heavy air cover, antisubmarine vessels, or mines that they utilized elsewhere. Although many submarines (including *Flasher*) were attacked there, only one submarine was lost in Lombok Strait during the war. That was the *USS Bullhead* (SS 332), lost with all hands on August 6, 1945, so very close to the end of the war.

Radar also picked up a friendly sub on the night of the 24th, that *Flasher* avoided. After reaching a point in the Indian Ocean about 160 miles south of the strait on February 25, she ceased daily submergences, but continued zigzagging as she headed for her new home "all ahead full." Her only contacts thereafter were friendly submarines, located by radar interference generated from their similar radar sets and frequencies.

Early on February 29 (Leap Year Day), 1944,

Flasher met her escort into Fremantle Harbor. The Commander, Submarine Division 162, and *Flasher's* relief crew officers boarded the sub before she made two runs across the magnetic range, and moored next to USS *Hake* (SS 256) and other subs nesting alongside the submarine tender USS *Pelias* (AS 14).

Whitaker's former boss from Brisbane, Ralph Christie, and his staff then came aboard. Christie was now an admiral, Commander, Submarines Seventh Fleet, and Whitaker's new commanding officer. After Christie left, the relief crew took over control of the boat, releasing *Flasher's* crew for "R and R" (rest and recreation).

The relief crew that took control of *Flasher* in Fremantle was headed by Lt. Cmdr. Manning Kimmel, son of Admiral Husband E. Kimmel, who became a scapegoat for the Pearl Harbor disaster. Lt. Cmdr. Kimmel was later lost along with all his crew on the submarine USS *Robalo* (SS 273).

On Saturday, March 4, the relief crew steered *Flasher* away from the *Pelias* and onto blocks positioned on the underwater railway tracks, to raise the sub into the repair yard. Two days later, *Flasher* was lowered down the railway blocks into the water to moor on the port side of USS *Hoe* (SS 258). (A year later a submerged *Hoe* collided with the submerged USS *Flounder* [SS 251] in a freak accident in the South China Sea off Indochina. Both subs survived the collision and the war. The same kind of underwater collision occurred between USS *Blackfish* [SS 221] and USS *Snook* [SS 279].[9A] It was an indication of how thorough the sub-

---

[9A] Robert F. Sellars, NSL Fact and Sea Story Book – 1993 (Annandale, Virginia: Naval Submarine League, 1993), p. 109.

marine coverage of enemy waters would become toward the later stages of the war, when independently operating American subs could bump into each other submerged in the open sea.)

As DuBois walked into headquarters at Fremantle, he saw Whitaker talking to Christie and several of his staff. When the men saw DuBois coming, they started laughing. DuBois, not understanding, looked to see if any of his clothes were unfastened. Then Christie said: "Ray, I heard you think we're the bravest bunch of bastards in the war!" Whitaker had TOLD them what DuBois said about their messages prodding *Flasher* to enter Verde Island Passage.

Flasher's typed war patrol report was due on arrival at Fremantle. In it, Whitaker complained of the torpedo and gun problems experienced, as well as the defectively designed electrical contact arms in the bow and stern plane control panels that failed *Flasher* on several occasions. (Electrically operated control of the extremely important bow and stern planes was a feature of early submarine production, but was discontinued by early 1944, as newer submarines were designed with more reliable hydraulic controls.)

The pitometer log on *Flasher* was also a sore point with Whitaker, since it constantly required repair, and gave unreliable speed readings, especially at slow submerged speed. Its accuracy was essential for dead-reckoning calculations. He suggested the trouble might be a sticky pump motor that the crew on *Pelias* could remedy. Whitaker also wanted the packing glands around the antenna mast tightened or replaced, as they leaked at deep submergence. The crew had not attempted to repair the leak during the patrol as it required removal of radar tuning equipment for access, and Whitaker preferred to live with the leak rather than jeopardize *Flasher's* radar equipment.

The patrol report also addressed the performance of radar and sound equipment. *Flasher's* SJ surface radar provided reliable readings on regular land features and freighters at 7½ miles, with reliable ranges on patrol boats and aircraft more in the 3½- to 4½-mile range. SD air search radar detected aircraft contacts at ranges as far away as 23 miles. Interference with the SD radar was noted in *Flasher's* patrol report, with line drawings showing the pictures the interference generated on the boat's primitive radar screen. This was important as it indicated probable enemy radar. Late in the war the Japanese would use more of their own radar and radar-detection finders to locate American submarines.

Sound gear was only effective up to three miles on the supersonic gear, and up to two miles on the sonic gear, although *Flasher* could hear up to 4½ miles on the sonic gear when the boat was rigged for silent running.

Whitaker gave his submarine a "4.0" for the habitability throughout the patrol, and commended the performance of his officers and crew as "very gratifying." *Flasher* had travelled over 10,000 miles just since Pearl Harbor, had consumed more than 108,000 gallons of diesel fuel, and had been on patrol for 54 days, 30 of which were spent submerged. She still had eight torpedoes aboard and plenty of supplies other than fuel, but her fuel tanks were almost dry.

Under Admiral Christie's authority, Flag Secretary P.F. Straub, Jr., commended *Flasher's* patrol, giving

her credit for more than 26,000 tons in enemy shipping sunk, awarding the Submarine Combat Insignia to the officers and crew, and commending *Flasher's* aggressiveness:

> The determination of the Commanding Officer to inflict the maximum damage on the enemy is well illustrated by the aggressive attack on 14 February in VERDE ISLAND PASS less than a mile from CAPE SANTIAGO which resulted in the sinking (of) a 7,000 ton freighter. While still being sought by the sunken freighter's escorts, he successfully attacked a second convoy that was standing in from CALAVITE PASSAGE and sank a 9,000 ton freighter loaded with oil.

Straub also condemned the sound-equipment failures noted by Whitaker and recommended their relocation or waterproofing to the Bureau of Ships.

Since leaving New London four months earlier, *Flasher* had travelled almost exactly halfway around the globe, passing through the Atlantic Ocean, Caribbean Sea, Pacific Ocean, South China Sea, Sulu Sea, Celebes Sea, Java Sea, Bali Sea and Indian Ocean. A hole drilled in New London, Connecticut, through the center of the earth to the surface on the other side would come closer to Fremantle, Australia, than any other city. Australia would be a new experience for most of the crew.

Flasher's crew was to enjoy numerous liberties in Fremantle and nearby Perth between patrols. Few wartime bases could rival the reputation that Perth and Fremantle generated during the war among Allied servicemen. Even the most dangerous submarine war patrol assignments were acceptable, it seemed, if the sub would only conclude its patrol in Fremantle.

Eager crewmen left the boat after their extended sea duty. When big Motor Machinist Andy Hale saw his smaller buddy, Radioman Randy Van De Veere, was headed over the gangplank to the dock, he shouted "Hey, Shorty! You goin' on shore leave now?" Leaving in the same party was Lt.(jg) McCants, who was as short, or shorter than Van De Veere. McCants stopped, turned to Hale, and responded sternly, "That's Shorty, *SIR*, to you!" It took a stunned Hale a second to realize the joke. Thereafter, men of the *Flasher* often addressed McCants as "Shorty, Sir," but only aboard the submarine, and then outside the hearing of Whitaker.

After each patrol, the crew had at least two weeks of liberty. Besides the girls, the parties, and the "gin mills," Fremantle and Perth offered other activities for the crew. There were also organized "rest camps" for the submariners, to try and keep them out of trouble. One of the Fremantle "Recreation Officers" was Brooklyn Dodger catcher Babe Phelps. Phelps was much appreciated by the crew for organizing softball teams and kangaroo-hunting trips for their free time.

Some of *Flasher's* single men would ultimately marry the Australian girls they met there. Some would not. One of Electrician Ross Brown's friends became very seriously attached to a very strait-laced young lady who, with her solemn parents, considered any tobacco and alcohol consumption dreadfully sinful.

When the sailor told Brown and the other shipmates of his engagement, and the fact his proposed in-laws already planned to follow him and his proposed bride home to the States after the war, the shipmates found a need to party. They got the young sailor blind drunk, loaded him with cigars, impregnated his clothing with smoke, and then dumped the nearly unconscious sailor on the lawn of his fiancée and her parents. That prevented one wartime marriage.

For their R & R, Glennon, McCants and Kristl were flown on Admiral Christie's seaplane to a rest-and-recreation camp 240 miles southeast of Fremantle, near Albany, Australia. There they hunted, fished, played cards and sampled the camp's fresh homemade bread. They were only supposed to be at the camp for a few days, but that was before the emergency at Fremantle developed.

On Wednesday, March 8, 1944, every member of *Flasher's* crew who could be quickly recalled from liberty was suddenly back at duty, to begin loading torpedoes aboard and preparing to get the boat under way. This was no easy task, as the boat had just begun her refit, and her periscopes had been removed for servicing ashore. Admiral Christie ordered *Flasher* and all other serviceable submarines to sea immediately to intercept an anticipated Japanese Fleet attack on Fremantle. With Glennon, McCants, and Kristl stranded in Albany, only Coffin and Burke were aboard to share the watch that Wednesday prior to the nighttime departure. Two Naval Reserve lieutenants and an ensign, James P. Hamlin, USNR, were drafted to replace the three missing officers.

After patrolling miserably in circles on the

rough seas for a week, the hastily scrambled emergency patrol finally concluded the evening of March 14. There had been no enemy sightings by any Fremantle submarines, or by the numerous aircraft involved in the searches. The Japanese attack turned out to be a false alarm, based on intelligence estimates of a probable sneak attack on Australia, combined with a routine report by Adm. Nimitz's son, Lt. Cmdr. Chester W. Nimitz, Jr., in *USS Haddo* (SS 255), of radar sightings of possible ships headed south through Lombok Strait.

Christie had sent the vital submarine tenders *USS Pelias* and *USS Orion* (AS 18) south to Albany to escape the expected Japanese attack. Once the threat of enemy attack evaporated, the three stranded *Flasher* officers boarded one of the tenders, and the two ships returned to Fremantle.

Transport on a surface ship was a strange experience for the submariners. Accustomed to waking for battle stations and emergency maneuvers at all hours, McCants suddenly awoke one night aboard the tender, alerted by his senses to an unknown danger. He glanced into the companionway, only to see the faces of Glennon and Kristl, who had also awakened and hit the deck. It was just the three submariners—nobody else was up—and there was no danger. The three submariners had all suddenly awakened because someone had turned off the tender's ventilation fan. Kristl commented that for years after the war he would wake up at the slightest noises, and would have trouble sleeping more than the three-hours-off, six-hours-on routine imposed during war patrols. He would also tend to get sleepy after six hours awake, which did not work well in his postwar, civilian life.

Flasher was returned to the relief crew after the emergency patrol. On March 18, she maneuvered back onto the keel blocks of the marine railway for a few hours' repair, before returning alongside Hoe and Pelias. The relief crew was replaced the following week by returning Flasher personnel, and the boat began to take on stores. The rest of the crew returned March 24, and Flasher cast off for exercises with HMAS Adelaide, a Royal Australian Navy cruiser. Sound tests were conducted March 25, before Flasher returned to Fremantle and released some of the temporary shore personnel from duty. After the sound tests, Flasher went back to the floating dry dock for work on her noisy propeller shafts.

Since Flasher was still within her six-month warranty period, a "Defect and Deficiency List" had been prepared during the first patrol. This list detailed uncompleted work by Electric Boat and problems with the diving plane controls, the pitometer log, binding in the number 1 periscope, and ineffective hydrogen burners. The Mark 18 electric torpedoes had required ventilation every four hours because the burners could not eliminate the dangerous hydrogen gas quickly. On March 25, with only one war patrol completed, the six-month warranty period expired. The Navy had retained $100,000 from the shipbuilding contract with Electric Boat, and now that the six months were up, EB requested the final payment. Based on documentation of uncompleted work, the Navy subtracted only $6,700 from the $100,000 due EB. Several of the defects in workmanship Whitaker reported were not EB's responsibility, and BuShips determined the others were not worth the paperwork processing costs, or were not clearly attributable to defective construction, rather than battle damage.

Only the troublesome pitometer log from the Pitometer Log Corporation merited any further subcontractor correspondence. That alone generated paperwork that continued for most of the rest of 1944, and resulted in a new pump finally being sent to Mare Island (*Flasher's* official Navy Yard now that she was in Australia) in October, 1944. The new pump was probably not installed on the sub in time to help her in the war.

March 28 found *Flasher* in exercises with the Australian fleet minesweeper *HMAS Dubbo*. *Flasher* made simulated attacks on the minesweeper, and *Dubbo* made simulated antisubmarine runs over the sub the next two days. *Flasher* followed this with further attacks on the submarine rescue vessel *USS Chanticleer* (ASR 7). Then she took aboard Commander Henry G. Munson to review drills with the cruiser *HMAS Adelaide*. Munson, already a successful submarine skipper, would later lead one of the war's hottest patrols aboard *USS Rasher* (SS 269).

During refit in Fremantle, *Flasher* received a new officer, Ensign James G. Hamlin, USNR. Hamlin, from Philadelphia, had been aboard *Flasher* during the short false-alarm patrol. He became her eighth officer, as he was an addition, not a replacement, to the complement. With Hamlin and Burke on duty, *Flasher* began taking on torpedoes and stores, fuel oil, and lubricating oil for her next patrol. She returned to the railway keel blocks twice to work on the noisy port propeller shaft.

CHAPTER 5

AIRCRAFT AND TORPEDO TROUBLES - *FLASHER'S* SECOND WAR PATROL

Because of the squealing propeller shaft, *Flasher's* departure for her second war patrol was delayed from March 31 to April 4, 1944. That afternoon she retested the port shaft. The noise level was finally acceptable, and she left Fremantle around 5 p.m. for her second war patrol.

During the voyage north, Whitaker assembled his officers to inform them of *Flasher's* assigned patrol areas. The sailing orders still allowed flexibility. He told them:

> I would like each of you to make an analysis of our patrol area and tell me what area you would want to patrol if you had the responsibility of saying so. Tell me which area within our big area... would be the most productive, and be ready to tell me why.

Whitaker had already studied the patrol reports of other submarines as well as his personal set of on-board encyclopedias, to learn the major traffic lanes the Japanese had to use to transport essential raw materi-

Chart of Second Patrol (April 4, 1944 to May 28, 1944 - by Author)

als and supplies. Usually the wardroom came up with areas that agreed with Whitaker's own choices, and those areas would be patrolled. This helped the morale of his junior officers, especially when *Flasher* was able to sink ships in the selected areas.

On April 6, *Flasher* experienced problems with electrical overloads when both the SJ surface radar and SD air-search radar were on. The switchboard was rewired to separate the radar power sources. This just delayed the problem four hours, when the SJ radar overloaded a generator again. The radars were interchanged, to put the less demanding SD radar on the weaker generator and the SJ radar on the stronger one.

Flasher's SJ radar had been upgraded during her refit at Fremantle by a new Plan Position Indicator (PPI). The PPI unit displayed ship contacts as if seen from above, with *Flasher's* position at the center of the rotating radar beam. Prior to this, the SJ radar screen produced only a pip at a single bearing on a horizontal line. The new screen was much better for visualizing and conducting attacks.

Surfaced and submerged training continued as *Flasher* headed north, with battle surface drill on the repaired 20mm guns, and submerged torpedo approaches. On the third day out a small electrical fire started in the forward engine room, causing a shutdown of the diesels and a switch to battery power. The fire was extinguished in five minutes with "no serious damage," and *Flasher* was back on two main engines within 15 minutes. She arrived at Exmouth Gulf, Australia, on the morning of the fourth day, having sighted only friendly submarines (*Gunnel* and *Crevalle*) and a friendly PBY (Catalina) airplane along the way.

Flasher's refueling at Exmouth was delayed two hours by a broken fuel barge pump. She topped off with 11,700 gallons to replace the fuel consumed since Fremantle, before departing around 2 p.m. Two hours later Whitaker called for battle stations surface, *Flasher* slowed to one third, and the gun crew fired off five rounds from the boat's four-inch gun. On April 8, another firing drill was conducted, expending 120 rounds of the 20mm ammunition and three from the four-inch gun. The boat continued a zigzag plan in the daytime but abandoned it at night.

She submerged 30 miles south of Lombok Strait the morning of April 10, to find an electrical power outage on the stern planes. As with the first patrol, the problem lay with the electrical control panels. The defects had not been solved during refit. While the short contacts complained of in the first patrol report had been replaced, the new contact arms were "too long and too rough." Whitaker stated "it has been necessary to station a watch on these panels during Battle Stations to ensure having power on the planes."

With *Flasher* submerged south of Lombok while repairs continued on the stern plane control panels, Whitaker held Captain's Mast. He had imposed no punishment during the first patrol on Joe Holmes for stowing away at Midway (after all, any wrong was committed against Midway, not *Flasher*), and this had not set well with the Navy brass. Pressure was put on a somewhat stubborn Whitaker to punish the torpedoman. Holmes had turned out to be an experienced, hard-working sailor on the first patrol, and Whitaker was afraid that if he did not impose some punishment, Holmes might be transferred off the *Flasher* after the second war patrol.

Holmes was told he could elect a formal court martial or stand Captain's Mast. Holmes quickly waived any formal proceedings. He was not charged with being a stowaway, or with dereliction of duty, or with desertion. Instead, Whitaker only charged him with being AWOL (Absent With Out Leave) for the three hours on January 10 when he had hidden under the torpedo room deck plates. Holmes' sentence was also very light, with a pay loss of $24 per month for two months, and a loss of any liberty for 20 days. The 20 days liberty restriction was typical of Whitaker's dry humor, since NOBODY on *Flasher* was to get any liberty for the six weeks it took to complete the war patrol. There was also a movement aboard to reimburse Holmes for the fine, but the sailor didn't want to upset the apple cart, and he asked that the collection idea be dropped.

The sub surfaced after dark to transit Lombok Strait. She then headed across the Java Sea on the surface, except for brief dives to escape enemy planes. Heading up Makassar Strait during the daytime, Whitaker decided to proceed in the probable enemy shipping lane between Balikpapan and Mangkalihat along the east coast of Borneo. He then changed *Flasher's* course to the northwest to follow the contour of Borneo toward Tarakan, sighting only debris and an enemy airplane on the way.

Flasher sailed through Sibutu Passage on the surface early on the morning of April 14, meeting the submarine *USS Haddo* with Whitaker exchanging pleasantries with Chester Nimitz, Jr., at dawn. Nimitz was Whitaker's friend from their service together on

Sturgeon. Haddo was experiencing a frustrating patrol, due to torpedoes that prematurely exploded, and deep-running torpedoes that did not explode. Nimitz was probably still unaware of the scramble at Fremantle caused in part by his radar contact a month earlier.

Because of the daylight, *Flasher* transited the narrow pass between Pearl Bank and Laparan Island submerged, and she stayed submerged until after dark that evening. Then she continued on the surface, changing course to the northeast to close on probable traffic lanes off the west coast of Mindanao, the second largest Philippine island.

Around 9:30 the morning of April 15, *Flasher* came alongside a 40-foot native sailboat bearing the name *"Toy."* Whitaker noted:

> This boat was found to contain seven scared Moros and about 20 sacks of Soy Beans which they stated they had obtained at Tawi Tawi and were taking back to Mindanao for food. They seemed to be very much afraid of our 20 MM guns which were pointed at them, but were unable to speak English until encouraged by a warning shot from a .45 pistol at which point their English improved rapidly. Gave them four or five packages of cigarettes, which they were most thankful for, and departed good friends.

McCants, Kristl and "two big sailors" comprised

the boarding party. When McCants fired his handgun overhead, the natives immediately spoke in clear English, although they had before feigned ignorance. Below deck they also had cattle. The Filipinos were far from land and lacked even a primitive compass, but were able to describe their heading by the stars and sun. Samples of the paper currency issued by the conquering Japanese in the Philippines were brought back on the submarine.

Flasher changed course to the northwest to pass submerged along the west coasts of Panay and Mindoro. At night she surfaced in Mindoro Strait and altered course due west toward Cape Varella, the easternmost tip of French Indochina (Vietnam). Whitaker decided to spend a few days patrolling an area in the South China Sea almost halfway between the Philippines and Indochina. After spending almost a week there patrolling on the surface, Whitaker "decided we have wasted enough time in this area. Headed for Cape Varella at one-engine speed, conducting surface patrol on route."

While headed for Indochina on April 24, *Flasher's* stern planes again failed during a routine trim dive. Whitaker "decided to remain submerged and make complete investigation." Personnel located the trouble again in the electrical control board and made repairs, after which the sub surfaced and proceeded as before.

Around dawn on the morning of April 25, Whitaker was rudely awakened by the diving alarm. *Flasher* was making an unscheduled running dive to 150 feet. The skipper scrambled to the conning tower.

"What the hell's the dive for?" he asked the

Sample Currency Issued by the Japanese for the Occupied Philippines
of the Type taken from Sailboat *Toy* (Author's Collection)

young officer of the deck.

The OOD responded "We had a radar contact, Captain, eight miles away, closing."

Whitaker said, "Really?"

OOD: "Yessir."

Policy aboard the boat was to turn on the SD air-search radar each morning. The many vacuum tubes in the primitive radar set took time to warm up and function properly. Chief of the Boat Felix Perkowsky had been watching the SD nearby as it warmed up.

"He's right, Captain. He sure was right, I saw it myself."

Suddenly there was a loud "BOOM!" as a "depth charge or large bomb" exploded not far away. The young OOD then proudly said to Whitaker, "Wasn't I?"

Not long thereafter sound picked up distant pinging, and smoke was sighted over the horizon. This proved to be a frustrating day for *Flasher*. The War Patrol Report describes her attempts to surface and close:

0726 Sighted smoke bearing 237° T. (Ship Contact No. 3). Believed ships to be on northerly course. Changed course to 310° T. to close.

0742 Sighted low wing monoplane (Plane Contact No. 5) bearing 020° T. distance about 4,000 yards and headed toward us. Went to 100 feet.

0805 At periscope depth. Discovered smoke had changed bearing to about 228° T. indicating ships on easterly course. Changed to intercept.

0825　Attempted to surface. Went to 48 feet and put SD out only to get plane contact at 2 1/2 miles (Plane Contact No. 6). Went to 130 feet expecting bomb but none came.

0842　Back at periscope depth.

0903　Started up to 48 feet preparatory to surfacing. Sighted plane bearing 151° T. distance about 8 miles (Plane Contact No. 7). Went back down to periscope depth.

0920　Surfaced on course 150° T. Sighted convoy by periscope bearing 197° T. with two low wing monoplanes searching above them. Decided to stay on surface and track from about 15 miles if possible. With two planes and masts of ships in sight, tracked on easterly course until 1010 when one plane headed for us and started coming in fast.

1010　Submerged with SD radar range of 10 1/2 miles. Went to 130 feet.

1039　At periscope depth. No ships or planes in sight.

1051　Came up to 48 feet and put SD radar mast up preparatory to surfacing. Plane contact 2 1/2 miles closing. Went down to 120 feet.

1111　At periscope depth.

1119　Sighted 2 planes bearing 130° T. Distance 7 miles headed in our direction. Went to 90 feet.

1132　At periscope depth.

1137　Sighted plane bearing 149°, at about 5,000 yards. Went to 90 feet.

1201　Sound heard light screws.

1206 Sighted gunboat type escort vessel at 3,000 yards, angle on bow 110° starboard. This escort apparently sent by planes to keep us down. His course is about 330° T. indicating that bearing of convoy was about 150° T. when he left it. His speed is about 20 knots. Decided from this that convoy is probably still on easterly course. Decided to remain at periscope depth and watch this fellow. He passed us and with range about 7,000 yards slowed down and commenced pinging.

1240 Escort passed out of sight bearing 307° T.

1337 Surfaced on course 105° T. with gunboat in sight by periscope astern at about 30,000 yards. Decided to try to regain contact with convoy. Our best dope indicates they are headed to eastward and it seems likely that they will cut back to northeast later this afternoon or tonight. Commenced search to eastward at 17 knots.

1627 SD contact 14 miles closing rapidly. Submerged.

1724 Surfaced. Continued search at 17 knots.

2330 It now seems that Japs have outguessed us as all efforts to regain contact have failed. Decided to continue search up to daylight position between Macclesfield Bank and Bombay Reef feeling that they are headed in this direction.

Flasher continued a night-long search for the convoy among the hazardous shoal areas southeast of Hainan, China, and northeast of Cape Varella, French

Indochina. Whitaker asked Exec. Ray DuBois how he would attack if they located the convoy in the dark. DuBois stated he would attempt to penetrate the screen so he could fire off all torpedoes in all directions from the center of the convoy. (Three months later, Red Ramage in *USS Parche* was to do just that, and became the first living submarine skipper to get the Congressional Medal of Honor.)

Whitaker agreed such an aggressive attack would be effective, but said he was interested in getting home alive, and it was just too dark and too shallow. Instead he indicated he would fire from a distance, without jeopardizing his ability to get away. This conversation, overheard by the crew, increased their faith in Whitaker. Their skipper might not speak to them once in an entire patrol, and he often went a whole patrol without visiting the compartments aft of the control room, but he had their unshakable confidence as a man who would sink ships and still get them all back to port.

Whitaker wanted everything to go perfectly, so he planned extensively before he proceeded. He often used DuBois as his sounding board for proposed tactics, and as a source for alternative tactics. During attack-training exercises after refits, Whitaker and DuBois would alternate command. Whitaker would lead one attack, then DuBois would be in charge. There was kidding about competition, with DuBois stating, "Let's show them how this is done." Then after the exercise was completed, DuBois would state over the general announcing system: "Rig ship for depth charge and stand by to build a little character." These activities may have fueled some of the crews' im-

pression that DuBois was the more aggressive of the two officers. Whitaker and DuBois were agreed on one subject though—they both wanted to sink ships and be around to sink more.

Mostly, however, Whitaker relied on his Executive Officer (DuBois and later Phil Glennon) to manage the submarine. His philosophy was that the Exec would run the boat, while he (Whitaker) would run the Exec. Prior to *Flasher's* commissioning in New London, Whitaker had told DuBois: "Ray, one of us has to be the S.O.B. and the other the good guy. *YOU* be the S.O.B." Whitaker's Exec was responsible for ensuring that everything went right, and for reading the riot act to the men when anything went wrong. "DuBois was hell on the boat, and a hell of a nice guy ashore," according to one of the junior officers.

Radioman Filippone recalled how he had accidentally missed the last timely bus back to the New London submarine base after a few beers near the EB boat yard, and it was DuBois who stopped his car and gave Filippone a ride. Sailors out after 5 p.m. were required to wear dress blues, but Filippone was still in his dungarees from duty at the fitting-out pier. When the sentry at the base gate started to hassle Vince, DuBois abruptly cut him off, told him Filippone had been with him, and drove on. DuBois also spent his shore time with the other *Flasher* officers between patrols.

By contrast, Whitaker was somewhat aloof while aboard, and he went his own way when the sub was in port (but so did most skippers, as they were separately billeted ashore at Fremantle).

The trust of the officers and crew in Whitaker

was reciprocated by Whitaker's trust in them. When *Flasher* needed to run tests on a squeaking shaft outside the harbor, Whitaker had no trouble letting DuBois take the boat out while he attended to matters ashore. Not many skippers would have done that, but Bull Wright had done the same for Whitaker on *Sturgeon*, and Whitaker never forgot it. And once when the Fremantle command required a wolf-pack report from Whitaker, he told Phil Glennon to prepare it. Glennon and Tom McCants worked up a combined report from the separate war patrol reports of the three wolf-pack subs over the next two days. Glennon then delivered it to Whitaker in front of Christie's Chief of Staff. Whitaker deliberately signed the report without reading it and said to the Chief of Staff, "There, that's the way I operate." Whitaker trained his men relentlessly, and then relied on them extensively.

Whitaker's search for the elusive Japanese convoy continued through the morning of April 26, between Macclesfield Bank and Bombay Reef in the middle of the South China Sea:

> Conducting search as before.
> 0700 Decided we had missed this convoy. Headed back toward Cape Varella. Regret missing this convoy, but their excellent plane coverage was too much for us. Type and number of planes indicated that they may have had an escort carrier with them. All the planes I saw looked much like our TBF and they were very fast.

In attempting to close on the convoy the previous day, *Flasher* had been chased down by planes eight separate times. Although the escorting aircraft carrier was never seen, everything indicated the presence of one. The only aircraft identified as forcing *Flasher* down were typical carrier-based planes: Nakajima B5N "Kates." Whitaker concluded that "there is much evidence that large convoys in the China Sea are now escorted by at least one escort carrier."

Flasher returned to the Cape Varella, Indochina, area and began patrolling about three miles off the coast submerged during the daytime and ten miles off the coast surfaced at night, hoping to discover ships hugging the coastline. Only small sailing craft were seen until the night of April 29 when:

2012   SJ radar contact bearing 260° T. range 15,800 yards (Ship Contact No. 4). This appears to be ship hugging coast on northerly course. Changed course to north and commenced tracking. There is a half moon and the visibility is good except for scattered rain squalls. It is not possible to see ship though, because of his nearness to coast.

2100   Closed in to 14,000 yards and found that there are two distinct targets. Tracking shows course to be 350° T. speed 7.5 knots. They are not zig zagging. Decided we would have to get ahead and make a submerged attack. Decided to dive about seven miles north of Cape Varella in about 40 fathoms of water. Commenced end around at two engine speed charging on two engines.

2230   Reached a point ahead of targets at range of

14,000 yards. Submerged and headed toward.

2245   Came up to radar depth and obtained range of 8,000 yards. Setup checks nicely with target course 350° T. speed 7.5 knots.

2253   Came up to radar depth and got range of 5,800 yards. Went to periscope depth and started pulling off track to eastward. Decided to get about 1800 yards off track and come around for bow shot in order to have six tubes available for three fish at each target. By this time could make out two medium ships in rough column. Could not see any escort. This seemed too good to be true, but could never find an escort. Sound conditions here are poor due to temperature gradients. Leading ship appeared to be freighter of about 4,500 tons with engines aft. Second ship was much larger freighter of about 6,000 tons. Headed in for 90° starboard track on leading ship.

2317   Fired three torpedoes at leading ship and immediately shifted to second ship, firing three at him. All torpedoes spread by periscope. One minute and five seconds after firing first torpedo observed hit just aft of MOT on leading ship. The second ship exploded with a tremendous flash and disappeared almost immediately. Believe this ship was loaded with ammunition.

2321   Had just shifted to first ship when first of three depth charges went off. Sound had reported fast screws bearing 020° relative during firing but did not stop firing to look since periscope had seen no escort. Third depth charge landed very close so went to 200 feet going ahead standard and turning rapidly. Escort's screws drew aft rapidly and faded out in direction of position where second ship had sunk.

2325   Heard distant explosion.

2333   Back at periscope depth. Escort appeared to be searching vicinity of sinking of second ship. Leading ship with one hit was dead in water and well down.

April 30, 1944

0000   First ship still afloat. Decided he would need another hit so commenced approach for stern shot.

0011   Made ready two tubes aft.

0015   With estimated range of 1500-2000 yards and with gyro on 180° and on steady course fired one torpedo aimed at center of target. Had checked to see that target bearing was steady so felt that we couldn't miss, but we did. Target now appeared to be on way sinking so decided to reload forward and wait until moonset at 0055 to surface and then finish him off if still afloat.

0040   Target sank.

0056   Surfaced. Nothing but land and escort at 2800 yards on radar. Cleared area to eastward at three engine speed charging on one engine. Decided to patrol center of our area on surface for next few days in vicinity of

previous contact.
0536 Submerged for trim.
0618 Surfaced. Will patrol for the day on the surface about 120 miles off Cape Varella at one
engine speed.

After the attacks and sinkings so close to shore, shipping would be re-routed around the area of the sinking, and antisubmarine activities there would be substantially increased. It made sense not to stick around.

Postwar analysis showed the vessels sunk the night of April 29 by *Flasher* were the river gunboat *Tahure* (644 tons) and the freighter *Song-Giang Maru* (1,065 tons). While Cmdr. John D. Alden was unable to verify *Flasher's* credit for the *Tahure* in time for his recent book, *U.S. Submarine Attacks During World War II*,[10] he later confirmed the sinking through his studies of Ultra reports. Ultra listed the vessel at 850 tons, as a Vichy French sloop.

JANAC confirmed the date, location, name of vessel (*Tahure*), and its ex-gunboat classification, tonnage and sinking by *Flasher*. So did former Navy Intelligence Captain W. Jasper Holmes, who described the vessel sunk by *Flasher* as the "ex-French gunboat *Tahure*," and as one of the Japanese combat ships sunk by American submarines in April, 1944, in his work *Undersea Victory II 1943-1945*.[11]

During *Flasher's* submerged approach on these

---

[10] Annapolis: Naval Institute Press, 1989.

[11] New York: Kensington Publishing Co., 1979, p. 62.

ships, her stern planes again failed to operate because of the control panel electrical shorts. The crew dismantled the Cutler-Hammer panel and determined that it was missing a stop pin. They fabricated and installed a new pin, after which the panel finally operated "satisfactorily."

Flasher patrolled well off Indochina the next day. After dark she ceased zigzagging to steady on a southeasterly course on the surface. Five minutes later, "sound reported loud noise bearing 305° T. similar to torpedo noise." *Flasher* immediately changed course and increased speed to two-thirds and then full to avoid the possible torpedoes from astern, but the noises were lost on a northwesterly bearing (329°).

The propeller noises were not only heard on the sound equipment, but by many aboard. When he heard the noise, Whitaker turned to the sound operator, "Baker! Didn't you hear that?"

Radioman Robert Allen Baker, a large, soft-spoken man, replied, "Yessir, I reported them."

Whitaker saw from eye contact with others that Baker was right, but told him to "make more noise!" next time. This was about as close as Whitaker ever came to backing down in a conversation.

On May 2 Whitaker decided to move into the eastern part of *Flasher's* patrol area to cover the traffic lanes to the northwest of "Dangerous Grounds," an area of very shallow, treacherous reefs. At noon lookouts sighted a possible periscope at 800 yards, causing a drastic course change and flank speed. The sighting turned out to be a stick, and speed and course returned to normal, even if pulse rates did not. This had occurred too soon after the torpedo incident to be taken calmly.

On the next morning, lookouts sighted smoke to the southwest. Whitaker felt the target was probably on a northeasterly course and so he attempted to "open out to the northeast to avoid being silhouetted by the sunrise, only to find that the target was lost." *Flasher* then reversed course, locating the target just after 7 a.m.:

0708　Regained contact and commenced tracking and end around at 19 knots. Found target to be on base course 275° T. and making about 15 knots. He is zig zagging very radically.

1000　Target now appears to have slowed to about 12.5 knots.

1002　We had reached a point about 80° to right of base course at about 35,000 yards range when target suddenly changed base course almost toward us. Slowed to estimated target speed and commenced tracking from ahead. Target appears to still be making 12.5 knots and now seems to be on steady course. The sea is so smooth that we feel a daylight periscope approach will be very difficult at best. At start of end around had three Mk. 14 torpedoes and one Mk. 18 loaded aft. At 0800 decided to load all tubes aft with Mk. 18 torpedoes. This had to be completed by 0830. Believed this might give us an excellent opportunity to take advantage of the good points of our four Mk. 18 torpedoes.

1047　Submerged, commenced approach from about 5,000 yards off target track to port at

Torpedo Exploding at Stern of *Teisen Maru* (Author's Collection)

estimated range of 30,000 yards. Commenced closing track.

1120　Target now identified as very large freighter of about 10,000 or more tons and is unescorted. He does not appear to be zigging, but expect him to start at any time.

1134　Am now about 400 yards off track on port bow of target at range of about 5,000 yards.

Desire to fire stern tubes so headed out for 80° port track.

1149 Fired four tubes aft spread by periscope. Lowered periscope kicked ahead and started turning rapidly to right to bring the bow tubes to bear.

1150-45 After torpedo run of 1700 yards, two Mk. 18's hit him well forward. They seemed to have little effect except to lower his bow a few feet and cause him to increase speed. Felt we had to stop him because if allowed to get away this time, he could possibly get air support before we could make another end around.

1154 With him firing at periscope with several guns of four or five inch, fired four torpedoes forward with large gyro angle, tracked about 110° port. As soon as he saw these Mk. 14 fish coming he made rapid turn to right and they all passed down his port side without hitting. He kept on turning right though and soon presented a 120° starboard track with torpedo run of about 2400 yards.

1159-30 Fired remaining two torpedoes forward spread widely by periscope. One of these was seen to run erratic.

1201 Torpedo hit within about five feet of stern of target. This stopped target dead in the water and we now began to relax even though he did not appear to be sinking.

1202 Commenced reload forward.

1211 Target did not appear to be sinking rapidly so fired another torpedo at him from forward. Allowed one knot speed. This was too much because at:

1212-30   Torpedo hit forward cutting off about 50 feet of his bow and taking with it his forward gun and gun crew who were still firing at our periscope and doing a fair job as they were coming close (one shell having landed about 20 feet away).

1218   Target now had about 10° down angle but did not appear to be sinking fast so fired one more torpedo from forward at 1500 yards. This torpedo circled out about 30° to the right then commenced turning left and finally hit the target in the bow. This finished him and he began to sink rapidly. The crew were already abandoning ship at this time.

1221   Target sank in vertical dive bow first. Four boatloads of about 100 survivors commenced rowing away. Much wreckage was left on the surface. Headed north to clear area a few thousand yards before surfacing. Commenced reload aft.

1401   Surfaced. Returned to scene of sinking to see if we could identify the ship. Picked up one life ring (without name) one bale of raw rubber, and a sample of Manila fiber. There were several hundred bales of rubber (both white and black) and boxes of Manila fiber on the surface. Found one sign in the wreckage with the German words RAUCHEN VERBOTEN printed on it. Took many pictures of wreckage and then cleared area to

Teisen Maru Dead in Water, with Bow Blown Away, and
Lifeboats Launched (Author's Collection)

eastward. Also found one hog (very fat) of
about 150 lbs. floating in wreckage. Having
been able to get no fresh pork in Australia
for patrol, it was a big temptation, but
thought of butchering aboard a sub caused
us to restrain ourselves.

Since one of the lifeboats fired at *Flasher*, Whitaker was asked about returning fire. He ordered the sub to pull away instead. Whitaker stated that *Flasher* was there to sink ships, not lifeboats, and "the survivors are in enough trouble already in the middle of the South China Sea—besides, they hadn't hit us."

Seaman Walt Lindberg and Signalman Corneau used a gaff to pull the floating bales and Manila fiber aboard. When they pulled in the sign, Lindberg and Ralph Heilstedt interpreted the German words "rauchen verboten" as "smoking forbidden." There was speculation by some of *Flasher's* crew that the rubber had been intended for Nazi Germany. The ship's course, westward toward the coast of Indochina with a cargo including Manila fiber and rubber, did not make much sense to the men of *Flasher*. The 5050-ton freighter was the *Teisen Maru*. Alden has identified the vessel as the previously named *Ursula Reckner*, and such a Dutch or German name may explain why a Japanese ship carried a Germanic "No Smoking" sign when sunk by *Flasher*.

Frank Kristl had no trouble identifying the bales as raw rubber since he had worked for Uniroyal before the war. Many of the men aboard kept pieces of the rubber and the manila fiber (used for rope or lines) as souvenirs.

Officers and crew of the *Flasher* could easily regret Whitaker's decision to forgo the fresh pork from the pig swimming in the South China Sea. Meats taken aboard in Fremantle for this second war patrol suffered in comparison to prior supplies from stateside and Pearl Harbor. Whitaker complained:

Our cooks were handicapped in preparing appetizing meals by the poor quality of beef received and by the lack of a variety of meats with which to make up the menus. Still very few aboard lost any weight on this score.

The food problem was raised a second time in the patrol report remarks:

The lack of good meats is still felt very keenly on patrol. The beef was poor, and we had no pork. It is strongly recommended that this condition be remedied as soon as possible.

Food supplied in Australia would occasionally receive adverse comment in future patrol reports. *Flasher* veterans would nonetheless remember meals on the sub as one of the best aspects of their wartime duty.

It had taken 12 torpedoes to sink the stubborn *Teisen Maru*. In 1944 a skipper could justify such an expenditure as long as the target sank. Had this occurred in 1942 during the torpedo shortage, Whitaker probably would have been sharply criticized or even relieved of command, due to the Navy's position in the early days of the war that the worthless torpedoes were infallible.

Even though the photographs were taken through *Flasher's* periscope, and on an overcast day, the pictures Lt. Kristl took of the sinking freighter were very good. The first picture (p. 143) shows the single hit within five feet of the ship's stern by the ninth or

Teisen Maru Sinking, with 15-Degree Down Angle and Much Smoke
(Author's Collection)

tenth torpedo at 12:01 p.m., causing the target to stop.
This first photograph also shows the ship's bow with
the raised forward gun emplacement that so nearly hit
the submarine, and kept firing accurately until it was
blown apart with the eleventh torpedo. The ship exhib-
its a mast-funnel-mast (MFM) layout with a split superstructure. These pictures also show the periscope's
horizontal and vertical marks for gauging mast heights

and ship length to compute distance, course, and speed for aiming the torpedoes.

The second photograph (p. 146) shows *Teisen Maru* after the eleventh torpedo, with the bow completely gone and the bow's down angle causing the stern to rise slightly. Boatloads of survivors can barely be seen amidships. The ship's forward mast has collapsed and the cables on it are twisted, apparently because of the bow damage. The two elevated gun emplacements astern the funnel and the one on the ship's aft section can be seen clearly. In the third photograph (p. 149) taken after the twelfth torpedo, the ship has a sharp, 15° down angle with the water apparently reaching the base of the funnel, and smoke from fires aboard is more pronounced. In the last photo (p. 152), only the latter fifth of the vessel remains above the surface, as she plunges down at a 45° angle. The lifeboats launched can be barely discerned at the water line to the right of center. *Flasher's* patrol endorsements showed the Fremantle brass were as impressed with the quality of the photographs as they were with the sinking.

(In Theodore Roscoe's excellent *United States Submarine Operations in World War II*,[12] two photographs appearing opposite page 451 (or page 457 in early editions) are credited to the submarine *USS Pargo* (SS 264). Roscoe must have used the wrong photos, since the photograph with the damaged bow appears to have been taken from *Flasher* of *Teisen Maru* either immediately before or immediately after the second photograph of her contained in this book. The ships

---

[12] Annapolis: Naval Institute Press, 1949.

and damage appear identical, and the guy wires on the forward mast are tangled exactly the same as appear in the second photograph.

Similar mix-ups occur with official Navy photographs. Supposed photos of the USS *Flasher* available for years from the National Archives were of a different, *Balao*-class submarine with the open periscope shears and Portsmouth-designed limber holes above the ballast tanks, features the *Gato*-class *Flasher* never had. As an result of this mix-up, Robert C. Stern's *U.S. Subs in Action*,[13] was apparently supplied the wrong picture for *Flasher*.)

Flasher's torpedomen in the aft torpedo room went to considerable trouble to remove and reload three of the tubes with battery-powered Mark 18 torpedoes for the initial four-torpedo salvo. Whitaker chose the electric Mark 18's as they caused no surface wake on their run to the target. Whitaker had noted the poor attack conditions caused by the abnormally calm seas. Submariners preferred a nice surface chop to hide their periscope's "feather" in the water and minimize the torpedo wakes. Wakes in the calm sea caused by steam bubbles from the Mark 14 torpedoes could easily have been spotted by the Japanese ship, and she could have turned to evade. When *Flasher* fired a second salvo using steam torpedoes, the damaged vessel did spot them and successfully evaded all four. The sub could not have joined the lone freighter in battle surface action as the freighter had several four- or five-inch guns to *Flasher's* one gun, and the merchantman's guns were

---

[13] Carrollton, Texas: Squadron/Signal Publications, Inc., 1983, p. 13.

Teisen Maru on Descent to Bottom, Showing Flotsam and Lifeboats Silhouetted Against Horizon (Author's Collection)

already loaded and manned, whereas *Flasher* would be a sitting duck while her single four-inch gun was readied for firing after surfacing.

Torpedo problems still haunted the American submarines, as shown by the one erratically running Mark 14 steam torpedo, and the fact that two hits with the Mark 18 electric torpedoes had little effect. As mentioned above, *Haddo* experienced numerous torpedo problems during this same period.

Even with these torpedo problems, *Flasher's* torpedoes were substantially better than those available to American submarines at the beginning of the war. Early in the war the Japanese disparaged the American submarine force and its torpedoes with good cause. Many of the Japanese ships reported submarine attacks or hits with American torpedoes that failed to explode. The Japanese had a far superior torpedo at the beginning of the war than anything developed by the Americans even by the end of World War II. Compared to the American's primary torpedo at the start of the war, the Japanese "Long Lance" torpedoes were faster, were more accurate, had longer ranges, and packed more explosive force than the best the Americans had to offer. Moreover, they detonated when they hit the enemy ship and left no tell-tale surface wake to alert the target in time to evade the torpedoes, or to mark the sub's location for enemy escorts and aircraft.

For the first year or two of the war the Navy's Mark 14 torpedoes had the following defects:

1. They were in short supply, due to their high cost ($10,000 apiece), their complicated design and need for hand crafting, and the Bureau of Ordnance's failure to increase production.

2. They consistently ran far deeper than set due to misguided Uhlan depth-setting gear and the effect of unbalancing, increased warhead loads, thereby missing their targets.

3. The super-secret, magnetic-activated Mark 6 detonator, of which the Bureau of Ordnance was so unjustly proud and defensive, often exploded prematurely or not at all.

4. The back-up contact detonator of the Mark 6

would crush on solid hits, jamming the firing pin before it could strike the primer, so it too was a dud.

5. The explosive payload was too weak.

6. Years of development had failed to produce a workable, wakeless electric torpedo (like the Germans were then using to deadly effect), or to produce a torpedo that did not betray the position of the submarine.

It is not surprising that many American submarine patrols at the beginning of World War II were unsuccessful. The torpedoes clanged against the side of the Japanese ships without exploding, or slid harmlessly underneath. U-boats had tried similar magnetic exploders at the beginning of the war with disastrous results. Unlike the Americans, however, the Germans quickly realized the defects in their torpedoes and court-martialed those responsible.

Admiral Christie in Fremantle was one of the last proponents of the magnetic exploders, and he required their continued use by Australian-based submarines long after they had been abandoned by all submarines controlled by Admiral Lockwood in Pearl Harbor. *Haddo's* luckless patrol by Chester Nimitz, Jr., had sounded the death knell of the magnetic feature, as even Christie finally gave up trying to fix it. Discovery of most Mark 14 torpedo defects and remedies occurred prior to *Flasher's* first patrol. This had taken two years of considerable uphill fighting against an uncooperative Bureau of Ordnance.

The United States had eventually produced an electric, wakeless torpedo during the war to supplement the Mark 14 steam torpedo. Development from a captured German electric torpedo was slow, and the final American product was inferior to the German model. The Mark 18 electric torpedoes supplied to *Flasher* (and fired at *Teisen Maru* with little effect) were temperamental.

Officers and crew of *Flasher* had attended lectures on the new Mark 18 torpedoes. Notes of the lecture are preserved, and contain much of the data and recommendations available to the wartime submariners. The Mark 18 electrics each weighed more than 3,000 pounds and cost around $4,000, which was a lot of money in 1943, but less than half the cost of the Mark 14 and 23 steam torpedoes. (The Mark 23 was basically a Mark 14 without the optional slow-speed setting.) The electric torpedoes cost less since they required less skilled labor to manufacture. They had been fired at Newport and ran as far as ten miles for a straight shot and 15 miles for a curved shot, but such distances, if achieved, were not relevant to combat. Most successful war shots were at a distance of under two nautical miles.

Seventy-two Exide lead acid battery cells in 36, two-cell sections were contained in each electric torpedo to power the 90 horsepower motor at 16,000 rpm. The cells had to be checked continually for gravity, acid level, voltage and grounds. Each battery of each torpedo also had to receive "freshening" charges once a week or more, depending on the surrounding air temperature. Each time the batteries in the torpedoes were charged, the explosive hydrogen gas emitted had to be closely monitored and "burned" off (consuming oxygen and producing more unwelcome water vapor in the submarine) by special, screened hydrogen eliminators or "burners." Improper ventilation during charging would create an explosive mixture. When

Flasher was on patrol the issue of proper ventilation procedure arose and the crew radioed for instructions. The answer came back one time that ventilation during charges was an absolute necessity. However, another message was received that ventilation during the charges would cause an explosion! Because of the extra maintenance hassles and the danger, *Flasher's* torpedomen wanted the electrics to be the first torpedoes launched.

Accuracy was another Mark 18 problem, as everything seemed to affect its performance. The Torpedo Data Computer (TDC) had to be readjusted each time *Flasher* switched between steam and electric torpedoes because of their different attributes. The electrics were supposed to have a 29.3-knot constant speed, but this decreased, as much as two knots, the shallower the torpedo's depth was set. Sea water temperature also affected the speed, with every ten-degree Fahrenheit decrease lowering the Mark 18's speed two-tenths of a knot. For each battery cell that had to be bypassed ("jumped out") on the torpedo, estimated torpedo speed decreased another quarter knot. A minor speed deviation could easily mean a missed shot, since the targets were almost always moving, and a hit was based on correctly placing the torpedo at the estimated location of the target after a run of one to two nautical miles. The electric torpedoes were also supposed to be shot not less than ten seconds apart, whereas *Flasher's* steam models were fired as quickly as six or seven seconds apart. These were all substantial handicaps and it was no wonder the electrics were resented by *Flasher's* crew.

The sub had fired seven torpedoes to sink the

Tahure and *Song-Giang Maru,* and another 12 torpedoes (with seven misses) to sink the *Teisen Maru.* This left her with only five torpedoes out of her original 24. Orders were received on May 4 to return to Australia. *Flasher* immediately headed east toward Mindoro Strait. Two days later, while she was south of Panay in the Sulu Sea, she sighted smoke from two ships:

1655   Sighted smoke bearing 345° T. On coming up to 60 feet found smoke to be coming from one ship at a great distance, but sighted masts of another bearing 350° T. Went to battle stations and commenced approach (Ship Contacts Nos. 6 & 7).

1719   Made out target to be large, four goal post freighter with minesweeper escort. Target found to be zigzagging radically about base course 160° T., speed about 13 knots. Decided to attempt stern shot as we have three torpedoes aft and only two forward.

1748   Fired three torpedoes aft with about 95° starboard track torpedo run about 1600 yards spread by periscope. Escort well up ahead. About one minute after firing, target was observed to be firing at torpedoes with several four or five inch guns. From where the splashes landed it appeared that all torpedoes passed astern. Freighter decks appeared to be filled with people. Believe we used too low speed, but find it hard to believe he could be making fifteen knots.

1751   Freighter dropped two depth charges.

1754   Torpedoes exploded at end of run. Escort

remained in vicinity pinging while freighter cleared area to eastward.

1757　Escort headed toward fairly close. Went to 150 feet.

1806　Back at 64 feet. Saw escort rejoining target to eastward.

1815　Sighted large hospital ship similar to ASAHI MARU coming up on same track freighter had passed over. We passed about 2,000 yards away headed on course 160° T. speed about 13 knots.

1828　Target sending signals probably to escort, but it looks more as if he is sending to Hospital Ship.

1847　Surfaced with SJ radar out of commission. Target bearing 100° T. range about 20,000 yards. Commenced closing at four engine speed.

1858　Saw much gunfire in direction of target.

1902　Sighted ship dead ahead at about 10,000 yards, apparently escort searching to rear of target. Reversed course and avoided.

1907　Escort no longer in sight. Reversed course and started closing again.

1908　SJ Radar back in commission. Picked up target bearing 127° T. range 25,000 yards. Hospital ship bearing 154° T. range 20,000 yards. Target appears to be on base course about 180° T. Commenced end around to starboard. Target found to be zigging radically and making about 15 knots.

2100　Target changed base course to 110° T. leaving us astern, all of our running having

gained us nothing. Decided to make end around to his port side. Commenced doing so keeping range at 20,000-22,000 yards and making 80% on four engines.

2314 Had almost reached port beam of target when we sighted Calusa Island bearing about 135° true, range 19,570 yards. It now became plain that target intended to pass Calusa close aboard and to the south. This would leave us to north of it. Decided to pass to north of Calusa and then cut down between Calusa and Cagayan Island.

2330 Was just about to head down between islands when we sighted small ship, apparently the escort, between the islands. This forced us to backtrack and pass to west of Calusa losing all the ground we had gained.

May 7, 1944
Tracking target as before. Started battery charge on auxiliary engine.

0015 On clearing Calusa found that target had changed base course to about 170° T. This gave us a 160° starboard angle on bow. Commenced end around to starboard at full power in order to get ahead about 0400. The moon is very bright so maintained range of about 20,000 yards.

0122 Sighted Hospital Ship bearing 176° true, range about 30,000 yards. This puts him in such a position that he will be practically on my track as I go around target.

0200 As we reached beam of target it became very

clear that this hospital ship was going to be very much in the way. He is in such a position that when we will have completed our end around he will be about 10,000 yards ahead of target and about 2,000 yards off his track to starboard. Sent contact report.

0239   Hospital ship bears 125° true, range 9,000 yards. In order to continue my approach I am forced to keep at about this range and pass through moon slick. Decided to do so in hopes that hospital ship would not see us or in hopes he would not warn target if he did. In the event that he did warn target, felt we would be justified in sinking him.

0358   Submerged 20,000 yards ahead of target, 10,000 yards ahead of hospital ship and about 2,000 yards off his track. Commenced approach.

0413   Sighted target bearing 337° T. It now appears that he has changed base course to 190° T. to pass hospital ship to westward. Headed in to close his track.

0420   Hospital ship passed at distance of about 1500 yards.

0430   It is now evident that we will be forced to fire at a long range. We believe we have excellent speed dope, and in any event we do not have time to make another end around before he reaches Basilan Strait, so feel we will have to accept long torpedo run.

0434   Fired our last two torpedoes with 90° port track estimated 3,000 yard torpedo run and one aimed at bow and one at stern of target.

0436-20 One torpedo hit target about midway between bow and MOT.[14] Estimate size of target to be about 7,500 tons.

0438 Escort headed toward at about 1,000 yards range. Went to 200 feet. The target seems to be firing every type gun you can think of. Sound is continuous crackle from his gunfire.

0440 Torpedo which missed exploded at end of run.

0454 Back at periscope depth. Escort still in vicinity at about 1500 yards. Damaged freighter is bearing 210° T. range about 4,500 yards and appears to be running in circles. He has a list of about 10° and a down angle of about 10°. Hospital ship is seen to be clearing area at best speed. Commenced closing damaged ship.

0530 Still had hopes that he would sink as he is apparently badly damaged, but about this time he succeeded in getting her headed in the general direction of Basilan at a speed of about 5 knots.

0615 Decided it was of no further use to keep after target as all our torpedoes are gone. So commenced opening out to northwest.

0630 Lost sight of target.

0757 Had just put SD radar up at 48 feet depth when we heard three explosions which had about the right interval for torpedo hits.

---

[14] Middle Of Target

> Hoped it was U.S. Sub. after our cripple.
>
> 0807　Surfaced and sent report of what we had done, hoping the boss might get someone on our cripple. Headed for Sibutu at two engine speed.

Based on *Flasher's* radio message, the *USS Bonefish* (SS 223) attacked *Flasher's* cripple, the 8,811-ton *Aobasan Maru* later that same day (May 7, 1944), off Basilan Island. *Bonefish* confirmed the freighter was down by the bow from prior damage, and was certain it sank following three torpedo explosions, but the stubborn Japanese ship survived and made it into port. She was finally sunk by Army aircraft before the end of 1944.

With no torpedoes left, *Flasher* headed to Australia, clearing Sibutu Passage and Banka Passage the following two days. Instead of travelling through Makassar Strait as before, she headed southeasterly through the Molucca Sea between Celebes and Halmahera, and the Banda Sea. On May 11, she passed through the eastern end of the Malay Barrier, between Sermata and the Babar Islands. While still 20 to 35 miles east of Sermata Island, *Flasher* was forced down by aircraft three times within two hours. Whitaker noted that the enemy plane must have been equipped with radar to locate the submarine repeatedly in the dark.

The different course south was occasioned by orders to proceed to Darwin, in northern Australia, instead of Fremantle. Since the patrol had lasted only a month, the Fremantle command decided *Flasher* could refuel and reload torpedoes at Darwin, and go

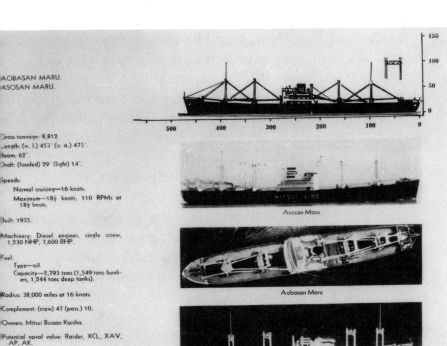

AOBASAN MARU.
ASOSAN MARU.

Gross tonnage: 8,812.
Length: (w. l.) 453' (o. a.) 475'.
Beam: 62'.
Draft: (loaded) 29' (light) 14'.

Speeds:
Normal cruising—16 knots.
Maximum—18½ knots; 110 RPMs at 18½ knots.

Built: 1935.

Machinery: Diesel engines, single screw, 1,230 NHP, 7,600 BHP.

Fuel:
Type—oil.
Capacity—2,793 tons (1,549 tons bunkers, 1,244 tons deep tanks).

Radius: 38,000 miles at 16 knots.

Complement: (crew) 47 (pass.) 10.

Owners: Mitsui Bussan Kaisha.

Potential naval value: Raider, XCL, XAV, AP, AK.

Remarks: Gunmounts—capable of mounting five 5" guns.
Vessels of this type reported operating as raiders in Indian Ocean.

Asosan Maru

Aobasan Maru

Aobasan Maru

Aobasan Maru (ONI 208-J)

back on patrol for two more weeks. There was another, top-secret reason for sending *Flasher* to Darwin and back out again. Navy Intelligence had learned from intercepted enemy radio messages the sailing instructions of an important Japanese auxiliary vessel, and *Flasher* was to intercept it.

After dawn on Saturday, May 13, *Flasher* picked up a pilot for Port Darwin, Northern Territory, Australia, mooring at the dock at 8:30 to take on eight torpedoes forward, four torpedoes aft, and 81,000 gallons of fuel oil. Darwin had been bombed by the Japanese earier in the war. A thoughtful Admiral Christie flew

Flasher's mail up from Fremantle, and provided cases of beer dockside for *Flasher's* crew, to help soften the lack of any shore leave. Whitaker made it clear there would be no mail or beer until the new torpedoes were loaded aboard, a laborious, time-consuming job which the highly motivated crew accomplished in record time. None of the crew had consumed any alcohol in over a month, and many drank too quickly too much of the warm, free beer. Some became incapacitated or got sick as a result, and it fell on the non-drinkers to get *Flasher* ready to leave the same afternoon. After the sub bounced once off the dock backing out, a worried Lt. McCants, a non-drinker, requested the helm and got it.

So *Flasher* departed Darwin without further incident that same afternoon for the Java Sea and the second leg of her second war patrol. While many aboard slept off the effects of drinks in Darwin, she passed back through the Malay Barrier around Sermata Island, and turned westward into the Flores Sea south of Celebes.

Flasher arrived to patrol on the surface ten miles southwest of Kapoposang Light, northwest of Makassar City, Celebes. On May 17, a fire broke out in the sub's Kleinschmidt water-distiller control panels in the forward engine room. It was extinguished within 15 minutes. Then, shortly after noon, just as predicted by Naval Intelligence:

> 1236   Sighted seaplane bearing 285° T. distance about 15 miles (Plane Contact No. 11). Believe he may be air coverage for some ship entering Makassar City. Feel that base course of ship entering Makassar City would

be about 120° T. Since this contact is to south of this bearing we believe we may be to north of his track. Changed course to 190° T.

1248 Sighted smoke bearing 279° T. (Ship Contact No. 10). Commenced closing track to south at 2/3 speed.

1305 Sighted masts of ship bearing 279° T.

1315 Slowed to take look. It is raining very hard and have lost sight of target. Continued closing to south as we still appear to be north of target track.

1328 Sighted plane in heavy rain very close.

1338 Heard light screws and pinging bearing 275° T. Still raining hard. Cannot see target.

1345 Sighted target bearing 259° T. at estimated range of about 3,000 yards. Could just make out outline of ship but identified him as KAMIKAWA MARU Type Seaplane tender. Unable to see escort. Angle on bow is about 80° port. Made ready six tubes forward.

1352 Target zigged away and gave us a 110° port angle on bow. Unable to get range, but estimate it at about 2500 yards. We were forced to make up our minds immediately whether to fire or not. Decided that I had to take a chance on this important target so with estimated range of 3,000 yards and estimated speed of 14 knots fired six torpedoes spread very wide by periscope. Hoped to get at least one hit, but they all missed. Went to 100 feet.

1358 Plane dropped bomb. Not close.

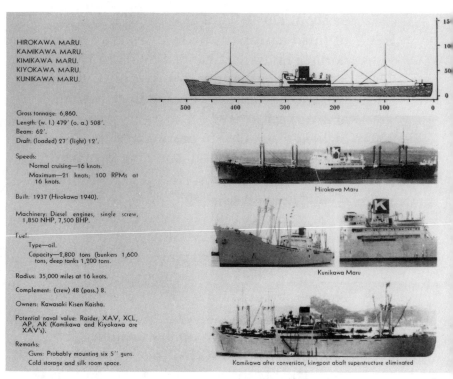

HIROKAWA MARU.
KAMIKAWA MARU.
KIMIKAWA MARU.
KIYOKAWA MARU.
KUNIKAWA MARU.

Gross tonnage: 6,860.
Length: (w. l.) 479' (o. a.) 508'.
Beam: 62'.
Draft: (loaded) 27' (light) 12'.

Speeds:
Normal cruising—16 knots.
Maximum—21 knots; 100 RPMs at 16 knots.

Built: 1937 (Hirokawa 1940).

Machinery: Diesel engines, single screw, 1,850 NHP, 7,500 BHP.

Fuel:
Type—oil.
Capacity—2,800 tons (bunkers 1,600 tons, deep tanks 1,200 tons.

Radius: 35,000 miles at 16 knots.

Complement: (crew) 48 (pass.) 8.

Owners: Kawasaki Kisen Kaisha.

Potential naval value: Raider, XAV, XCL, AP, AK (Kamikawa and Kiyokawa are XAV's).

Remarks:
Guns: Probably mounting six 5" guns.
Cold storage and silk room space.

Hirokawa Maru

Kunikawa Maru

Kamikawa after conversion, kingpost abaft superstructure eliminated

Kamikawa Maru (ONI 208-J)

1400	Escort getting close. Went to 200 feet.
1405	Escort shifted to short scale and headed in on firing run.
1407	Escort passed directly overhead with us kicking ahead at about 5 knots and turning.
1407-10	Depth charges started going off. Five depth charges all very close but apparently astern.
1408	Continued to avoid keeping escort astern. Found out that pit log will not house.
1513	At periscope depth. Sighted mine sweeper type escort astern at about 4,000 yards. Went to 150 feet.

1539   At periscope depth. Nothing in sight.
1828   Surfaced. Headed for Eastern Java Sea at 15
       knots.

Despite *Flasher's* failed attack, the seaplane tender was eventually neutralized. American subs sank six of Japan's seaplane tenders and damaged a seventh beyond repair. Aircraft sank and severely damaged the only other two Japanese seaplane tenders prior to war's end, so they were all removed from service.

The following day *Flasher* resumed her course to the south-southwest at standard speed. Six miles to the west, she sighted another submarine which turned out to be the *USS Rasher*. These two Fremantle-based subs would end the war with two of the most successful wartime records. In the JANAC report of 1947, the top-ranked *Flasher* would be a scant 330 tons ahead of the second place *Rasher* in total enemy tonnage sunk without assistance. The 330-ton figure is less than the 500-ton minimum for ship sinkings considered by JANAC. (*Flasher* would get another 4,333 tons, sharing half credit with *Crevalle* for sinking the 8,666-ton *Tosan Maru*, bringing *Flasher's* overall total to 104,564.) When met by *Flasher*, *Rasher* was in the middle of a typically hot patrol in which four Japanese ships would be sunk. *Rasher* was as effective as any U.S. submarine in World War II, but received little of the limelight she deserves.

Flasher continued to the west, headed for the traffic lanes off Surabaya, the major Java port occupied by the Japanese. On the morning of May 19, she obtained another target:

0308   SJ radar contact bearing 318° T. range 17,500

yards (Ship Contact No. 11). Commenced tracking and found target to be on steady course 065° T. at 7.5 knots. Commenced end around at 19 knots.

0514   Arrived 13,500 yards ahead of target and on his track. Slowed to target's speed and changed course to 065° T. in order get a more accurate speed check. Target speed checks nicely at 7.5 knots, course at 065° T.

0537   Submerged at beginning of morning twilight 13,350 yards ahead of target. Headed for target.

0553   Sighted target by periscope at 8,500 yards. Appears to be small freighter of about 2,000 tons with stack aft. He looks high in the water so set torpedo depth at six feet.

0606   Target still on straight course. Headed out for stern tube shot -- 90° starboard track.

0622   Fired three torpedoes from stern tubes torpedo run about 1200 yards.

0623   Felt sure we couldn't miss this one, but we did. He kept on steady course for one minute and fifteen seconds after firing and then gave us a 180° angle on bow. I feel sure these torpedoes passed under target. Watched torpedoes by periscope and tracked them with sound gear and everything indicates that torpedoes ran deep.

0706   Surfaced and headed towards eastern part of Java Strait at two engine speed. Sighted many sailboats.

1349   SD radar contact at 12 miles (Plane Contact No. 13). Submerged.

1825   Surfaced. Heading for eastern part of Java
       Sea at 15 knots.
1915   Received orders to return. Commenced
       making 17 knots.

The words "to Fremantle" were obliterated on
the patrol report at the 1915 hours entry, probably for
security reasons. Submarine names were also obliterated in war patrol reports, but often survived in the
deck log.

Flasher submerged the morning of May 20 for
her approach to Lombok Strait, surfacing that evening
five miles north of the strait's entrance, and proceeded
through it. The following two days she sailed south
through the Indian Ocean toward Fremantle.

On May 23, *Flasher* received urgent orders to
help rescue the disabled *USS Angler*. *Flasher* changed
course to the north-northwest, abandoned zigzagging,
and went all ahead flank speed (18 knots). *Angler* experienced tainted drinking water during a prior patrol
and her skipper, Robert Olsen, requested the tanks be
checked and flushed during refit. Olsen felt that excessive chlorine used to clean the tanks may have settled
in the tank walls. This was not done by departure
time, but *Angler's* division commander reportedly told
Olsen that, if he didn't want to take the *Angler* back out
as it was, somebody else would.

A bad depth-charging of *Angler* in Sunda Strait
between Sumatra and Java may have shaken the chlorine loose to mix with the water supply, since right
after that the *Angler's* crew all got sick. Olsen then had
insufficient able-bodied personnel to man the ship on
the surface. Besides *Flasher*, the submarine *Crevalle* (SS

291) and the patrol-plane tender *USS Childs* (AVD 1) raced to *Angler* to provide fresh water and assistance.

Angler was in need of a baker and an auxiliaryman, so Baker Charles "Ski" Ezerosky and Motor Machinist Mate Bill Beaman were told to get their gear together to be transferred at sea to *Angler*. An auxiliaryman like Beaman was responsible for maintaining the extensive air-pressure systems, hydraulic systems, and numerous other complex systems essential to operation of the submarine. The two men were standing by with their belongings in the control room when they learned, to their relief, that their services aboard the other sub were no longer required.

As *Angler* did not need the help from all three vessels, *Flasher* and *Crevalle* were excused after three hours, and they proceeded on to Fremantle. On May 26, *Flasher's* gun crews again trained on the 20mm weapons, firing 60 rounds from each gun to make sure they still worked prior to refit.

On May 28, *Flasher* moored at the north wharf in Fremantle to be relieved by the Submarine Squadron Sixteen Relief Crew under Commander Henry G. "Hank" Munson. Munson had witnessed *Flasher's* exercises before the second patrol, and would soon lead *Rasher* on one of the greatest submarine patrols of the war. In 65 days on patrol, *Flasher* had travelled 13,649 miles and consumed over 150,000 gallons of fuel oil.

Whitaker had a list of problems to be addressed during refit. Most importantly, *Flasher's* pit log still gave her problems despite repairs during the previous refit.

Substantial defects were also noted by Whitaker in the preparation of seven of the 36 torpedoes carried

on *Flasher's* second war patrol. (*Flasher's* normal 24 torpedo complement had been supplemented by the 12 taken aboard at Darwin.) One of the torpedoes had a leaky exhaust valve that caused the torpedo's after body to flood, three of the torpedoes had non-functioning gyro setting mechanisms, two torpedoes clearly ran erratically, and one torpedo (overhauled by the submarine base at Midway Island) had a sluggish depth engine and missing gasket that caused the after body to flood. All but the last of these torpedoes had been overhauled by the sub tenders *USS Orion* and *USS Pelias*. Whitaker was sure the three torpedoes that missed the freighter May 19 did so because they ran deeper than set. That made ten defective steam torpedoes out of the 32 Mark 14's she carried. However, seven defects were identified and corrected by *Flasher's* rigid pre-launching routine, and there were no dangerous circular runs.

In addition to the steam-torpedo problems, *Flasher* had problems with the four Mark 18 electric torpedoes whenever more than one was recharged. Because electric torpedoes required fully charged batteries, each had to be periodically recharged during the patrol. *Flasher* was unable to adequately dissipate the highly volatile hydrogen gas generated by charging the Mark 18 batteries, so the crew had to resort to frequent ventilation of the torpedoes, a consequential loss of battery acid, and an increased incidence of grounds.

Whitaker observed that during the second patrol *Flasher* experienced "excellent performance of personnel," which he attributed in part to a lack of transfers after the first patrol. If his comments were designed to discourage crew rotation by the Fremantle command, they were unsuccessful, since about ten of the crew would be transferred during the coming refit.

Captain J.B. Griggs, commander of Submarine Squadron 12, gave *Flasher* a glowing patrol endorsement, highlighting "the same splendid aggressiveness that characterized the first patrol of this ship." Griggs congratulated the officers and crew, commended their outstanding morale, noted that electrical problems with the radar power sources and the PPI transformer would be fixed, and indicated deficiencies in charging the Mark 18's and eliminating hydrogen would be remedied during this refit. The Fremantle Torpedo Station was ordered to check into the very poor condition of torpedoes that had been issued *Flasher*.

In a second memo, Admiral Christie concurred in Griggs' endorsement and praised the "persistence of FLASHER during the chase of a convoy on 25 April," even though *Flasher* had been unable to make any attack due to air cover. Christie could recognize a good effort despite the lack of sinkings from that convoy. *Flasher* was awarded the Submarine Combat Insignia for her second successful patrol and was credited with sinking 20,065 tons of enemy shipping. Christie was also able to specifically identify *Flasher's* April 29th freighter as the *Song-Giang Maru* (1,065 tons) based on Naval Intelligence and confirmation from Vichy Radio. By a third endorsement from Commander, Seventh Fleet, *Flasher* was congratulated for a successful war patrol. Despite the intensive enemy air coverage, torpedo problems, and numerous misses, *Flasher's* second patrol had been a good one, netting three confirmed sinkings and one damaged freighter.

The relief crew steered the *Flasher* onto keel

blocks and she was hauled out of the water for two days. While *Flasher* was high and dry, on June 4, the Allies were capturing Rome on the other side of the world. Two days later, on D-Day, June 6, 1944, the troops landed in Normandy, France.

Flasher's relief crew included a naval reserve officer, Ensign F.B. ("Kiko") Harrison, who would soon join the sub's crew for the rest of the war. *Flasher's* regular crew reported back June 10, to replace the relief crew. Some personnel were detached to other duties, and the boat received replacements. One departing sailor was Seaman Andrew Harry Brokovich, who had berthed in a raincoat under *Flasher's* leaking "soft patch." His name would stay with her for the rest of the war, though, as *Flasher* men would "Pass the Brokovich" whenever they wanted ketchup, the sauce he allegedly used with every meal.

One replacement was Cook Angelo LaPelosa. LaPelosa was to become one of the most popular men aboard, well-known for his great food, his quick wit, and his confrontations with the shore patrol while on "R & R." To his shipmates he would be known as "Wop," a name the tough Italian-American would use to introduce himself, and proudly bore. The name was never used derogatorily. Among his *Flasher* shipmates, and many other submarine veterans, he was legendary. At the end of the war *Flasher's* crew presented him with the boat's original battle flag.

Flasher ran maneuvering exercises, sound tests, and the magnetic range on June 11. She suffered and repaired a steering casualty the same day. Deep submergence tests were conducted on June 13 along with surfaced and submerged training exercises. On June

Flasher's Original Battle Flag, Presented to
Cook Angelo LaPelosa by the Crew (Author's Collection)

14, Ensign Harrison formally reported aboard for duty
as a sudden replacement for Lt. Tom Burke. Burke had
broken a bone in his right foot and would miss *Flasher's*
third war patrol. Harrison assumed some of Burke's
duties, including those of the Plotting Officer during
approaches. Jim Hamlin took over Burke's duties as
Communications Officer.

On June 16, *Flasher* took aboard Commander
Frederick B. Warder as training officer. Warder was
the aggressive skipper of the *USS Seawolf* (SS 197) in the
early, dark days of the war, earning the nickname
"Fearless Freddy." A meticulous professional, Warder
timed *Flasher's* training maneuvers with a stopwatch.
After timing several dives to periscope depth, Warder

told Whitaker, "Reuben, this diving officer does a good job. Fact is, some of the fastest diving I ever saw. How about putting in another diving section?"

This was no small request, as it would involve a turnover of the diving personnel manning the planes and manifolds, and would disturb the regular watch schedules. *Flasher* had four different diving sections.

Whitaker said, "Fine, if you want it done, but the whole watch section is about to be relieved in 30 minutes, and we'll be diving after that."

But Warder wanted to proceed his way. "Well, why don't you go ahead now? I want to see how they compare with this section."

Seeing that Warder was going to want all four diving sections timed, Reuben countered, "Captain, I'll be glad to do it, but it's not going to make any difference—they all dive the same way, in the same time."

"Like HELL they do." said Warder.

"Yessir, they do."

"Well, I'd like to see another section on it."

So it went. Whitaker changed the diving sections and dives were timed. The third section was put on and timed, as was the fourth section. After all the sections were timed, Warder turned to Whitaker and said, "You know, this is the first submarine I've been on where it doesn't make any difference who's diving—it dives with exactly the same diving time." *Flasher's* five dives for Warder that day were not *exactly* the same, but they varied only slightly, officially clocked at an average of just under 40 seconds, to reach the 80-foot diving depth.

June 16 through 18 were spent diving, training and making practice approaches on *HMAS Dubbo*, with

Commander Warder aboard. Warder, later head of the Submarine School in New London, would credit *Flasher* as having the "best trained crew" he had ever seen in a submarine.

Working late the day prior to departure, several of *Flasher's* crew had their final night ashore delayed by many last-minute duties and patrol preparations. When they were finally released for liberty that evening, they hurriedly left the boat to make the best of the few hours remaining. The sailors, including Signalmen Doty and Corneau, headed over the gangplanks from sub to sub and up to the tender, over and through the tender to reach the gangway to the dock on the tender's opposite side. At the top of this last gangway they were stopped by a shipshape young duty officer, who found them all "out of uniform" because of scuffed shoes, a missing stripe, or, in Doty's case, a T-shirt.

The tired and dejected sailors, deprived of their last liberty ashore, trudged back to *Flasher*. Soon, however, they were summoned by Whitaker, and told to follow him back to the tender. There Whitaker asked the junior duty officer for permission "for my men and me to go ashore." The young officer still refused to let the sailors by, pointing out the various technical defects in their dress. Whitaker then disappeared into the tender, to return with a senior staff officer, a captain, who said to the young duty officer, "Lieutenant, would you PLEASE let these men go ashore?" Thus, Corneau, Doty and friends finally got their liberty.

CHAPTER 6

KARIMATA STRAIT AND THE
FIRST WOLF PACK -
FLASHER'S THIRD WAR PATROL

On June 19, 1944, Captain Griggs of Submarine Squadron 12 came aboard *Flasher* to present awards and the Submarine Combat Insignia to her officers and crew. After a comment during the awards presentation that *Flasher's* crewmen performed well despite lapses in their dress code, Whitaker announced that maybe his men didn't look too good, but they "were the finest group of men to go to sea with."

Shortly before departure at 5 p.m. for her third war patrol, Whitaker picked up *Flasher's* orders and dropped them off for Exec. Ray DuBois to look over. They required *Flasher* to travel up Makassar Strait off the east coast of Borneo, proceed westerly across northern Borneo through Balabac Strait between Borneo and Palawan Island, and into the South China Sea. While there was clear intelligence the Japanese had mined Balabac Strait, some submarines had successfully transited it, and the Fremantle command wanted the strait utilized.

DuBois had gone through Balabac on *USS Snapper* in 1942, and the strait had not been easy then. Now it was mined. One theory for transiting the strait successfully was to race through while the tide was

Chart of Third Patrol (June 19, 1944 to Aug. 7, 1944) (by Author)

running, and the tethered mines would tip over in the current, allowing more clearance for the subs. DuBois thought it was crazy to risk so dangerous a passage when better, much safer passages into the South China Sea were available by travelling around the south of Borneo, or up through the Sulu Sea past Mindoro.

Whitaker said: "Ray, we'll be one of three submarines going through Balabac."

"I don't care how many submarines are going through Balabac," responded DuBois. "It's stupid to go through there when there are other ways to get to the patrol station."

"Oh, shit!" Whitaker said, then asked, "What do you want to do?"

"Get the orders changed."

Whitaker said "Oh shit" again. Getting orders changed was a near impossibility, but Whitaker went back and somehow got a different route that avoided Balabac Strait. *Flasher* was to proceed to the South China Sea on her third patrol by way of Karimata Strait between Borneo and Sumatra. Karimata Strait was a dangerous route, as it had large areas of shallow water and mines, but for Whitaker and DuBois it was far better than Balabac.

USS Robalo (SS 273, pronounced "Robe'-el-low") had been moored alongside *Flasher* at Fremantle. She would depart three days after *Flasher* on June 22, also on her third war patrol, under Cmdr. Manning Kimmel. (Kimmel had been in charge of *Flasher's* relief crew after her first patrol.) Kimmel also received, but had apparently not challenged, orders for Balabac Strait. *Robalo* was able to pass through the deadly strait successfully into the South China Sea.

On her return through Balabac on July 26, though, *Robalo* struck a mine and sank. Some of the crew survived the sinking only to die while in Japanese custody. Clay Blair indicates in *Silent Victory* that American Intelligence learned *Robalo's* helpless survivors were brutally murdered by their Japanese captors in supposed retaliation for American air attacks on Palawan.

Two weeks after *Robalo's* sinking, the *USS Flier* (SS 250), built next to *Flasher* at the Victory Yard and commissioned three weeks after *Flasher*, met the same fate. On August 13, 1944, she struck a mine in Balabac Strait and sank. Over a dozen crewmen escaped the sinking *Flier*, but only about half of these were able to swim or float to a nearby island. One of the survivors was the executive officer, Lt. James W. Liddell, Jr. Liddell, who had been blown through the conning tower hatch by the blast, was a former shipmate of DuBois', and had been with DuBois on *Snapper* in 1942 when they made it through Balabac. The few *Flier* survivors were eventually rescued by *USS Redfin* (SS 272).

In the fall of 1944, the Navy held an inquiry in Fremantle into *Flier's* sinking. No inquiry was conducted for *Robalo* because there were no witnesses to her loss. Admiral Christie was officially cleared of any blame in *Flier's* sinking, but the loss of two submarines in a row due to orders through Balabac Strait probably contributed to his abrupt transfer later that year by Admiral Thomas C. Kinkaid. Christie and Kinkaid had disagreed on other matters. (Kinkaid was also the uncle of Manning Kimmel, skipper of *Robalo*.) Admiral James Fife would replace Christie at Fremantle in

December, 1944, just as he had earlier replaced him at
Brisbane, to Whitaker's chagrin. Balabac Strait was
abandoned as a passage by the Americans.

Out of the Victory Yard's first four boats, only
Dace (SS 247) and *Flasher* remained after less than a
year of service, as both *Dorado* and *Flier* were now lost.
Had Whitaker and DuBois not resisted *Flasher's* orders
to go through the strait, she might have been sunk as
well.

After dark and the completion of night-training
exercises with *HMAS Dubbo* off Fremantle, *Flasher*
released her escort and proceeded north toward
Exmouth Gulf. Transit to Exmouth Gulf was uneventful except for sightings of friendly aircraft and submarines *USS Puffer* (SS 268) and *USS Rasher*. (*Puffer* had
suffered and survived a severe depth charging in
Makassar Strait the previous October.)

Flasher arrived at Exmouth the morning of June
22, to moor alongside the fuel barge. During her
three-week refit in Fremantle, the No. 4 main ballast
tank had been converted to a fuel tank to increase her
fuel capacity and ability to stay on station during patrol. No one remembered the new tank in Fremantle
prior to departure, so *Flasher* had to take on almost
30,000 gallons of fuel to fill it and replenish the diesel
fuel used since Fremantle.

She also arrived with a sailor who had acute
appendicitis, only to find the station's Navy doctor
absent. After considering and rejecting several alterna-
tives, the station commander dispatched a "Kingfisher"
airplane to find and retrieve the doctor from the Australian "outback." In his patrol report, Whitaker lauded
the personal efforts of the station CO as deserving

"much credit for the manner in which he takes care of submarine interests with his very limited facilities." *Flasher* departed that afternoon, leaving Electrician Markom G. Spencer, Jr., in good hands.

Another of *Flasher's* electricians, Blaine Knop, provided the boat's lookouts with dolphin insignia for the jackets they wore now on the cooler June nights. (The northern hemisphere's summer months are winter for the southern hemisphere.) He made a stencil of the submarine qualification emblem, and used the yellow paint aboard to stencil it on their jackets. The emblem was a hit, and it wasn't long before Lt. McCants discovered that Knop was the boat's artist. Soon McCants made his way back to the maneuvering room, jacket in hand, to get his stenciled too. Knop wisecracked that, alas, the insignia were just for the lookouts. McCants, smiling, proceeded to explain that *gold* dolphins were technically reserved for officers (*silver* dolphins were for enlisted personnel). Also, the jackets were all U.S. Navy property that Knop had defaced, and the yellow anti-fouling paint was to be used only on the hull. "So," asked McCants, "are you going to stencil my jacket or not?" Knop did.

Back on *Flasher* after missing her second patrol, was Signalman Charles Joseph Moore, *Flasher's* poet. Moore characterized his shipmates' lot as an unlucky one, both afloat and ashore:

LIFE ON A SUBMARINE
Life on a submarine isn't so funny,
Plenty of cash but what good's the money.
Out to sea two months at a time
With no place to spend even a dime.

When that run is finished and you're finally back,
They pay you money 600 at a crack,
You shove off on liberty full of good cheer,
And four hours later you're chocked full of beer.

A week on the beach you're nearly a wreck,
Living in gin mills, sleeping on deck.
That girl that you met, she's really a honey,
She has lots of experience and most of your money.

Fourteen days later, well why mention that,
Your eyes are all bloodshot, your wallet is flat.
Then back to the ship you sorrowfully roll,
Soon you're out on another patrol.

Oh! life on a submarine isn't so funny,
Plenty of cash but what good's the money.
Right now, yes I swear it, when we get in this time
I'm going to send home every little thin dime.

     The submarine headed north on the surface during the trip to Lombok Strait, conducting training as before, with brief battle stations surfaced the afternoon of June 23. Diving after dawn on June 25, *Flasher* was unable to make any headway against the strong southerly current flowing through the strait. That evening she surfaced in virtually the same spot where she had submerged, despite proceeding against the current underwater for over 12 hours.

     Under cover of darkness, she began to transit the strait at flank speed on the surface. *Flasher* attempted to pass an enemy patrol boat to the east until running into a second one, so she changed course to pass west of both craft, coming within three miles of Nusa Besar Island. The enemy boats never sighted the camouflaged submarine.

Clearing Lombok shortly before midnight, *Flasher* changed course to the north-northeast to pass east of the Kangean Islands. She then curved westward, sighting sailboats and submerging for enemy plane contacts the following two days.

For the next 1,000 miles, *Flasher* would be operating in enemy-controlled waters that were not as deep as her own hull length (312 feet). Much of the water depth was only 200 feet, dangerous for submerged operations, and too shallow for evading enemy antisubmarine attacks.

Having travelled westerly across the length of the Java Sea, *Flasher* entered and transited Karimata Strait, between Borneo and Sumatra, the evening of June 27. As the sub neared Japanese-held Singapore, she was forced down in the shallow waters by two plane contacts, before sighting smoke shortly after 6 p.m. on June 28:

1812   Sighted smoke bearing 311° T. (Ship Contact No. 5). Commenced closing at four engine speed.

1920   Sighted mast bearing 300° T. and much smoke in this direction indicating a large convoy. Change in bearing of smoke and change of range indicates convoy headed for Singapore on course of about 295° T.

1953   Radar Contact on last ship of convoy bearing 303° T. range 19,500 yards. Commenced end around to starboard as we would have the best water in this direction.

2100   Found that convoy had about 13 large ships with several small ones believed to be escorts. Ships appeared to be in four groups with about three merchantmen in each group, and with an escort on each side of each group. It was evident that we would have to attack in water of not more than 25 fathoms. It also appeared that we could only make one attack as the convoy was close to really shallow water to the northwest and we felt sure they would seek the protection of this shallow water after the first attack. The Commanding Officer was reluctant to make a submerged moonlight attack in this depth of water. It was also considered that a surface attack offered the best opportunity of doing the most damage to the enemy. We also hoped we would be able to evade on the surface after our attack and thereby avoid a lot of trouble for ourselves. We therefore decided to wait for moonset at 0055.

2209   Arrived on desired station about 40° on the starboard bow of leading group of convoy at range of 17,000 yards. Decided to remain here until moonset. Convoy base course checks at 295° T. speed 9.75 knots. The leading group of three ships contained two of the largest ships in the convoy. We therefore decided to attack these two large ships.

June 29, 1944

0052   Heavy clouds covered moon which was

about set anyway. Went to battle stations and commenced approach for attack. Picked up escort on starboard bow of leading ship at range of 7,500 yards. Continued to keep bow pointed at escort. With range of 4,000 yards on escort, and with him directly ahead, he gave us a zero angle on bow. Since convoy has also zigged toward, did not feel that he had seen us, but felt we had to get out from in front of him so changed course to left with full rudder and put him on our starboard quarter. Kept him in this position until range started to open at 3,000 yards. At this time convoy has zigged away and we had an angle on the bow of about 65° starboard on the leading ship, range about 5,500 yards. Came right with full rudder and headed in for 90° starboard track. This course would pass us about 2,000 yards astern of escort. Had just headed in when we picked up another escort on port bow at 4,500 yards. Felt we could complete attack before he could worry us. With gyro angles about zero and torpedo run to leading ship about 3,500 yards the first and second ships were almost overlapping, with the second ship about 700 yards closer than the leading ship. From this position fired three torpedoes at leading ship with 1° offset and immediately fired three at second ship with 1° offset. On completion of firing commenced reversing course to right with full rudder and at flank speed. Had hoped to fire stern

tubes at third ship but this did not develop
as he had fallen too far astern. Two minutes
and twenty five seconds after firing first torpedo, a torpedo hit the center of the first target. Immediately thereafter a torpedo hit
just forward of the stack on the second target. Two other hits were then observed on
first target, one forward and one aft. A second hit was then observed on the second target about midway between his MOT and
stern. The first target, with three hits was
seen to break in two and sink almost immediately. The second target with two hits
appeared to have stopped, and commenced
firing a gun aft. No splashes were seen and
I doubt if he knew where we were. Commenced evading on the surface at full power.

0121 Leading escort started dropping depth
charges.

0124 With range of 5,500 yards heard and observed heavy explosion on damaged ship
followed by cloud of black smoke. When
smoke began to clear away, could no longer
see ship, nor could we find him on radar,
only one ship of leading group still being in
sight. He was well to the left of smoke and
had turned his stern to us. The remainder of
the convoy had also turned away and were
headed in the direction of the "really shallow water." Since escorts were between us
and the convoy and since it became evident
we could not reach an attack position before
they were protected by shallow water, we

decided to clear the area and head for our patrol station. One officer (the engineer officer) had been detailed to do nothing but watch the targets. He identified the first as a large freighter of about 8,000 tons and the second as a large transport of about 10,000 tons. The Commanding Officer was well occupied with details of the attack and can only state that they both appeared to be large ships with the second definitely larger than the first. The second appeared to have a considerable amount of superstructure and is believed to have been a passenger-freighter type.

0552　Submerged. Decided to remain submerged today because of our attack and because of our nearness to Singapore.

1915　Surfaced, heading for patrol area at two engine speed.

Flasher had fired six Mark 14 steam torpedoes from her forward torpedo room with contact exploders and torpex, a more powerful explosive than the earlier TNT. The sequence of firing was tubes 3-4-5-6-1-2, at five- to eight-second intervals. Range was 3,625 yards for the large cargo vessel, a long shot. Estimated range was 3,000 yards on the second ship, a large cargo-transport. The first five torpedoes fired were hits, with only the last torpedo from the No. 2 tube a miss. Whitaker described the first target as a loaded cargo vessel with the mast-kingpost-funnel-kingpost-mast (MKFKM) construction, and the cargo-transport vessel as a mast-funnel-kingpost-mast-kingpost (MFKMK)

Two Views of Lower Portion of Periscope (Navpers 16160)

vessel resembling *Heian Maru,* a Japanese seaplane tender.

Fremantle credited *Flasher* with sinking two ships the night of June 29 off Singapore, those being a 7,500-ton cargo ship and a 10,000-ton transport "similar to *Heian Maru.*" Postwar analysis by JANAC showed that the cargo vessel was the 6,079-ton *Nippo Maru* (or *Niho Maru*). No postwar credit was given for the sinking of the larger cargo transport, indicating *Flasher* may have only damaged the second ship. JANAC gave no credit for damage—JANAC's published report only confirmed outright sinkings.

Alden indicated in *U.S. Submarine Attacks of World War II* that *Flasher* may have caused heavy damage to the enormous *Notoro*. His subsequent research of Ultra intercepts confirmed this, and revealed that *Notoro* had to be towed into Singapore. Built in 1920 as part of the *Shiretoko*-Class oilers, the 14,050-ton *Notoro* was modified as a seaplane carrier in 1924, then reconverted in 1942 to a fleet tanker when Japan needed tankers more than seaplanes. While the *Notoro* did differ in configuration from the *Heian Maru*-type vessel Whitaker described as the second target that night, the differing configurations are easily reconciled. This was only one of several very damaging attacks *Notoro* survived during the war, but which effectively removed her from the Japanese war effort. *Flasher* would have missed this convoy altogether had she taken her original assigned route through Balabac Strait.

　　Flasher surfaced the evening of June 29 to charge batteries and proceed northward across the large, shallow continental shelf between Indochina and Borneo, running on two engines at 15 knots while charging with the other two engines. She remained on the surface the following day, passing about 45 miles west of Natoena Island early in the morning and finally entering deeper waters. The boat arrived in her patrol area in the South China Sea between Indochina and Manila, Philippines, shortly after dawn on July 1.

　　This third patrol would be different since *Flasher* was part of Fremantle's first "wolf pack," along with *USS Crevalle* (SS 291) and *USS Angler* (SS 240). The Pearl Harbor command had already initiated wolf packs and considered the use of three or more subs patrolling together successful. Unlike Pearl Harbor's packs, Fremantle's wolf packs would never bear the official nicknames of her ComSubPac counterparts, such as "Blair's Blasters" or "Hydeman's Hepcats," etc.[15] Also, Fremantle did not assign the pack command to a squadron commander (as was the initial Pearl Harbor practice), but let their early wolf packs proceed under the senior of the three sub captains. As senior commander, Whitaker was in charge of the first Fremantle wolf pack. This was the third war patrol for *Flasher*, and the fourth for both *Crevalle* and *Angler*.

The three subs proceeded at different times to the patrol area, travelling separately to avoid congestion through narrow straits such as Lombok. *Crevalle* and *Angler* were supposed to depart shortly after *Flasher*, but *Angler* damaged her starboard prop on June 24 and had to return to Fremantle for repairs. Continuing a patrol with a noisy propeller would have been suicidal. *Angler's* repairs were completed and she finally left Fremantle on June 29.

When *Flasher* arrived in the patrol area on July 1, she was to wait several days for *Crevalle*, and an estimated two weeks for the waylaid *Angler*. Whitaker decided to patrol alone in the center of the South China Sea at a point where probable enemy traffic routes between Saigon and Manila would intersect with a north-south route between Singapore and Japan. Nothing developed the following two days as *Flasher*

---

[15] William J. Ruhe was exec. of *Crevalle* at the time, and reports the pack did call itself "Whitaker's Wolves," with the following code names for the three skippers: "Dumbo" for Whitaker, "Patsy" for Cmdr. Walker in *Crevalle*, and "Goatfish" for Cmdr. Hess in *Angler*. For this and other details of the patrol, see Ruhe, *War in the Boats*, Washington: Brassey's, Inc., 1994.

patrolled, zigzagging on the surface around this theo-retically rich patrol area. Lookouts sighted an oil-drum raft the afternoon of July 3, and the crew used it for 20mm gun training, expending 300 rounds. Whitaker justified the ammunition expenditure as "these were quite large and heavy drums and considering them a menace in our area, decided to try to sink them." Even after all the gunfire, the drum raft did not sink imme-diately, but Whitaker felt sure it sank after *Flasher* left the area.

Shortly before midnight *Flasher* arrived for a surface patrol about seven miles off Hon Doi, Indo-china, but saw only sailboats, small coastal freighters of 700 to 800 tons, and a 200-ton trawler, all of which Whitaker rejected as unworthy targets. It turned out Whitaker was right to be choosy, as he would need all his torpedoes for much better targets. If *Flasher* had attacked small freighters, she could have sunk more ships by war's end, but not the total shipping tonnage she achieved. Also, once any target was attacked, en-emy shipping would avoid the area, and antisubma-rine activities (especially air cover) would make the area dangerous.

Flasher surfaced after dark July 7 and moved out from the land to conduct her night surface patrol. An hour later she would have her first significant contact since the attacks near Singapore:

2030   SJ Radar Contact bearing 229° T. range 14,300 yards (Ship Contact No. 14). This ship was close to Hon Doi and was seen to be headed north. Commenced tracking. Moon is about full but it is overcast and raining. Will have to make surface attack.

2055 Picked up escort on starboard beam of target. This escort was very active and never maintained any fixed station for long.

2201 SJ Radar Contact bearing 000 T. range 6,500 yards (Ship Contact No. 15). Believed this to be small sail boat but it was raining hard and he was dead ahead so was forced to avoid. This put me back on beam of target at 13,000 yards.

2220 Target has Cape Varella abeam to port about 2500 yards.

2315 Arrived at point about 6500 yards ahead of target and about 1000 yards off his track to starboard. As we have eight torpedoes aft and ten forward, decided to fire aft. Slowed to let target overtake us. Still raining although it is fairly bright, feel we can get away with night attack all right.

2329 Set tubes aft on four feet just in case target is shallow draft. We know nothing about him at this time as we haven't seen him.

2340 Sighted target at 4350 yards with about 10° starboard angle on bow. Commenced working around for stern shot, keeping stern to target. Target appears to be medium freighter of about 4,000-5,000 tons. Wish that tubes were on six feet, but will not change them now.

2354 Fired four torpedoes aft with 2° divergent spread. Target course 345° T., speed 9.6 knots, track 75° starboard, torpedo run 2100 yards. Escort at this time was well back on starboard quarter of target and well out of way. One torpedo was seen and heard to hit target almost under the foremast. Another was seen and heard to hit midway between MOT and stern. This one threw up a cloud of sparks. With escort astern at about 2700 yards, commenced heading out slowly watching for target to sink.

2357   Escort commenced racing about wildly trying to find us. Am sure he never saw us.

2400   Target was seen to sink and at the same time disappeared from radar at range of 3,000 yards. Commenced clearing area.

July 8, 1944

0003   Escort commenced dropping depth charges, a total of 10 depth charges being dropped.

0022   Lost escort on SJ radar. Commenced heading back to patrol station off Hon Doi.

Two of the Mark 14-3A steam torpedoes and two of the Mark 23 steam torpedoes were fired, all carrying contact exploders and torpex. Whitaker had good track angles, ranging from 74° to 78°, and a good shooting range of 2,300 yards. The target was identified as a medium freighter "similar in outline and length to the *Tarusima Maru*, ONI 208-J (Rev.) Page 102, with single AM escort." The freighter was identified after the war as the 3,557-ton *Koto Maru No. 2* (or just *Koto Maru*), built in 1927 and requisitioned by the Japanese government earlier in the war.

The following day was spent submerged, and under increased enemy air activities. The planes

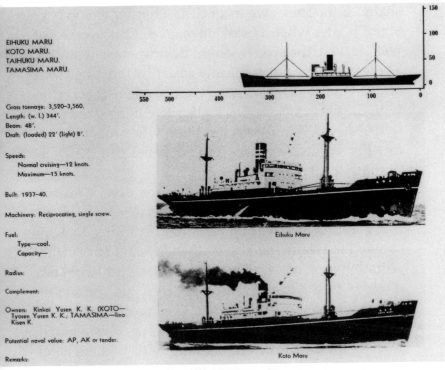
EIHUKU MARU.
KOTO MARU.
TAIHUKU MARU.
TAMASIMA MARU.

Gross tonnage: 3,520–3,560.
Length: (w. l.) 344'.
Beam: 48'.
Draft: (loaded) 22' (light) 8'.

Speeds:
    Normal cruising—12 knots.
    Maximum—15 knots.

Built: 1937–40.

Machinery: Reciprocating, single screw.

Fuel:
    Type—coal.
    Capacity—

Radius:

Complement:

Owners: Kinkai Yusen K. K. (KOTO—
    Tyosen Yusen K. K.; TAMASIMA—Iino
    Kisen K.

Potential naval value: AP, AK or tender.

Remarks:

Eihuku Maru

Koto Maru

Koto Maru (ONI 208-J)

dropped numerous bombs, but none close to *Flasher*. The same pattern continued for the next two days, with heavy enemy air coverage and almost no small coastal traffic, all apparently the result of the sub's successful attack on July 7. Japanese aircraft including Rufes, Idas, Sallys, and Jakes, all sought the submarine. Continued hunting in this area would now be difficult, but *Flasher* remained, conducting night surface patrols and diving each morning for periscope patrols during daylight.

One morning Signalman Corneau was high above *Flasher* performing the pre-dawn ritual of cleaning the periscope lenses and greasing the periscope shafts. If the lenses were not clear, Frenchy would hear about it later when *Flasher* dove, and if the grease not well packed, the scopes would drip water when used. These jobs were not made any easier by the rough seas and the noisy, high winds. Corneau had checked in with the Officer of the Deck prior to climbing the periscope shears, but he was forgotten when lookouts below him sighted a closing enemy plane and the OOD urgently ordered a dive.

Oblivious to the plane and the dive, Corneau had just decided to rest from his tasks when he noticed that *Flasher's* bow was under water. A frantic look aft showed the stern was rising. Frenchy could not swim, although even an excellent swimmer would have been doomed in the heavy seas. He threw his grease gun and equipment over the side and scrambled at record speed down the shears to the conning tower hatch. Luckily for Corneau, although the OOD had the hatch lanyard in his hand, he had not yet yanked the hatch cover closed. Corneau leapt down the hatch and, without catching a single rung of the ladder, hit the conning tower deck below. Then the hatch slammed shut and the boat slid under the waves. From then on, whenever he had to go up to service the periscopes, Corneau provided each OOD with a whistle to blow in case of a dive.

(Corneau was luckier than one former shipmate, who was transferred from *Flasher* in 1943 following his injury in a car accident. The sailor was put on a later-built Electric Boat submarine after his release from the hospital, only to drown when he failed to come down from the lookout post when the boat dove. An autopsy disclosed he had suffered undetected ear damage from the auto accident, and this had prevented his hearing the diving alarm.)

Other than airplane sightings, *Flasher* saw little enemy traffic in the area, and ignored three north-bound coastal vessels of about 150 to 350 tons apiece. The evening of July 11, *Flasher* surfaced after dark and headed for a new patrol station offshore. She switched places with *Crevalle*, which arrived July 5, and patrolled to the east while the two boats waited for *Angler*. *Crevalle* continued the submerged inshore patrols. The next morning *Flasher* arrived at her new station 90 miles off Indochina, at a probable Saigon-to-Takao traffic route. Later that day, *Angler* finally arrived and patrolled a short distance south of *Flasher*.

After dawn on July 13, *Flasher* sighted two ships to the east-northeast and began closing at 15 knots. Whitaker became worried when he realized he might be closing too fast, so he reversed course and began to open out, only to lose the convoy. *Flasher* again changed course and closed slowly. At this point the sub was sighted, an escort and a patrolling "Mavis" seaplane raced toward her, and she dove before finishing her contact report to *Angler*. As soon as *Flasher* submerged, she changed course 80° to port, and when the Mavis dropped her bomb, *Flasher* was already far removed from the targeted diving point.

For the next hour, *Flasher* played cat and mouse with a pinging minelayer-type escort, which at one point passed directly over her. Whitaker commented, "Don't see why he didn't stop and play with us." Over the following three and a half hours *Flasher* surfaced three times, only to be driven down each time by air-craft. Finally, she surfaced shortly before 2 p.m. and sent *Angler* the estimated course and location of the convoy. No attempt was made to notify *Crevalle,* as her inshore patrol assignment meant she would be submerged and unable to receive radio messages. *Angler* and *Flasher* were unable to regain contact with the convoy by noon the next day, so Whitaker ordered new patrol stations for the two boats and abandoned the search.

The next few days *Flasher* patrolled northeast of her prior patrol area, in the center of the South China Sea. The wait for a target here proved to be deadly dull, with only two very long range radar reports of possible planes. It had been more than ten days since *Flasher's* last offensive action and there had been few sightings. The crew became noticeably irritable. While not everyone lost his sense of humor, enough pet peeves surfaced to make things uncomfortable for all aboard. To make things worse, visibility had become poor and the seas rough. After four days on her new patrol station without a single significant contact, Whitaker radioed *Crevalle* to learn whether she had any sightings, but the other sub had had no luck either. This was enough for Whitaker, who decided Fremantle's first wolf pack was wasting its time in the present search area:

2315 Sent the boss a message expressing doubt as to whether traffic here warranted the continued employment of three submarines. It appears to me that we aren't having much luck and I feel that maybe there are better areas.

The following morning, July 19, found *Flasher* still waiting in the same unproductive location, experiencing rough weather and poor visibility, when at:

1046   Sighted ship as it came out of poor visibility, bearing 050° T. range about 15,000 yards. The Officer of the Deck (Ensign Hamlin) used very sound judgment and sounded the diving alarm immediately thereby preventing us from being sighted (Ship Contact No. 18).

When the enemy was sighted, Ensign Jim Hamlin had "pulled the plug" without even checking with Lt. Snap Coffin, just a few feet aft on the cigarette deck. Coffin had to wait with the others for an explanation, after scrambling down the hatch as *Flasher* slid below the waves.

1052   Identified contact as KUMA Class Cruiser escorted by one destroyer on his port bow. Angle on bow of cruiser is zero. Commenced approach. Set torpedo depth 12 feet.

1103   Target zigged 30° to right. Headed in for bow shot. Target making 185 RPM. Estimated him at 18 knots.

1106   Target gave us about a seven degree port angle on the bow with us headed across his track. Went ahead full and came right for stern shot. His range now about 2,500 yards. It is going to be close as to whether we get around and squared away in time.

1110   Commenced firing stern tubes on track of

about 120° port. Didn't mean to let him get this far by but we were too slow. Fired four torpedoes with about 1400 yard torpedo runs, about 30° left gyro angle, with estimated speed 17 knots. Spread by periscope. Was forced to "take her down" at this point as destroyer escort was on our port beam at about 500 yards with a zero angle on the bow. Don't think he saw us but he sure looks mean.

1110-58　Heard one torpedo hit followed about ten seconds later by another one.

1114　Destroyer started dropping depth charges, all pretty close.

1118　Destroyer dropped last of 15 depth charges in initial attack. Spent the next hour and twenty minutes trying to outguess the escort. He always appeared to be fairly close but apparently didn't have good contact as no further charges were dropped during this period.

1240　At periscope depth. Sighted cruiser dead in water bearing 207° T, range about 6,500 yards. Destroyer is patrolling up and down this side of him. Cruiser is down by the stern and has a good port list. He has considerable yellow smoke coming up aft and his mainmast has disappeared. Commenced approach for bow tube shot.

1318　It appears now that cruiser may have a slight bit of headway, so set him up for three knots. He could not possibly be making more speed as we have been making only four

Flasher's Torpedo Striking the Imperial Japanese Navy Light Cruiser Oi (by Author)

knots and have been closing him nicely with a 120° port angle on the bow.

1326　Had intended to close in to about 1500 yards but at this point with range to cruiser of 3200 yards, and with destroyer headed for us at about 2,000 yards, decided to go ahead and fire. Fired four bow tubes spread by periscope with half a target length between torpedoes. With this setup I didn't see how we could miss, but we did. Spread should have taken care of at least a 3 knot speed error.

1327　Went deep as destroyer continued to close rapidly. The sea was very rough by this time and it is possible that these torpedoes, set at ten feet, did not perform properly.

1335　Destroyer commenced dropping depth charges none of which were very close.

1345　Destroyer dropped last of thirteen depth charges. Spent next two hours getting out from the immediate vicinity of destroyer.

1548　Periscope depth. Sighted cruiser bearing 135° T, range about 9,000 yards. Also saw destroyer in vicinity of cruiser. Cruiser is apparently still dead in water. Commenced another approach. It now became necessary to reload forward as we only had torpedoes left in tubes Nos. 1 and 2 and they had been flooded so long that I didn't trust them. Depth control was too uncertain at periscope depth due to rough seas, so was forced to run at 150 feet during reload. This was bad as I could not look. The reload was complicated by the fact that two of my four remaining torpedoes were lined up for tubes Nos. 1 and 2 which were already loaded. We were forced to move these torpedoes down to tubes Nos. 5 and 6 by chain fall. This process took an awful long time and we were trying to keep to a minimum of noise.

1608 From now until 1630 heard what appeared to be much gunfire in direction of cruiser. Also heard two heavy explosions that we could not identify.

1651 Sighted destroyer bearing 139° T. range about 7,000 yards. Cruiser not in sight. This is about the position cruiser was last sighted. Continued to close last known position of cruiser. Destroyer remained in this vicinity.

1744 Destroyer took departure on course about 245° at high speed.

1756 Watched destroyer disappear bearing 253° T. on course about 245° which would head him for Saigon. By this time we were in vicinity of last known position of cruiser. Sighted some floating debris including oil cans and drums. It is possible that cruiser might have sunk or that destroyer might have sunk him. Also realize that he may have gotten underway and that destroyer might have been left behind to worry us. With this in mind decided to conduct search for him after surfacing.

1907 Surfaced. Sent ANGLER a message and told him to search for cruiser in sector 240-270 from last known position. Also told him we would search to south of course 240° T. Also

told CREVALLE to assume cruiser headed
for Saigon and to take course to intercept.

When the first torpedo hit, Cook Hidetaro
Wakahara of the Imperial Japanese Navy was in the
cruiser's galley below decks, and roughly amidships,
preparing the noon meal. The lights went out immediately and the ship listed, making movement deep in
the pitch-dark cruiser dangerous and difficult. Then a
second torpedo hit. Wakahara was somehow able to
navigate topside to the forward area through hatches
and up ladders, where he found men leaping into the
water. The aft two-thirds of the 500-foot cruiser broke
away and immediately sank.

Having heard that sinking ships sucked those
nearby in the water down with them, Wakahara leapt
as far away from the bow section as he could, into the
oily seas below. He became covered in the fuel or oil,
but was fished out by an escort, only to collapse on
deck. He awoke much later to find himself lying
among corpses of his former shipmates. (One of 330
Japanese sailors rescued following *Oi's* sinking,
Wakahara married a Japanese-American student after
the war, and moved to Southern California. The *Oi*
survivors' association to which he belongs held a
reunion in Japan on July 19, 1994, the 50th anniversary
of the sinking.)

Uncertain whether the cruiser had sunk, the
wolf pack searched for the cruiser that evening, until
Whitaker decided to give up shortly after midnight.
They needn't have bothered, since the *Kuma*-class light
cruiser *Oi* of the Imperial Japanese Navy lay more than
two miles below, on the bottom of the South China Sea.

Hidetaro Wakahara of Light Cruiser *Oi*
(Courtesy of Mr. and Mrs. Wakahara and Mr. Terry)

Flasher had fired four steam torpedoes from her stern tubes. The two newer Mark 23 torpedoes missed forward and aft of the cruiser, while the older Mark 14-3A torpedoes were hits. At a close range of 1,200 yards, *Flasher* had hit 50 percent of her hurried shots at an escorted warship making an estimated 17 knots in rough seas with frequent course changes. The four bow shots at the crippled cruiser were fired at a target with an estimated speed of only three knots, but at almost triple the range, or 3,400 yards, and all four of these carefully aimed torpedoes missed.

Japanese cruisers were named after rivers in Japan. The Oi River flows south through a valley into the Pacific midway between Tokyo and Nagoya. The light cruiser *Oi* was completed in 1921, and was relegated to training duties following the controversial 1930 London ship limitation treaty, along with her four sister ships of the *Kuma* class. Officers (including Minoru Genda, the pilot who planned the Pearl Harbor attack) served or trained on *Oi* in her two decades of service prior to the war. During the growing Japanese militarization of the late 1930's, she and the rest of her class were reactivated, refitted and modernized.

Oi was believed to have seven 5½-inch guns, eight torpedo launchers, 80 mines, 24 depth charges and a catapult with seaplane, according to Office of Naval Intelligence (ONI) Publication 41-42 as available to *Flasher* in 1944. However, after several years of planning by the Japanese high command, *Oi* had been secretly converted at the Maizuru Naval Arsenal, and by 1942 was armed with 40 of the deadly Long Lance Japanese torpedoes in 10 four-torpedo launchers, along with four deck guns. *Oi* and her sister ship *Kitakami* became the world's most heavily armed, high-speed torpedo cruisers, equipped with the world's best torpedoes. The two cruisers were designed to lead the attack on the American fleet expected to confront the Japanese.

After Pearl Harbor, there was no U.S. fleet left to directly challenge the Japanese Navy. *Oi* became part of the "Main Force" that unsuccessfully attempted to invade Midway in April, 1942. With Guadalcanal and a sudden need for beach-assault craft, *Oi* was sent to

Truk and utilized as a high-speed transport, carrying troops, supplies and six Daihatsu 46-foot landing craft. Along with destroyers and submarines, *Oi* helped reinforce embattled Imperial army forces in the Solomons and New Guinea. In 1943, she and *Kitakami* were sent to operate out of Singapore.

ONI 41-42 had indicated *Oi's* "underwater protection very good" but two of *Flasher's* torpedoes had penetrated this and she went to the bottom. Naval Intelligence Captain Jasper Holmes reported in *Undersea Victory II* that the accompanying destroyer was able to rescue almost two-thirds of *Oi's* crew, prior to *Oi's* sinking five hours after the attack.[16]

Following the patrol, *Flasher* was given 5,100 tons credit for sinking a *Kuma*-class cruiser, in one of the rare wartime underestimations of tonnage. *Oi's* displacement was increased to 5,700 tons by JANAC. In fact, her standard displacement had increased to 5,860 or 5,870 tons with the 1941 modification to a torpedo cruiser, and her trial displacement was around 7,000 tons.

When sunk, *Oi* was in the middle of the South China Sea headed to the southwest, apparently to rejoin the Imperial Japanese Fleet at Singapore. Three months later, when the fleet sailed for the greatest naval engagements in history at Leyte Gulf, it would be without the assistance of the Imperial Japanese Navy's Light Cruiser *Oi*, her many Long Lance torpedoes, her five-inch guns, and her substantial antiaircraft batteries, due to the actions of the *USS Flasher*.

The three-sub wolf pack received orders the

---

[16] New York: Kensington Publishing Co., 1979, p. 109.

Naval Intelligence Photo of Light Cruiser *Oi*
(Naval Historical Center)

evening of July 21 to move closer to the Philippines. The pack proceeded to their new position slightly northwest of Manila, with *Flasher* approximately 30 miles offshore, and *Crevalle* and *Angler* located due west of her at 20-mile intervals. Nothing happened until the third day, July 24, when airplane contacts repeatedly forced *Flasher* down. Because of the planes, Whitaker ordered submerged daylight patrols for the pack.

The enemy aircraft harassment was probably due to Japanese radar, since the Japanese were employing more and better radar and radar-homing devices against the submarines. Many subs operating close to Japan already used their SD air search radar infrequently, and then only in short bursts to avoid Japanese homing on the radar signal.

Late on the afternoon of the 24th, *Flasher* met with *Angler* to get spare vacuum tubes to repair *Flasher's* malfunctioning surface (SJ-a) radar. The tubes failed to correct the unit's transmitter, but the problem was traced to a defective condenser, which was replaced. The radar was fixed in time for a contact early the next morning, when at:

0555   Received contact report from ANGLER reporting 10 ship convoy on course about 310° T. Set course to intercept.

0700   Sighted smoke bearing 216° T. distance about 15 miles. (Ship Contact No. 19). Sent contact report to ANGLER and CREVALLE. Commenced tracking and commenced pulling ahead of convoy.

0722   ANGLER told us that base course of convoy was 335° T. speed 8. This checked with us except that convoy speed seemed a little faster.

0752   Received message that ANGLER was diving.

0755   Sighted large flying boat bearing 060° T. distance 10 miles and headed towards us. (Plane Contact No. 23). Sent aircraft plain language contact report while diving. This put us in a bad spot about 20,000 yards off convoy track. Decided to head in on normal approach course at high speed. Commenced doing so.

0841　Took look and sighted smoke and tops of ships. We are holding bearing pretty well and believe we can get in if battery holds out.

0857　Went to battle stations.

0915　Counted 14 large ships in convoy plus a large number of good escorts ranging from destroyers down to PC boats. At this time it looked as if we might get in for a shot on an end ship. Convoy was arranged in two columns of about five ships each with a third column of what appeared to be the most important ships in the center. The center column was seen to contain two or three large tankers and an escort carrier bringing up the rear. Could see a few planes on his deck, but he had none in the air.

0926　Sighted escort close with small angle on bow. Kept heading in. It seemed that every time I took a look from now on I had an escort close aboard.

Even in the middle of danger, Whitaker would sometimes exhibit his wry sense of humor. Knowing the periscope was already on low viewing power, a setting obvious to anyone who looked at the periscope controls, he quipped, "I'm shifting to low power—that escort's scaring me on high power." How such humor went over with the tense group in the conning tower is anybody's guess. Auxiliaryman Bill Beaman also recalls Whitaker reporting the bow wake of an escort actually washing over the periscope.

0949   Decided I would have to take a look although one escort appeared close aboard bearing about 230° Relative. Raised periscope just in time to watch escort pass over after torpedo room. While we were frantically getting periscope out of sight the after torpedo room reported fast screws passing over. This upset our plans as we felt we might have been sighted. Was forced to go to 100 feet so we would have a little start on him if he started dropping them. At this point I couldn't tell anything from sound. There were screws and pinging in all directions.

0956   Made observation and found a destroyer about 400 yards away but with large angle on bow. Found that convoy had changed base course without our knowing it due to our high speed running to get in. We now found that the whole convoy had passed over us. Could have fired long-range shot at this point with about 120 track but as we only had six torpedoes and as ANGLER and CREVALLE still had not attacked, decided to wait and make another end around. Commenced tracking convoy submerged. His patrol plane is still with him. Course now about 010° T, speed about 10 knots. This is a convoy of large, fast ships. I don't believe there is a ship present of less than about 6,000 tons.

1156   Surfaced and commenced trailing.

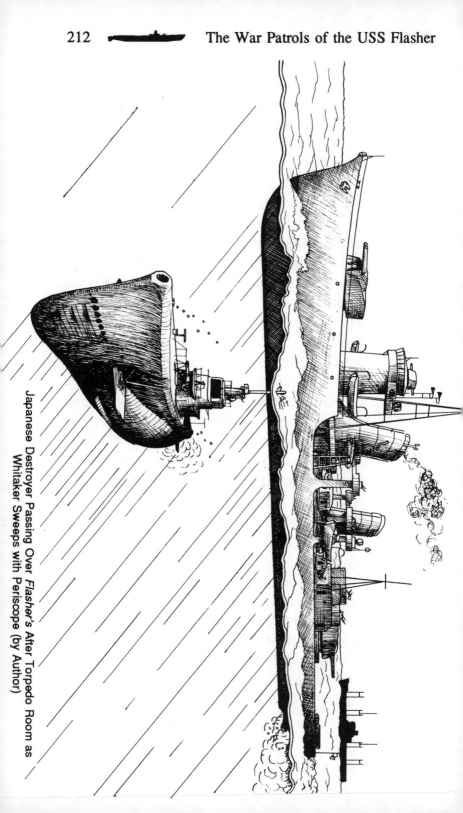

Japanese Destroyer Passing Over *Flasher's* After Torpedo Room as Whitaker Sweeps with Periscope (by Author)

1205   Visibility closed in and we lost sight of convoy. Decided it would be impossible to make end around in this weather. Decided to trail.

1222   CREVALLE reported she was ahead and commencing attack. Our SJ radar being back in operation, decided to close in slowly hoping to get radar contact.

1450   Heard two loud explosions followed by many more. Decided CREVALLE had made attack and is getting worked over. Sound believes best bearing is now 330° relative. Can now hear loud pinging in this direction. Commenced closing at high speed as I believed convoy would now alter base course and felt we had to see them if we were to regain contact.

1554   Sighted smoke and masts of convoy bearing 031° T. distance about 14 miles. Changed course to head for them. Angle on bow about 180°.

1558   Sighted escort bearing 330° T. at range of about 14,000 yards with about zero angle on bow. Submerged. Don't think he sighted us as visibility was poor, but did not want to get sighted at this point. After diving found that there were two escorts apparently searching for CREVALLE. Put our stern toward them and commenced opening out.

1704   Escorts no longer in sight, but can still hear their pings. Surfaced.

1707   Sighted escort astern. Submerged to keep from being sighted. Continued opening out.

1725　It commenced raining very hard. Took advantage of reduced visibility and surfaced. Put on four engines and opened out from escorts. Sent our best dope to ANGLER.

1742　Decided we were well clear so changed course to head for convoy.

1803　Sighted escort bearing 290° T. He appears to also be joining convoy. The visibility was poor in our direction, so turned our tail toward him and soon lost him. Still trying to regain contact at four engine speed.

1820　Told ANGLER that CREVALLE and escort were about 30 miles behind convoy. It appears that FLASHER will have to regain contact as ANGLER and CREVALLE appear to be pretty well out of the picture.

2048　Was afraid we had lost contact for good, but at this point we picked them up bearing 060° T. range 22,000 yards. Sent Contact report to CREVALLE and ANGLER and commenced tracking and working toward port bow of convoy. I felt that I had to wait to attack until one of the other boats got contact, especially in view of the fact that I only had six torpedoes.

2207　Sent contact report giving enemy course 020° T. speed of advance 11 knots. He seems to be making 12 knots through water. We are just fooling around, tracking and charging batteries.

2254　Sent contact report giving enemy course 005° T. speed of advance 11 knots.

July 26, 1944

0005   Sent another contact report.

0105   Sent another contact report giving enemy course as 030° T. speed of advance 11 knots.

0130   Convoy apparently stopped zig zagging. Visibility poor with many rain squalls.

0140   ANGLER reported contact. Sent message that we were commencing attack and started in. We are now 10,000 yards from leading ship in port column and about 4,000 yards off his track.

0201   It now seems that we will have to fire at about a 60° track and even so we will be close to two escorts.

0209   Changed course to 150° T. and headed in for 60° port track at 10 knots.

0211   With torpedo run about 3,000 yards and with one escort on port bow at 2,500 yards and with one on starboard bow at 2,000 yards commenced firing forward. Fired three torpedoes at second ship in column and then shifted and fired three at third ship. Used 1° divergent spread.

Flasher was still on the surface, relying for protection on the darkness and her camouflage paint. After firing the torpedoes, Whitaker yelled down from the bridge: "All ahead flank! Right full rudder!"

In the conning tower below, DuBois quickly countermanded Whitaker's order, calling out: "Left full rudder!"

Whitaker then yelled down: "Ray! What the hell's going on?"

DuBois responded: "You have a destroyer to starboard! You're going to run into him going right!" DuBois, standing near the SJ radar PPI scope in the conning tower, could see better where all the enemy ships were located, than could Whitaker in the darkness. So *Flasher* turned left:

> Went ahead flank and commenced turning left with full rudder. The range to the escort to starboard is now 1800 yards and he has about 20° starboard angle on bow. This puts us inside of him. Came to course 030° true, this being the convoy base course. We are now in good position to act as an additional escort, but feel that I cannot get out until we pull ahead a little. One minute and fifty eight seconds after firing first torpedo, observed and heard first hit just forward of center of first target. This was followed by a second hit well aft on first target. About 10 seconds later a torpedo was seen to hit the second target just aft of the center.
>
> 0214 We were feeling pretty good as we had hit both our targets and especially as the range on the escort astern had opened to 1900 yards and we had as yet not been detected. At this point however, our feeling of security came to an abrupt end when the whole scene was lighted up as bright as daylight by the explosion of a tanker in the center column. One of our torpedoes which had missed the second target hit this large target about amidships. The ocean appeared full of ships

and we were in an uncomfortable position. We cleared the bridge immediately and started down.

When the tanker exploded, those topside were stunned by the brilliance of night turned to day, and a sea full of enemy ships. Whitaker ordered "Dive! Dive!" and lookouts scrambled down. Next-to-last down the hatch was McCants, followed by Whitaker. In his haste, McCants missed the ladder, falling eight feet to the conning tower's hard, steel deck. Whitaker did the same but fared better, as he landed on McCants instead of the steel decking. Recovering, McCants exclaimed, "My God it's DAYLIGHT up there!" While it wasn't funny at the time, the sight of *Flasher's* stunned, normally very proper skipper sitting on one of his junior officers was the subject of later ribbing aboard the submarine. As *Flasher* submerged, the patrol report reflects:

> By the time we hit fifty feet we could hear shells landing all around where we had been. We felt that we must have been seen and went to three hundred feet turning at high speed, and expecting an immediate depth charge attack. Although many high speed screws passed over us, and although escorts were pinging in our vicinity for a long time, it appears that they still thought we were on the surface as they dropped no depth charges. We were giving out a tremendous cloud of smoke when we submerged, and I believe that they were firing at

our smoke thinking that we were still on the surface. We took a southerly course to clear the vicinity in order to surface and trail.

The massive 16-cylinder diesel engines on *Flasher* did not smoke normally, but changing speed by pouring on the power, especially when all of the engines were not fully warmed up, generated an enormous amount of white smoke. It made the Japanese think *Flasher* was there on the surface.

0326   With much pinging and fast screws heard in the vicinity of damaged ships, came to periscope depth. Periscope observation showed tanker bearing 043° T, range about 8,000 yards still burning brightly and low in the water. This appears to be very large tanker, but it is almost completely covered by flames. Two escorts were seen to be in the vicinity of the tanker but somewhat to the left of it. Continued to open out.

0355   Came to radar depth and picked up escort at 4500 yards, bearing 049° true, range closing. Went back to periscope depth.

0407   Heard two distant explosions. Believe this is ANGLER making attack.

0413   Came to radar depth. Picked up escort at 6,000 yards astern. It is still pretty light from burning tanker but believe we can surface.

0418   Surfaced. Picked up two escorts astern at about 7,000 yards and also another contact 10° to left of tanker at 15,000 yards. Kept opening out tracking other contact. Found him to be dead in the water.

0445   Tried to contact ANGLER and CREVALLE to give them dope on damaged ship, but they did not answer. Decided to remain in vicinity and dive at daybreak to close damaged ship and tanker to see what happened to them and in hopes of trailing.

0511   Submerged and headed for damaged ships with tanker still burning brightly.

0525   At periscope depth. Large damaged ship in sight, but tanker cannot be sighted, nor can any fire or smoke from it be seen. Feel sure it has sunk. Continued to close damaged ship. There are two escorts in the vicinity of this ship. He is dead in water and they are searching all around him.

0700   Our large, damaged freighter appeared to get up steam and get under way about this time. He stood off on northerly course at about five knots. Continued to close last position of tanker, but he was not to be found. Am positive he sank.

0932   Commenced opening out to south.

1027   Heard two explosions followed by two more and then at intervals until 1050 by many more explosions.

1030   Saw high, wide cloud of brown smoke on last bearing of our target. Feel sure one of the other boats got him.

1037   Sighted plane in vicinity of smoke on last bearing of freighter. (Plane Contact No. 24). This freighter was a very large, four goal post type of about 8,500 tons. He had a good list and was well down by the stern. He was a MKFKM type of about 475 feet in length. He is identified as the Asosan Maru type. Our second target was seen quite plainly in the light of the burning tanker prior to diving. He was a medium looking vessel of the MKFKKM type of about 500 feet length. He had a Raked bow and a cruiser stern. He is identified as the Hirokawa Maru type of 6,872 tons.

1227 Surfaced.

1232 Sighted plane bearing 340° T. distance 16 miles. (Plane Contact No. 25). He closed to 12 miles then went out of sight. Decided to head for barn as ANGLER and CREVALLE are still down and we have no more torpedoes. Also feel it would be impossible to regain contact with convoy at this late time.

1915 ANGLER reported two hits on large merchantman.

1950 Told the other two what we had accomplished and also that we are headed for barn. Told Walker on CREVALLE to take charge of Wolf Pack.

2020 CREVALLE reported sinking three ships one of which had been previously damaged. Feel this was ours as he reported sinking it at 1030. Our time indicated 1027. He also stated this to be a very large merchantman.

Flasher's torpedoes were aimed at the second and third freighters in the convoy's port column, hitting them and also the third tanker in the center column. The tanker had been loaded with refined fuel or volatile crude oil produced in Southeast Asia. It exploded so brilliantly that it illuminated the submarine for all of the Japanese gunners in the surrounding convoy. Christie gave *Flasher* credit for sinking a large, 10,000-ton tanker, whereas she sank a substantial, but medium tanker, *Otoriyama Maru* (or *Otorisan Maru*) of 5,280 tons. Alden's research indicates Ultra intercepted a radio signal from a convoy member, *Mayasan Maru*, identifying the torpedoed tanker. Tankers were vital to the Japanese, who began the war against America, in part, to get oil. The convoy had been headed toward the Formosa Strait and Japan.

The freighter *Flasher* crippled and *Crevalle* later sank was the *Tosan* (or *Tozan*) *Maru*, a passenger-cargo vessel of 8,666 tons. The two subs were each given wartime credit for half the estimated 8,800 tons, or 4,400 tons apiece. After the war, *Flasher* and *Crevalle* were each (again) officially given half credit for the sinking, exactly 4,333 tons apiece. JANAC, however, listed joint sinkings separately. Therefore, while *Flasher* is generally cited as sinking 100,231 tons of enemy shipping, this figure still understates by 4,333 tons the total tonnage she sank. *Flasher's* total tonnage per JANAC was, therefore, 104,564 tons.

Other submarines were credited with joint sinkings, shared with other submarines or allied aircraft. *Jallao*, for instance, was given half credit for destroying *Tama*, a light cruiser similar to *Oi*, but this is not apparent from the list of her individual sinkings. JANAC lists 29 enemy warship and merchantman sinkings credited to joint actions by submarines, or submarine-aircraft combinations. Theodore Roscoe's

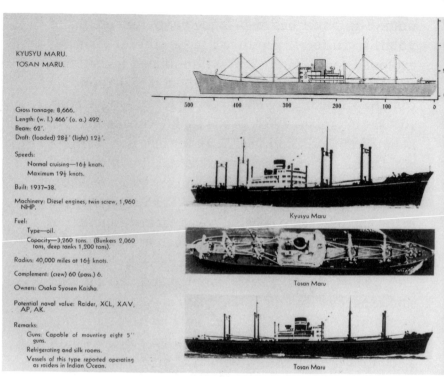

KYUSYU MARU.
TOSAN MARU.

Gross tonnage: 8,666.
Length: (w. l.) 466' (o. a.) 492 .
Beam: 62'.
Draft: (loaded) 28½' (light) 12½'.

Speeds:
    Normal cruising—16½ knots.
    Maximum 19½ knots.

Built: 1937–38.

Machinery: Diesel engines, twin screw, 1,960
    NHP.

Fuel:
    Type—oil.
    Capacity—3,260 tons. (Bunkers 2,060
        tons, deep tanks 1,200 tons).

Radius: 40,000 miles at 16½ knots.

Complement: (crew) 60 (pass.) 6.

Owners: Osaka Syosen Kaisha.

Potential naval value: Raider, XCL, XAV,
    AP, AK.

Remarks:
    Guns: Capable of mounting eight 5''
        guns.
    Refrigerating and silk rooms.
    Vessels of this type reported operating
        as raiders in Indian Ocean.

Kyusyu Maru

Tosan Maru

Tosan Maru

Tosan Maru (ONI 208-J)

United States Submarine Operations in World War II[17] shows the combined sinkings, but Lockwood, Blair and others generally omit credit for joint sinkings in their figures.

Whitaker only claimed "damage or probable sinking" for the second freighter, but *Flasher* was credited by Christie with its sinking. JANAC failed to give this credit to *Flasher*, so the target must have survived the attack despite damage. Alden indicates that the 6,863-ton *Kiyokawa Maru*, a seaplane carrier, was dam-

---

[17] Annapolis: Naval Institute Press, 1949, pp. 564-565.

aged in the attacks of July 26, but he was unsure which of the three subs in the wolf pack had inflicted the medium damage reported in the Japanese records. Whitaker identified the damaged target as a mast-kingpost-funnel-kingpost-mast (MKFKM) freighter similar to the 6853-ton *Hirokawa Maru* as shown on page 73 of ONI 208-J (Rev). This description fits the *Kiyokawa Maru* closely.

Angler was credited by Christie with damaging one *Asosan Maru*-type freighter. The Fremantle command credited *Crevalle* with sinking three freighters in addition to the *Tosan Maru* on the patrol. *Crevalle* was given JANAC credit for sinking the *Aki Maru* of 11,409 tons (on July 26), and the *Hakubasan Maru* of 6,650 tons (on July 28, after *Flasher* departed the area), but not her two other claims. *Angler* was not given any postwar credit for a sinking in the attack of July 26. As stated earlier, damage to Japanese shipping, no matter how extensive, was not considered by JANAC, only confirmed sinkings.

It is not clear whether any of the three vessels JANAC denied *Angler* and *Crevalle* fit the description of *Kiyokawa Maru*. However, Alden's subsequent research indicates that an attack by *Angler* at 4:58 p.m. (Japanese time—"I" or "Item") corresponds with Ultra confirmation of a torpedo hit in *Kiyokawa Maru's* No. 2 hold, and that the damaged seaplane tender made it to Takao, Formosa. *Crevalle's* two claims were of a *Kaga Maru*-class freighter and an *Amagisan Maru*-type freighter. *Crevalle* made an attack at 5:33 p.m. Japanese time. The repaired *Kiyokawa Maru* was finally sunk off Nagasaki in 1945, probably after hitting a mine.

Flasher's six torpedoes were fired from the forward torpedo room, and consisted of four Mark 14-3A steam torpedoes and two Mark 23 steam torpedoes, all using the contact exploders and an eight-foot depth setting. As before, Whitaker fired the bottom four tubes first and the top tubes one and two last, possibly to minimize surface wakes immediately in front of the sub's bow until the last second. The two freighters were 3,000 yards away, which was a relatively long range, and the tanker *Flasher* sank was at an estimated 4,000 yards, one of the sub's longest shots. It is doubtful Whitaker would have intentionally fired at such a range. Other subs obtained hits on non-targeted ships when there were overlapping targets sailing in close columns. Skippers preferred such target formations, unless the closer ship was an escort running "interference" for a more important ship.

Separate reviews were given each submarine's patrol report, as well as an endorsement for the wolf pack's performance. Commander Submarine Squadron (Subron) 18, Captain Eliot H. Bryant (who had participated in *Flasher's* Board of Inspection survey), outlined the pack's performance during the attacks and remarked:

> The attack by the group on the large convoy off the Philippines on 25-26 July 1944 was outstanding, both as to results obtained and to method of execution. In the face of heavy air and surface coverage, all submarines pressed home their attacks in a manner which reflects great credit on the courage and skill of the three commanding officers and

their ships.

Admiral Christie had similar comments in his endorsement of Fremantle's first wolf pack. He noted:

> FLASHER regained contact with the convoy after dark, but refrained from attacking until at least one other submarine had also gained contact, since she had only six torpedoes remaining. This proved to be a sound decision. It is unlikely that either of the other ships could have regained contact without the excellent information provided by FLASHER at frequent intervals.

Flasher sailed out of her patrol area the morning of July 27, headed for Mindoro Strait. She transited the Sulu and Celebes Seas and Makassar Strait on the surface, except for brief submergences to avoid aircraft. On July 31 she submerged with the lightening sky at a point about 12 miles off Cape William in Makassar Strait, to surface that evening about 25 miles southwest of Cape Mandar.

John Precup and a young torpedoman from the forward torpedo room switched watches for the night of July 31. Precup took the torpedo room watch while the lanky young sailor took Precup's forward port lookout station by the periscope shears. South of Makassar Strait he spotted the flaming exhausts of three Japanese Mitsubishi "Nell" bombers only three miles away, flying only 800 feet above the water. He yelled and Lt. Glennon hollered, "Clear the bridge!

Diving Control Station with Stern and Bow Plane Wheels, Depth Gauges, and Gyro Compass (Navpers 16160)

Dive! Dive!" Everyone scrambled down as *Flasher* dove to escape the bombers. The torpedoman scrambled down the ladders to the conning tower deck and then the control room deck with the other lookouts, before heading aft, forgetting that as Precup's replacement, he was supposed to take Precup's position manning the bow planes on a dive.

As he was walking aft, he heard Chief Perkowsky in the control room exclaim, "Where's the bow planesman!?" The planes had been rigged out and *Flasher* was in a steep dive without a planesman. It took several minutes to recover depth control of the boat. The next day the torpedoman was called to Glennon's room, where he explained what had happened. Glennon was not upset with him over the incident, but made it clear how that kind of oversight risked the lives of all aboard. It was drilled into all submariners that "There's room for everything aboard a submarine—except a mistake." It would be many years before the young sailor stopped worrying about the one bad slip he made aboard *Flasher* during the war.

Luckily for the sub, the three Nells never spotted her. While camouflage and the darkness made the submarine's hull difficult to spot at night, phosphorescent wakes could reveal the sub to the enemy. Enemy aircraft were extremely difficult to spot at night. In order to detect aircraft, nighttime lookouts had to either spot the exhaust glow or notice something had blotted out a star. By the time the sound of an aircraft reached the lookouts, it was too close and too late to dive.

Flasher later surfaced to proceed to a point north of Lombok Strait to await nightfall and a surface transit of the dangerous strait at three-engine speed. She avoided a small patrol boat in the darkness, and completed her passage shortly before midnight.

One day out of Fremantle, on the morning of August 6, *Flasher* exchanged calls with the outbound submarines USS *Hake* (SS 256) and USS *Harder* (SS 257). *Hake* had sunk seven vessels during the first six months of 1944, including the 9,547-ton, aircraft transport *Nigitsu Maru*, and a destroyer. *Harder*, beginning her sixth war patrol under the famous Commander Sam Dealey, was already one of the deadliest American subs of the war. Before the month was out, she and her entire crew would be lost to Japanese depth charges off the west coast of Luzon, in the same area patrolled by *Flasher* in each of her first three patrols. In less than 30 days Fremantle had suffered three stunning losses of *Robalo*, *Flier* and *Harder*. Only eight of the 249 crewmen on the three subs survived.

Flasher arrived at Fremantle the morning of August 7, 1944, having completed her extremely successful third patrol. In his patrol report, Whitaker commented on the poor weather, especially during the latter part of the mission, when monsoon weather caused "rising seas and swell from the southwest, poor visibility, and overcast skies." Whitaker countered the poor visibility with substantial reliance on his SJ-a radar. The overcast skies and poor visibility also meant navigational problems, and *Flasher* went for one period of nine days with only two star sightings. DuBois had relied on less-accurate sun sightings and dead reckoning for navigation.

Even in the middle of the South China Sea, improper navigation could get you grounded or killed. The South China Sea is full of dangerous bank, shoal and reef areas to the north (Paracel Island Reefs and Macclesfield Bank), the south (Charlotte Bank, Scawfell and Luconia Shoals, etc.), and the east (Truro and Scarborough Shoals and Dangerous Ground, an area about the size of Colorado). Enemy shipping often used shallow water to escape from Allied submarines, preferring the navigational hazards to torpedoes, and knowing the subs had to surface to avoid grounding.

Sun sightings with a sextant could provide *Flasher* with a close approximation of her present position so long as it was possible to spot the sun through the cloud cover. Multiple star sightings would give more precise navigation, but still depended on relatively clear skies. Intermittent sighting of distinctive landmarks was the best way to obtain a navigational fix, but land and distinctive land features were not readily available except when patrolling close to a shoreline with prominent features that matched chart references. The United States lacked good charts of much of the enemy-controlled waters, and most of the dangerous shoal areas in the South China Sea are far removed from any land. Also, the Japanese were not about to leave navigational aids (beacons, lighthouses, etc.) functioning for the Allies. They could illuminate such guides when signaled by their own shipping, but the rest of the time the devices were dark.

Whitaker complained (as he had after the first two patrols) of the inaccurate and erratic pitometer log. *Flasher's* crew relied on the pit log for dead reckoning navigation. With infrequent star sights, an unreliable pit log made it difficult to know exactly where *Flasher* was. In his endorsement of the patrol, Acting Commander Subron 12, (J.F. Madden) noted "the continued unsatisfactory performance of underwater logs is a source of embarrassment to submarines and will continue to be until some substitute is furnished or a better supply of replacement parts becomes available."

The patrol report also noted increased antisubmarine activities by the Japanese:

> The convoy encountered on July 25 had the largest number of escorts I have ever seen with one convoy. They were all modern escorts and ranged in size from

destroyers to PC boats. These escorts showed no indication of having radar. All convoys encountered had air coverage during daylight, and in general enemy air search on this patrol was stronger than previously encountered. Our evasion tactics consisted of taking advantage of the good temperature gradients present and easing away, hoping we hadn't been picked up.

Whitaker noted that all of the escorts and destroyers were employing "pinging" as their search method, i.e., active sonar which generated a "ping" sound to reflect from the sub's hull and disclose its location.

Underwater evasion by *Flasher* was complicated by excessive noise from vibrating lookout hoops, designed to support lookouts from *Flasher's* periscope shears. The loops had been welded once by the *USS Pelias* crew and once by Submarine Repair Unit 137, but the welds didn't hold. New welds would be made during refit.

On July 6, while *Flasher* was patrolling submerged off the coast of Indochina, her hydrogen detector fan had disintegrated and a jury-rigged substitute was arranged. Similarly, the auxiliary engine was disabled by a jammed outboard exhaust valve on July 26, when the wolf pack successfully attacked the large, 14-ship convoy. The critical hydrogen detector and the malfunctioning exhaust valve would be additional matters addressed during the refit.

Each day in the patrol area, *Flasher's* radiomen

had experienced "jamming" by Japanese radio stations that caused problems, particularly when "new numbers were being sent." *Flasher* was nevertheless able to receive all "serials" (messages) intended for her.

Despite problems encountered by SubPac submarines operating close to Japan with enemy homing on SD radar emissions, *Flasher* was able to utilize her SD-4 air search radar over 500 hours during her third patrol, apparently without any appreciable enemy homing activity. *Flasher* utilized her SJ-a radar almost 700 hours during the same patrol. Requested improvements and repairs made to both the SD and SJ radar proved useful during the patrol, and the power-supply problems of the second patrol were not repeated. The single failure of the SJ-a radar just before the July 26 convoy attacks was *Flasher's* only radar casualty and this was repaired prior to the attacks.

Flasher's sound equipment had been able to detect and determine the bearing of small coastal freighters at ranges from three to four miles, and pinging from escorts at up to 15 miles. This meant a pinging enemy destroyer or escort could easily give away the position of a convoy, actually attracting Allied submarines. Escorting planes could also be counterproductive, as far-off circling aircraft could advertise an otherwise-unseen Japanese convoy below.

Whitaker noted that the quality and variety of meats received for the third patrol were a marked improvement over those of the second patrol. He hoped to have an ice cream freezer installed during the upcoming refit.

As to living conditions, Whitaker commented "habitability except for two periods of silent running was very good." Those two periods were during *Flasher's* evasion attempts after attacking the Light Cruiser *Oi* on July 19 and the large convoy on July 26. Whitaker consistently understated the strain and severity of the depth-charging ordeals and evasion of enemy antisubmarine forces during *Flasher's* patrols. His description of *Flasher's* worst depth chargings to date was that the charges were dropped "fairly close" or that the depth charges "landed pretty close and shook us up a bit" (both remarks as to the attacks on February 14, 1944).

Referring to depth-charge attacks on *Flasher*, Tom McCants later wrote, "Once I remember saying the Twenty-Third Psalm about 43 times in 45 minutes—and that was with the Lord's Prayer too!" Frenchy Corneau similarly recalled that the noise or pressure from close depth charges was so powerful that "I could feel the pain all over my skin."

Life was substantially more strained aboard a front-line submarine than commanders were willing to admit in their war-patrol reports, which they knew were going to be spread throughout the Navy. This applied to *Flasher*. Author Clay Blair noted that after the third patrol Whitaker and DuBois were "physically and mentally drained." The stress on everyone aboard a World War II submarine was unrelenting. The constant threat from enemy (and "friendly") air, surface and submarine forces began the moment a submarine left on patrol and did not lift until the sub was safely back in port. Danger from "operational" mishaps, such as accidental flooding, fires, running aground, or mechanical, electrical or hydraulic failures that prevented the boat from surfacing, were always present. Submarines were lost to these "operational" failures during both peacetime and wartime, making submarine duty dangerous even without the enemy. Submariners were paid hazardous duty pay, and they earned every cent.

If a submarine got into trouble while on patrol, the probability was that every man aboard would die. Any crewmen who escaped a damaged or sinking sub would drown unless they were picked up by the enemy. Given the options of drowning or capture, some preferred to drown. Japanese treatment of prisoners of war was barbaric and reports of such treatment, in addition to incidents such as the Pearl Harbor surprise attack, alienated the Americans. (It may now be fashionable to state war crimes and atrocities are only revealed for the defeated nation, but the evidence of U.S. treatment of Japanese prisoners bore no relation to the evils inflicted on Allied prisoners by the Japanese military.[18])

Stress of command on men like Whitaker and DuBois may have been as aggravating as stress generated by the enemy. World War II submarines were complex and imperfect machines requiring a crew of 80 highly skilled individuals to keep them operating for a full war patrol. As shown in the patrol records, mechanical and electrical failures were the rule rather than the exception, even on a brand-new sub like *Flasher*. While the submarine captain had the strain and responsibility of all decisions, the executive officer had a

---

[18] Haruko Taya Cook and Theodore F. Cook, *Japan at War, an Oral History* (New York: New Press, 1992), and Saburo Ienaga, *The Pacific War - 1931-1945* (New York: Pantheon Books, 1978).

crushing burden of day-to-day operations, coupled with the important navigational duties.

Compounding these responsibilities was the knowledge that every aspect of the submarine's operations during the war patrol was to be reviewed by everyone up the chain of command. Career naval officers knew that 50 copies of the patrol report would be disseminated throughout the service. It was common for early war patrols during World War II to be the subject of unfounded criticisms and second-guessing by desk-bound commanders, captains, and admirals. Further, *Flasher's* third patrol had involved Whitaker's additional responsibilities as head of Fremantle's first wolf-pack operation, coupled with frustration over trying to coordinate with her sister subs, and *Flasher's* exposure to more enemy ships and planes than on her first two war patrols combined.

The patrol experiences led Whitaker to recommend aggressive priorities for wolf-packing submarines:

> In Wolf-Pack operations, it is imperative that all submarines engaged make every effort to keep in contact with the enemy. On the night of July 25, the FLASHER regained contact about 2100 and was then forced to remain inactive for a period of almost five hours until at least one other submarine had contact. It is realized that enemy action may possibly prevent submarines from remaining in contact during daylight. However, when darkness comes all submarines should

use maximum speed to close up. It is believed that even battery charging should remain secondary until contact is regained. In this connection, it is pointed out that the Auxiliary engine can be used to good advantage for charging while seeking to regain contact. After contact is regained, each Commanding Officer is then free to take whatever time he considers absolutely necessary for charging his batteries before he attacks. During this time he can at least trail and thereby perform a useful function. On the night of July 25, if this vessel had been blessed with a large load of torpedoes, the Commanding Officer would probably have been forced to attack before other submarines had regained contact in the hopes of getting in several attacks before dawn. In this event, had the FLASHER been run down and kept down after the initial attack, all the advantages of a wolf pack would have been lost.

Whitaker was obviously not pleased with having to wait for the other subs.

Flasher had spent 50 days on patrol, fired all her torpedoes, and burned 120,244 gallons of diesel fuel in travelling 12,153 miles (the equivalent of four coast-to-coast trips across the United States), leaving her tanks almost dry, with only 5,607 gallons when she arrived at Fremantle.

The acting Subron 12 Commander, J.F. Madden,

commended *Flasher's* commanding officer, officers and crew for "an excellent and most aggressive patrol." Nevertheless, while Madden commended *Flasher's* attack on a cruiser, he gave no credit for any cruiser sinking.

Whitaker told Christie about the cruiser attack and said, "I BELIEVE I sank him Admiral, but I can't swear I did."

Christie waited patiently as Whitaker told him why he thought the cruiser had sunk. When Whitaker finished, Christie grinned and said "You sank him. He was the Light Cruiser *Oi*." Christie had received confirmation *Oi* had sunk from decoded Japanese messages.

Loss of an Imperial Japanese Navy cruiser was a hot topic in coded communications with the Empire. Christie's endorsement, dated August 30, 1944, also acknowledged the sinking of a *Kuma*-class light cruiser by Flasher:

> 1. The Third War Patrol of the U.S.S. FLASHER was conducted in the SOUTH CHINA SEA. Strong blows against Japanese merchant shipping were struck in the vicinity of SINGAPORE, CAPE VARELLA, and CAPE BOLINAO. A Light Cruiser of the KUMA Class was sunk north of DANGEROUS GROUND.
>
> 2. In her characteristically resolute and determined fashion FLASHER skillfully and aggressively attacked the enemy at every opportunity. The cordon of escorts surrounding two exceptionally

well protected convoys was penetrated and hits obtained on all ships attacked. An excellent fire control organization is indicated.

3. The night surface attack on the SINGAPORE bound convoy is particularly noteworthy since it was conducted in water of about twenty-six fathoms sixty miles from the entrance to SINGAPORE STRAIT.

4. The decision of the Commanding Officer to delay his night attack on the convoy off CAPE BOLINAO until other boats were in contact, and the frequent contact reports, enabled CREVALLE and ANGLER to locate the convoy and sink three large AKs just before dawn.

5. The Commanding Officer distinguished himself by his competent tactical command of the Coordinated Group consisting of FLASHER, CREVALLE, and ANGLER. Seventy nine thousand six hundred tons of enemy merchant shipping and a Light Cruiser were sunk by this attack group.

6. The ASOSAN MARU which was damaged in attack No. 4, was sunk a few hours later by CREVALLE. The gross tonnage, 8,800 tons, is being divided evenly between FLASHER and CREVALLE.

7. This patrol is designated as

"successful" for purpose of award of Submarine Combat Insignia.

8. The Force Commander takes the greatest pleasure in heartily congratulating FLASHER ('s) Commanding Officer, Officers, and Crew, on this outstanding patrol, in which the following heavy damage was inflicted on the enemy:

SUNK

1-AP	(Similar HEIAN MARU-EU)	10,000 Tons	(Attack No. 1)
1-AK	(Large-EU)	7,500 Tons	(Attack No 1)
1-AK	(Medium-EU)	4,000 Tons	(Attack No. 2)
1-CL	(KUMA Class-EC)	5,100 Tons	(Attack No 3)
* 1-AK	(ASOSAN MARU Class-EC)	4,400 Tons	(Attack No. 4)
1-AO	(Large-EU)	10,000 Tons	(Attack No. 4)
1-AK	(KIROKAWA Class-EC)	6,900 Tons	(Attack No. 4)
	Total	47,900 Tons	

* Half credit shared with CREVALLE

(Signature) R.W. CHRISTIE

The terms "AP," "AK," and "AO," referred to transports, freighters, and tankers, respectively. "CL" refers to a light cruiser. "EU" meant "Estimate—Uncertain" whereas "EC" meant "Estimate—Certain."

Admiral Kinkaid's Chief of Staff, H.W. Graf, wrote "Commander Seventh Fleet is deeply gratified by the aggressive character and masterly execution of U.S.S. FLASHER's Third War Patrol" and he congratulated *Flasher's* personnel for an "eminently successful mission." The separate wolf-pack endorsement by Commander, Seventh Fleet noted: "Despite the fact that the preponderance of damage to the enemy in this joint operation was inflicted by one submarine, it is apparent from the total that the pack system is extraordinarily effective." Such endorsements required that all copies on board "be destroyed prior to entry into enemy-controlled waters."

At noon on August 7, *Flasher's* crew was relieved by Lt. Cmdr. D.G. Baer and his crew, and left the boat for two weeks' leave. On August 12, the relief crew moved the sub into the dry dock for two days of repairs and maintenance. With the flooding of the dry dock *ARD 10* the morning of the 14th, *Flasher* was waterborne in 40 minutes, and left to moor alongside the dock. More than 7,000 gallons of lubrication oil and almost 80,000 gallons of diesel oil were loaded on the 17th, and on the morning of August 21 Whitaker and the regular crew returned to take over from the relief crew.

The same day, August 21, DuBois and Lt.(jg) Frank Kristl were detached from *Flasher* and transferred to Submarine Division 182 (ComSubDiv 182). Both officers had been aboard since the sub's commissioning the year before.

DuBois' leave from *Flasher* was supposed to be temporary, as he was Whitaker's and Christie's choice to take command of her after *Flasher* returned from her fourth patrol. Whitaker would have completed ten war patrols after *Flasher's* fourth patrol, and he told Christie he thought he could use a break stateside, after which he could return to the war zone for more action.

DuBois, awarded a well-deserved Silver Star and two Legions of Merit for his wartime performance, was not to assume command of *Flasher* as planned.

Instead, he would go to New London to assume command of the *USS Mackerel* (SS 204). DuBois would return to the Pacific at his request the following year, as captain of the *USS Barbero* (SS 317), and leave for patrol in a group of subs that included *Flasher*. In Fremantle, DuBois asked permission for a quick trip stateside, which was summarily denied, although others with substantially fewer war patrols than DuBois were granted such trips. The command in Fremantle may have been displeased with DuBois for suggesting *Flasher's* orders through Balabac Strait for the third patrol be changed. Because of his battle-front experience, however, DuBois could, and did, put in for rotation to duty stateside, a request Fremantle granted.

About 30 years later, Whitaker told Author Clay Blair, Jr., that he thought DuBois made a mistake by sitting out the fourth patrol.[19] Actually, the Fremantle command had wanted DuBois to sit out the fourth patrol. However, DuBois had decided against waiting in Fremantle to take over command of *Flasher*, if it meant shabby treatment. DuBois' transfer stateside certainly never hurt his career, since he, like Whitaker, ultimately became an admiral.

Frank Kristl would meet with *Flasher* again in 1945, after serving on *Angler*. The senior lieutenant aboard *Flasher*, Phil Glennon, became her new Exec. Lt. Snap Coffin continued as Engineering Officer and took over Glennon's position as the boat's First Lieutenant. Lt. Tom Burke, absent from the third patrol with a bro-

---

[19] *Silent Victory*, Clay Blair, Jr., Philadelphia: J.B. Lippincott & Co., 1975, p. 73. One of the best, and most complete, histories of the submarine war in the Pacific.

ken foot, returned to make *Flasher's* fourth patrol, serving as Communications Officer as before. Lt. McCants took over Glennon's responsibilities as Gunnery and Torpedo Officer, a position he held on the training sub *USS Marlin*. Kiko Harrison continued as Plotting Officer.

Several others were temporarily or permanently transferred ashore, and would not make the fourth patrol. Chief of the Boat Felix Perkowsky left for other duties. Some of the crew believed the veteran chief had agreed to help Whitaker with *Flasher*, on condition it would be for only three patrols. In those patrols he had left his indelible stamp on *Flasher's* personnel. Replacing Perkowsky as COB was Chief Torpedoman Bill Pearce, also experienced, and a veteran of *USS Growler's* patrols.

Signalman Corneau, who was small to begin with, had suffered adverse reactions during submergences, had been unable to eat, and had lost 20 to 30 pounds on the third patrol. During *Flasher's* fourth patrol, he worked with the refit crews, and narrowly missed transfer to *Bonefish* (SS 223), which wanted him as a signalman. Corneau appealed to the officer in charge that he had to get back on *Flasher*. He was able to return to *Flasher* for her fifth patrol and never experienced any recurrence of the third patrol maladies. (*Bonefish* was sunk the following summer, and all aboard perished.) "Dynamite" Bartl, Mack Foxx, and Stanley Joseph Paczkowski, Jr., also sat out the fourth patrol but returned for *Flasher's* fifth patrol.

Muster the morning of August 22 disclosed numerous new crew members and a new officer, Ensign J.E. (Eddie) Atkinson from Pine Bluff, Arkansas. Eddie became *Flasher's* Assistant Engineering Officer. *Flasher* held fire drills that day and then departed for Gage Roads to take aboard sound test personnel. She failed her sound tests, as her starboard propeller continued to make noise. On August 23 she reentered *ARD 10* for the six-hour job to replace the prop. The morning of August 24 revealed three sailors absent over leave. *Flasher* left the dry dock to begin aircraft radar exercises, sound tests to check the new prop's cavitation noises, and practice torpedo approaches. The morning of August 25 she returned to moor alongside *Crevalle* again, and received her three overdue sailors.

During the cavitation tests, the sound test personnel drew curves reflecting *Flasher's* noise level at different speeds and gave copies of the data to Whitaker "for use during evasive action." He now had valuable information on how much noise *Flasher* made at various submerged speeds, as she maneuvered to evade Japanese escorts.

On August 26, *Flasher* began exercises off Fremantle, initially assisting in antisubmarine training exercises. She entered Gage Roads Channel after dawn the following morning to pick up Commander Creed Burlingame, from ComSubDiv 162. Burlingame had demonstrated his competence as a sub skipper earlier in the war in the very successful *USS Silversides* (SS 236). *Silversides* served throughout the war with distinction, sinking 23 vessels (per JANAC), and survived to go on exhibition in Muskegon, Michigan.

With Burlingame aboard, *Flasher* conducted torpedo approaches and frequent battle stations drills. After firing an exercise torpedo the following morning, she returned to moor alongside *Crevalle*, and to hold mast for a fireman who missed *Flasher's* training departure. The fireman was tried, sentenced, fined, and transferred to Submarine Repair Unit 137 the same day.

After a medical officer found hoarded crackers (and a few insects) in one of the boat's mattresses, he ordered all mattresses aboard burned. Also the doctor tossed one sailor's badly mildewed shoes into the bay, and the skipper had to help the sailor, in galoshes, get past the tender duty officer so the young man could get new shoes. That afternoon *Flasher* was sealed and thoroughly fumigated in a two-hour process. Torpedoes, stores and fuel were loaded on August 29, and *Flasher* was ready for departure.

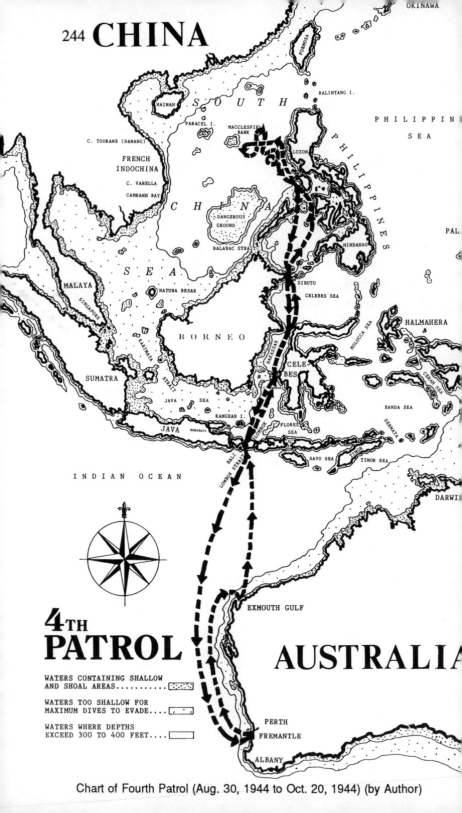

Chart of Fourth Patrol (Aug. 30, 1944 to Oct. 20, 1944) (by Author)

CHAPTER 7

TROOP SHIPS AND DEPTH CHARGES - *FLASHER'S* FOURTH WAR PATROL

*F*lasher began her fourth war patrol shortly after 5 p.m. on August 30, 1944, headed toward her patrol station in the South China Sea. As with the last patrol, Whitaker would supervise a three-sub wolf pack, this time to consist of *Flasher*, *Crevalle*, and *Lapon* (SS 260). Like her pack mates, *Lapon* was by now a veteran, having sunk at least eight vessels in five patrols. In 1943, she had daringly entered the Sea of Japan with the subs *Permit* and *Plunger*. The three subs would proceed independently to the patrol area. Substantial problems would be encountered before this jinxed wolf pack could assemble.

The first boat to leave Fremantle was *Flasher*, with *Crevalle* scheduled to depart September 1 and *Lapon* to leave September 4. On her familiar course northward to Exmouth Gulf and then Lombok Strait, *Flasher* continued training exercises. She entered Exmouth the morning of September 2 to refuel, topping off before departing early that afternoon. At a wreck located off Vlaming Head, Australia, *Flasher* held a gun drill with the crew firing 13 rounds from the four-inch deck gun.

A Coca-Cola machine installed during refit appeared to be a real morale booster. To ready the drink machine the Coke syrup was poured in and the water tank in the refrigerated space below deck was charged with carbon dioxide. At least that was how it was supposed to work. One time the valve from the drinking water system to the Coke machine's water tank was accidentally left open, so that when the tank was pressurized with carbon dioxide, the sub's drinking water became carbonated. Carbonated water by itself was not a problem, but the mixture apparently reacted with the water system's copper pipes to generate green drinking water. In addition to the color, anyone drinking the water immediately vomited. This minor emergency was solved when the entire system was flushed clean.

The daylight hours of September 5 were spent submerged 15 miles south of Lombok Strait, fighting the strait's strong southerly current. *Flasher* surfaced after dark to race through at four-engine speed, completing the transit in two hours. The same problem was encountered the next day, when she attempted to pass between Cape Mandar and Cape William in Makassar Strait after dawn, and found the southerly current too strong. She surfaced shortly after 9 a.m. to try the run on her diesels, but was driven down by Mavis and Sally bombers within a half hour. Shortly after noon Whitaker tried it again, this time successfully.

As *Flasher* was finishing her transit of Makassar Strait and entering the Celebes Sea on September 8, enemy plane sightings drove her down twice and serious mechanical problems began to trouble the sub. Leaks developed on the exhaust systems for both No. 1 and No. 2 main engines, a situation that grew worse as the patrol continued. Whitaker was worried that the noise and sparks caused by the leaks would endanger *Flasher*

on any night-surface attacks when the diesels were used. He felt this was disastrous and recommended the exhaust systems be completely replaced after each patrol if inspections during refit were inadequate to detect weaknesses.

As if this were not enough, *Flasher's* No. 3 main engine exploded as she approached Sibutu Passage and the nearby Japanese naval base. The engine's crankcase door blew off and the aft engine room filled with smoke. This occurred September 9, bringing the sub to a stop. *Flasher* secured the No. 3 and No. 4 main engines while proceeding on No.1 and No. 2 (the ones with the bad exhausts). *Flasher* used No. 4 main engine for charging batteries, but it was intermittently out of commission while repairs were effected on the blown No. 3 engine.

Repairs on the blown main engine were completed prior to dawn on September 10. Disassembly and inspection of the enormous diesel engine showed one of the cylinders contained a cracked piston with scored wrist pins and bushings, caused by improper installation of bearings by the relief crew during the last refit. By putting the bearings in reverse order on the connecting rod, all lubrication to that piston and rod was shut off and the parts were ruined. It was amazing the General Motors engine performed as long as it did before blowing. *Flasher's* crew replaced the connecting rod, piston, and all bearings and rings, after which the engine performed satisfactorily.

Lapon, arriving at about this time at Exmouth Gulf for refueling, also experienced engineering problems, and was delayed there an extra day for repairs. *Lapon* was making her first war patrol under a new skipper, Lt. Cmdr. D.G. Baer.

The problems of *Flasher* and *Lapon* were nothing, however, compared with those of *Crevalle*. After passing through Lombok Strait, Crevalle had just surfaced from a morning "trim" dive when the boat unexpectedly plunged beneath the waves, with two men still topside, and the hatches into the conning tower and control room wide open. The seas closed around the sub and thundered down the open hatches until someone was able to close the control room hatch. This still left the men in the conning tower unable to close the hatch to the bridge and facing almost certain death, when the bridge hatch finally closed as the sub passed 150 feet. It is thought Ensign Howard J. Blind freed the hatch retainer as the boat went under, so that it could close under the mighty force of the sea pressure.

Crevalle plunged down at a sharp angle and probably would have been another unexplained war loss, if Motor Machinist Robert Yeager not "ordered" the maneuvering room to reverse the props to stop the sub's fatal descent. Yeager's actions serve as testament to the demands that qualified submariners have initiative, and know their boats from bow to stern, rather than just their specialty. *Crevalle's* catastrophe was evidently caused by momentary inattention to the main ballast tank vents.

A badly shaken and water-logged *Crevalle* surfaced to rescue one of the lookouts, but Ensign Blind was lost. Blind was posthumously awarded the Navy Cross, and Yeager received the Silver Star for his quick actions. Because of major damage, the highly vulnerable *Crevalle* headed back to port, ultimately to proceed for a complete overhaul back in the United States. *Bone-*

fish (SS 223) was eventually ordered to replace *Crevalle* in the wolf pack.

Whitaker had *Flasher* deviate from her shortest course north to Mindoro Strait, in order to scout islands in the Sulu Sea. While proceeding submerged toward the coast of Panay in the northeastern Sulu Sea on September 11, the first substantial enemy vessel of the patrol appeared:

1639   Sighted ship bearing 146° T., range 16,000 yards. (Ship Contact No. 1). Went to battle stations and commenced approach. Angle on bow about 25 port. It appears that we will get in easily. Do not understand lack of escorts or air coverage.

1650   Target identified as a large hospital ship of about 8,000 tons. Discontinued attack.

1830   Surfaced, headed north for deep water along West Coast of Panay.

Flasher proceeded through Mindoro Strait into the South China Sea, having sighted numerous planes on her northward transit and having spent several hours watching activity at a "newly discovered landing strip" used by the Japanese near San Jose, Panay.

Arriving on station September 13, Whitaker decided to patrol on the surface off Cape Calavite, in and around the Verde Island Passage where *Flasher* had sunk ships on her first patrol. Shortly after dawn, however, the SD air search radar showed a plane contact, and Whitaker reconsidered. It would be better to patrol submerged that day.

In the evening, *Flasher* received orders by radio

to cover the approaches to Manila "with reconnaissance our primary mission." When he intercepted orders from *Haddo* to sister ship *Hake* for *Hake* to move north of Cabra Island, Whitaker decided to move *Flasher* in to cover the northern approaches to Manila abandoned by *Hake*. There followed several days of enemy plane and patrol boat sightings, but no targets. As *Hake* was leaving her patrol area north of Cabra Island, *Flasher* tried that area on September 17, again without luck, so Whitaker decided to move back to a point west of the fortress island of Corregidor. *Flasher* submerged there before dawn on September 18, for a periscope patrol. It was not long before she encountered a very dangerous, very formidable, Japanese naval force:

0824 Sighted plane bearing 242° T., distance about 4 miles. (Plane Contact No. 16). This was a twin float plane and believe he may be searching ahead of convoy.

0906 Sighted mast of ship bearing 275° T., range about 20,000 yards. (Ship Contact No. 5).

0913 Again sighted our float plane over ship. Had believed the mast might only be a patrol vessel until this time, but now feel sure it is a convoy.

0917 Went to battle stations. Knowing this convoy is headed for Manila, we can tell from his true bearing that we are about on his base course, so our problem is fairly simple. The sea is rough, so feel sure we will not be sighted by plane.

0926 Target identified as large MARU with four

destroyer escorts. He appears to be a very new ship and looks very modern. He has two destroyers at a range of 1500-2000 yards, one bearing about 60° on each bow. The other two destroyers are well out at a range of 3000-4000 yards from him and possibly a little sharper on the bow. They are all pinging and if their equipment is good, we will have trouble getting through. Sound conditions are excellent. We picked up screws of the convoy at about 14,000 yards by JP.

0929   Target zigged toward giving us small angle on bow at about 11,000 yards. We headed for him.

0938   Target zigged 30° to his left giving us 20° starboard angle on bow at 6,000 yards.

0942   Range 4,350 yards. Target appears to be covered with people. Believe he is a loaded transport. He seems to have hundreds of people around his rails, possibly acting as periscope lookouts.

0945   Coming right with full rudder at 2/3 speed, heading in for 90° track. Target has zigged away giving us 70° starboard angle on bow. The near starboard escort is very close to us on our starboard bow. Probably as close as three hundred yards, but his angle on the bow is about 70° starboard. Had intended to fire six torpedoes, but cannot get number three tube ready. (See Note under Casualties).

0947-20   Still swinging right. Commenced firing forward with about 15° right gyro, about 90°

starboard track, torpedo run about 2750 yards. Fired torpedoes at about 8 second intervals. Spread torpedoes by periscope. First torpedo aimed just abaft MOT, second just forward MOT, third about half a ships length ahead of bow, fourth half a ships length astern, and fifth at MOT. Hoped to get at least three hits. Used target speed 11 knots. Due to nearness of escort and due to the fact that the plane was close aboard, decided to go deep. Headed for 300 feet turning left at standard speed.

0949 Heard first torpedo hit followed at 7 1/2 second intervals by two more hits and then after 15 seconds by the fourth hit.

0950 Near escort has passed astern, but now have outer screen coming in fast from dead ahead. Shifted rudder to full right to try to get off his track.

0953 We didn't manage it. He passed overhead, going down our whole length, and dropped four beautiful ones. These charges were close and really shook the boat, breaking many light bulbs and doing other minor damage. We were at 325 feet at this time and I believe they were above us. Commenced avoiding at 2/3 speed with destroyers milling around and pinging all over the place. Headed out on westerly course.

1000 Explosion heard. Not close.

1001 Hear many sounds characteristic of ship sinking, bearing 008° T. by sound. This would be in the correct direction.

1010-30   Heard another explosion.

1012-30   Another explosion. Destroyers are pinging astern but don't appear to be trying too
hard to find us.

1035   Commenced coming up to periscope depth.
Would have started up sooner, but water
was so high in forward torpedo room bilges
that we could not take an up angle for fear of
grounding our sound training motors. Something should be done about this situation.

1050   Forward torpedo room reports that they
have the water under control, having been
using the buckets efficiently for the last half
hour. Destroyers still appear well astern and
act as if they might be picking up survivors
rather than hunting for us.

1114   Periscope observation showed two or three
destroyers in vicinity of attack. They are apparently picking up survivors as they are
remaining in the same vicinity. The float
plane is circling them, flying very low and
every once in a while he increases altitude
then turns and dives down as if to indicate
presence of something on water.

Whitaker described the target as a freighter used
as a transport, estimated at 8,000 tons with a composite superstructure, a mast-kingpost-funnel-kingpost-
mast (MKFKM) layout, flush deck, cruiser stern and
raked bow. It had to have been important, since the
single vessel warranted four destroyers and one float
plane as escorts. *Flasher* had sunk the 5,350-ton *Saigon
Maru*, completed in 1937 and listed in ONI 41-42 as an

"auxiliary cruiser" of the Japanese Navy. *Saigon Maru* was one of 14 merchant ships absorbed into the Imperial Japanese Navy in preparation for war. She became an armed merchant cruiser in August, 1941, and was redesignated as an auxiliary gunboat in January, 1944. It was intended that she would be an "armed merchant raider" like the Germans were using in the Atlantic. *Saigon Maru* had been heavily armed, with 500 mines and four 4.7-inch deck guns.

When *Flasher* returned to periscope depth, the escorts were apparently recovering survivors from the water. As before, *Flasher* had fired a combination of Mark 23 and Mark 14-3A steam torpedoes with contact detonators. The torpedoes had been set at 10 feet, 12 feet above the target's estimated 22-foot draft, and fired at approximately 2,500 yards, with gyro settings ranging from 11° to 17°.

In Phil Glennon's opinion, the depth charging suffered after the sinking of *Saigon Maru* was *Flasher's* worst of the war. The boat was badly shaken, with flooding in the forward torpedo room from excessive venting of the torpedo tubes. *Flasher* had also been forced down to 325 feet, just beyond her design depth, and about the deepest her patrol report would admit. *Saigon Maru* had been an important Japanese transport loaded with troops. No doubt the loss of their important charge had infuriated the escorts. Whitaker continued to watch them:

1201   Lost sight of destroyers. When last seen they were still in vicinity of attack with float plane still circling them.

1420   Sighted float plane for last time, still circling

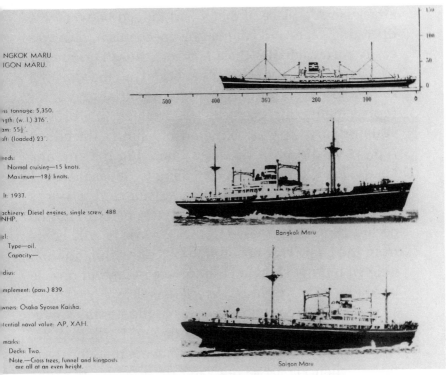

NGKOK MARU.
IGON MARU.

ss tonnage: 5,350.
ngth: (w. l.) 376´.
am: 55½´.
aft: (loaded) 23´.

eeds:
  Normal cruising—15 knots.
  Maximum—18½ knots.

lt: 1937.

achinery: Diesel engines, single screw. 488
NHP.

el:
  Type—oil.
  Capacity—

dius:

mplement: (pass.) 839.

wners: Osaka Syosen Kaisha.

tential naval value: AP, XAH.

marks:
  Decks: Two.
  Note.—Cross trees, funnel and kingposts
  are all at an even height.

Bangkok Maru

Saigon Maru

Saigon Maru (ONI 208-J)

in direction of attack.

1835   Surfaced about 20 miles northwest of Cabra Island. Discovered that depth charging has ruined the performance of our SJ radar. It appears to be all right but it just doesn't pick up anything. Headed for Cabra Island to make a better check.

2138   Definitely determined that the SJ radar is out. Commenced conducting patrol covering traffic lanes west of Manila.

Torpedo tube No. 3 would not fire during the

attack since a piece of metal had lodged between the operating gears and jammed the mechanism. This was easily corrected after the attack and caused no further problems. The depth charges knocked out the vital SJ-a radar, however, and after numerous trial-and-error replacements, the problem was isolated to a broken resistor card. It was removed but not replaced, as repairs would have required removing the antenna head. This Whitaker was unwilling to do, as it would endanger the boat. Without the resistor card, *Flasher's* SJ-a radar was only half as effective as before, and the occluded range increased from 350 yards to 1700 yards from the boat. This meant that objects within about a mile would not show on the surface radar, but objects beyond a mile would be detected as before.

A message from *Flasher* as to the sinking somehow started a rumor in Fremantle and Perth that the sub itself had sunk. Some in Perth were therefore surprised when *Flasher's* crew later returned for rest and recreation. Luckily, this rumor never reached the U.S. and the crew's families.

On September 19, the day following the sinking of *Saigon Maru*, Whitaker watched through the periscope from seven miles as a submarine hunter-killer group of three *Mutsuki*-class destroyers came out to search for *Flasher*:

> These destroyers appear to be searching for the submarine that made the attack here yesterday. The three destroyers are in a line making about 20 knots and appear to be making a thorough antisubmarine search off Manila Harbor...

(By this point in the war, there were only three remaining *Mutsuki*-class destroyers out of the original 12. One of these would be sunk two days later in the air attacks on Manila, while the other two would be sunk on December 12 north of Cebu, by PT boats and Marine aircraft.)

Whitaker began to worry if his attack the prior day would endanger *Haddo* nearby, as she was to perform lifeguard duties in this vicinity on September 21 and 22. (During the war, American submarines rescued over 500 U.S. pilots from the water and enemy-held islands, including future President George Bush, while on these "lifeguard" assignments.) *Flasher* was also ordered to conduct lifeguard duties, but those would be farther north, off Cape Bolinao. Whitaker decided not to reveal *Flasher* to the enemy unless a really impressive target showed, as the exposure would be counterproductive to *Haddo's* important lifeguard duties.

That evening *Flasher's* first wolf-pack partner, *Lapon*, arrived on station. Whitaker directed her to conduct an inshore patrol "along the coast of Luzon in the vicinity of 16° N" while *Flasher* would patrol off Cape Bolinao after finishing her lifeguard duties there.

Before dawn on September 20, *Flasher* dove for the radar technicians to work on the lower antenna assembly, where the problem had been isolated. Whitaker ordered the 110-foot depth as he felt *Flasher* would be too vulnerable on the surface with the lower mast assembly off, in case a sudden bomb or depth charge attack ruptured the top seals and left "nothing to keep the water out." By 8:30 a.m. repairs to the radar had been completed, at least as far as Whitaker was willing to allow in the middle of a war patrol.

Flasher arrived at her lifeguard station off Cape Bolinao the evening of September 20, in time for the carrier strikes planned on Manila for September 21 and 22. Early on the morning of the 21st *Flasher* sighted a well-lit hospital ship, later identified by *Lapon* as the *Tsugara Maru*.

Around 1 a.m. on September 22, *Flasher* received a message from *Lapon* that she was attacked by five enemy escorts following an Allied plane attack on a nearby convoy. *Lapon* was able to give an analysis of five ships damaged or sunk by the aviators in what *Lapon* called the "Battle of Palauig Point." In the boat's patrol report, Lt. Cmdr. Baer summed up as follows:

> No praise can be too great for the aviators who executed this attack. Their accuracy was remarkable and the swiftness with which the second wave followed was surprising. LAPON is not grateful for the four destroyers escorted by the single patrol vessel that they left behind.

The Navy's Task Force 38, fortified with no fewer than 12 aircraft carriers, had launched an impressive air raid, sinking about 100,000 tons of Japanese shipping in and around Manila Bay. It was a drastic change for American aircraft to control the sky over any part of the South China Sea, even if only temporarily. Other than guerrillas in the hills, the submarines had been the only Allied presence in the area since 1942.

Lapon later reported she had regained contact

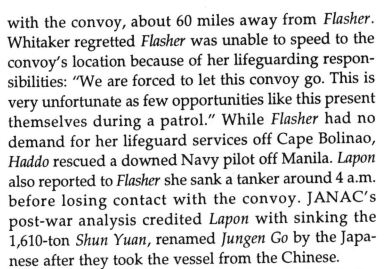

with the convoy, about 60 miles away from *Flasher*. Whitaker regretted *Flasher* was unable to speed to the convoy's location because of her lifeguarding responsibilities: "We are forced to let this convoy go. This is very unfortunate as few opportunities like this present themselves during a patrol." While *Flasher* had no demand for her lifeguard services off Cape Bolinao, *Haddo* rescued a downed Navy pilot off Manila. *Lapon* also reported to *Flasher* she sank a tanker around 4 a.m. before losing contact with the convoy. JANAC's post-war analysis credited *Lapon* with sinking the 1,610-ton *Shun Yuan*, renamed *Jungen Go* by the Japanese after they took the vessel from the Chinese.

The next few days were uneventful for *Flasher* and *Lapon*, except for sightings of enemy planes and small coastal freighters. On September 25, Whitaker ordered the two boats to try different areas for a while. *Flasher* arrived on station the following morning, commencing surface patrols and submerging to wash out her No. 4 main ballast tank after converting it from fuel to sea water. The tank had to be flushed clean to avoid leaving fuel oil traces on the surface, allowing the Japanese to trail *Flasher*.

Switching the tanks from fuel to sea water was easier said than done. With *Flasher* surfaced in enemy waters, Motor Machinist Bill Beaman had to go topside and then disappear down into the dark, cramped, and slick areas under *Flasher's* metal deck superstructure, maneuvering through the narrow spacing over the pressure hull, and often wading knee-deep in water. He then mechanically disconnected the main vent valve linkages, removed two locking rings holding the vent valves closed, replaced the valve linkage, and then stowed the locking rings. If the submarine had to dive because of enemy planes while Beaman and others were working inside the superstructure, they would drown. Luckily, there were no planes.

On September 26, *Flasher* received orders for the wolf pack to remain east of 118° east longitude until October 9. *Flasher* and *Lapon* exchanged messages and met to adjust their SJ transmitters. The boats utilized the SJ-a radar units for communicating by "keying" the transmitters, as well as for surface-search radar.

Whitaker decided since the two boats had steamed this far west, they would wait until noon on the 27th before complying with their new orders. It was a fortunate decision. September 27 proved to be an event-filled day:

0532 Sighted two ships bearing 325° T. These appeared to be two battleships with about 30° port angle on the bow. Put stern to them and went ahead on four engines trying to open out to make an end around. Was afraid we would be sighted in early morning light. (Ship Contact No. 11).

0540 Sighted smoke bearing 170° T. This made it evident that we could not make end around on battleships. There was no time to encode a message to the LAPON, so sent them a plain language message of sighting ships and submerged.

0555 Unable to sight battleships, but sighted smoke bearing 169° T. (Ship Contact No. 12).

0559 Believe we are well to the west of this convoy's track as his base course here should

be about 015° T. Came to normal approach course and commenced closing track.

0628   Still closing track. Identified contact as 8-10 ship convoy arranged in two columns with several escorts, including at least two destroyers. Commenced making approach on passenger vessel which is leading ship of near column. He appears to be a medium AP of the MFM type. He has at least three passenger decks and an awful lot of superstructure.

0646   One tanker appears to be in center of formation and two more tankers in far column. We cannot get to them.

0721   With angle on bow about 35° port and range about 3500 yards, came left for fifty port track. Hope to hold on long enough to swing left for larger track later, but port leading destroyer is on our starboard beam fairly close with about a 20° port angle on bow.

0723-30   Target range 3,000 yards. No change in course. Destroyer has now given us a zero angle on the bow, range 1000 - 1500 yards. Feel we must either fire now or probably lose all opportunity of doing so. Decided to fire only four torpedoes as other ships of column are about in line and at greater range.

0724-30   Commenced firing forward. Target speed 7 knots, track 50° port. Torpedo run about 2400 yards. Fired four torpedoes at seven second intervals spread 1/2 ships length between tracks. Spread by periscope.

0725-30   With destroyer on our starboard beam with zero angle on bow and range about 1,000 yards, decided to go deep. Thought of firing four stern tubes at him, but did not have time to turn for down the throat shot. Went to 330 feet. One minute and thirty-seven seconds after firing, heard one hit. Forty-four seconds later heard another definite hit. The first hit checked well for the third torpedo which was spread well forward, and later events indicated that our speed estimate was low. The second hit does not check in time for a hit on the transport as time between hits was 44 seconds and firing time was only 22 seconds. There was another ship astern of our target however, and at somewhat greater range, but with a small angle on the bow. The time for the second hit checks well for a hit by the first or second torpedo on this target or on a target in the far column. The LAPON who was tracking this convoy on the surface later reported seeing one ship explode and also said that she saw a flash with white smoke on another ship.

0728   The first of 15 fairly close depth charges went off.

0729-28   Three fairly close charges.

0734   Commenced hearing very loud breaking up noises in direction of first target. These noises were heard throughout the ship and were the loudest the commanding officer has heard in ten war patrols.

0739   Seven more depth charges, not close. Avoid-

ing to southeast.

0806   Commenced coming up slowly as escorts seem to be not too close.

0844   Periscope observation shows two escorts bearing 034° T., range about 8,000 yards. These fellows appear to be looking for survivors. Headed away from them to get clear and surface.

0943   Escorts apparently have picked up all hands as they commenced dropping single depth charges, apparently to keep us down. They dropped about 16 between now and the time we surfaced at 1102.

1042   Lost sight of escort. Still hear their pinging.

1101   Heard distant depth charge.

1102   Surfaced. Masts of two escorts still in sight by periscope on surface. Opened out at full speed.

1130   Lost contact with escorts. Commenced searching for convoy on original base course as we have no idea which way they went. Making 18 knots on four engines.

1544   We should be ahead of convoy now, but have not sighted them. Headed over towards Lingayen Gulf to intercept them if they changed course that way. Also feel they may head in and anchor overnight.

1810   Received message from LAPON indicating convoy headed for beach at 1200 today. We changed course to head for entrance to Lingayen Gulf in the hope of intercepting them. LAPON reports sinking large tanker and large freighter.

During the war *Flasher* was credited with sinking one medium AP (transport) on the morning of September 27, as well as damaging a second, unknown vessel. JANAC, of course, was only concerned with sinkings, so it did not credit damage. However, it did credit *Flasher* with sinking the 6,374-ton *Ural Maru* the morning of September 27. She was an auxiliary ship of the Imperial Japanese Navy, 406 feet long at the water line, with a maximum speed of 18½ knots, and a cruising speed of 15½ knots. She was built in 1929, and is pictured in ONI 41-42 in her earlier hospital-ship configuration. *Ural Maru* was apparently headed from the Philippines to Hong Kong at the time of its sinking, based on the convoy's course.

After *Flasher's* attack on the morning of September 27, *Lapon* conducted an end around and closed on the convoy, claiming the sinking of a large cargo vessel and a large tanker. *Lapon* did not surface and radio *Flasher* with the course and location of the convoy, however, until after dark. *Lapon's* wartime credits for the cargo vessel were not supported by JANAC, but she was credited with the sinking of the 5,599-ton tanker *Hokki Maru* around noon on the 27th.

In his recent work on submarine attacks, John Alden was unsure whether *Flasher* or *Lapon* should properly be credited with sinking the *Ural Maru*. It appears clear, however, that (1) Whitaker identified *Flasher's* target as a medium transport of the mast-funnel-mast type "having an exceptionally lot of superstructure with at least three passenger decks;" (2) *Ural Maru* matched Whitaker's description; (3) *Flasher* was credited during the war with sinking such a transport; and (4) Whitaker reported hitting the transport, and

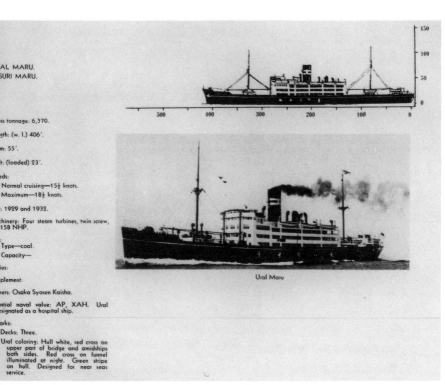

IRAL MARU.
ISSURI MARU.

Gross tonnage: 6,370.
Length: (w. l.) 406'.
Beam: 55'.
Draft: (loaded) 23'.

Speeds:
    Normal cruising—15½ knots.
    Maximum—18½ knots.

Built: 1929 and 1932.

Machinery: Four steam turbines, twin screw,
    1,158 NHP.

Fuel:
    Type—coal.
    Capacity—

Radius:

Complement:

Owners: Osaka Syosen Kaisha.

Potential naval value: AP, XAH. Ural
designated as a hospital ship.

Remarks:
    Decks: Three.
    Ural coloring: Hull white, red cross on
    upper part of bridge and amidships
    both sides. Red cross on funnel
    illuminated at night. Green stripe
    on hull. Designed for near seas
    service.

Ural Maru (ONI 208-J)

watching the escorts at 8:44 a.m. looking for survivors in the water. Conversely, *Lapon's* attack did not occur until noon, and *Lapon* never claimed or alleged she had attacked a transport. *Lapon* claimed attacks on a cargo vessel and a tanker, and the tanker has been identified as the *Hokki Maru*. *Lapon* also was on the surface at the time *Flasher* attacked, and saw one ship explode and the other issue a flash and white smoke at the time of *Flasher's* attacks.

Lapon's claimed freighter was supposed to be a "Large AK," the same type as *Hawaii Maru*, of 9,480 tons. She had a M-K-F-K-M configuration, an old-style plumb bow and counter stern, a 475-foot length, a

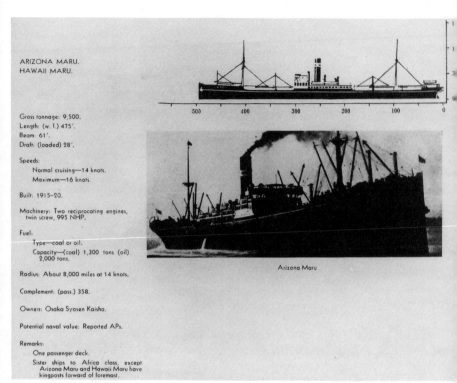

ARIZONA MARU.
HAWAII MARU.

Gross tonnage: 9,500.
Length: (w. l.) 475'.
Beam: 61'.
Draft: (loaded) 28'.

Speeds:
  Normal cruising—14 knots.
  Maximum—16 knots.

Built: 1915-20.

Machinery: Two reciprocating engines,
  twin screw, 995 NHP.

Fuel:
  Type—coal or oil.
  Capacity—(coal) 1,300 tons (oil)
    2,000 tons.

Radius: About 8,000 miles at 14 knots.

Complement: (pass.) 358.

Owners: Osaka Syosen Kaisha.

Potential naval value: Reported APs.

Remarks:
  One passenger deck.
  Sister ships to Africa class, except
    Arizona Maru and Hawaii Maru have
    kingposts forward of foremast.

Arizona Maru

Hawaii Maru, Type Attacked by *Lapon* (ONI 208-J)

one-deck composite superstructure, and was built before 1920. *Flasher's* target, however, was claimed as a "medium AP." *Ural Maru* was a third smaller than *Hawaii Maru* at 6,370 tons, with an M-F-M configuration, a raked bow, a cruiser stern, a 406-foot length, a three-deck superstructure, and was much newer. The two ships should not have been mistaken for one another, especially in daylight attacks. The available data supports the *Ural Maru's* sinking by *Flasher* and not by *Lapon*. Based on his continuing research since publication, including Ultra confirmation from the Japanese of the time of the torpedo hits, Alden also agrees that *Ural Maru* was sunk by *Flasher*.

Although JANAC did not assess damage to ships that did not sink, Alden did, and he indicates Japanese records showed the *Tachibana Maru*, a 6,521-ton tanker, experienced light damage consistent with that time and location. Indeed, *Flasher* received wartime credit from Fremantle for damage to a second unknown vessel as a result of the September 27th attack, and the visual verification of the hit by *Lapon*. Alden's post-publication Ultra research has also confirmed the timing of *Flasher's* torpedo hits on *Tachibana Maru*. Although she was able to continue on her way, the tanker was sunk less than two weeks later in a night surface attack by the *USS Sawfish* (SS 276), several hundred miles to the north.

The convoy's base course had been northward when *Flasher* attacked, so Whitaker searched to the north. However, the convoy's base course had changed to the east, but *Lapon* was unable to surface after her attack and radio *Flasher* of the course change. By the time *Lapon* did communicate, the convoy was gone. In his Coordinated Attack Report, Whitaker remarked that this convoy was lost because the wolf pack lacked a third submarine:

> A minimum of three submarines should be used in a coordinated attack group. This was well demonstrated on September 27th when both Flasher and Lapon lost contact with a valuable convoy when a third submarine in the group could have maintained contact while the first two made attacks.

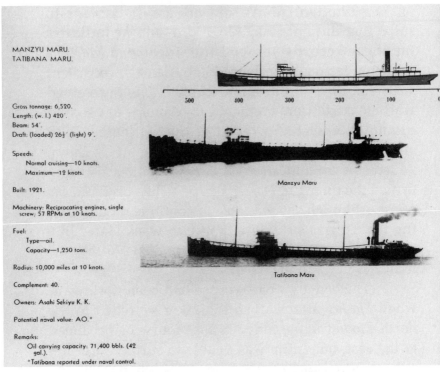

MANZYU MARU.
TATIBANA MARU.

Gross tonnage: 6,520.
Length: (w. l.) 420'.
Beam: 54'.
Draft: (loaded) 26½' (light) 9'.

Speeds:
    Normal cruising—10 knots.
    Maximum—12 knots.

Built: 1921.

Machinery: Reciprocating engines, single
    screw; 57 RPMs at 10 knots.

Fuel:
    Type—oil.
    Capacity—1,250 tons.

Radius: 10,000 miles at 10 knots.

Complement: 40.

Owners: Asahi Sekiyu K. K.

Potential naval value: AO.*

Remarks:
    Oil carrying capacity: 71,400 bbls. (42
        gal.).
    *Tatibana reported under naval control.

Manzyu Maru

Tatibana Maru

Tatibana (or *Tachibana*) *Maru* (ONI 208-J)

On September 29, *Flasher* repeatedly tried to contact the submarine *Bonefish*, which was to replace the unfortunate *Crevalle* in the wolf pack. Whitaker needed to provide *Bonefish* with the wolf pack's new assigned location. After failing numerous times, Whitaker radioed the Fremantle command to reach *Bonefish* and have her radio *Flasher*. Contact was finally made on September 30. Almost a month after *Crevalle* had originally departed Fremantle, there would finally be three subs in the wolf pack. Prior to joining the pack, *Bonefish* had already inflicted medium damage on the enormous, 17,000-ton tanker *Kamoi* and sunk a small tanker.

After sinking *Ural Maru*, *Flasher* sighted numerous float planes and a *Chidori*-class torpedo boat that she pursued, but could not catch. Whitaker felt this dangerous antisubmarine vessel was worthy of torpedoes. Destroyers had been elevated to high-priority targets after the United States realized that Japan had a shortage of convoy escorts. While not a destroyer, this type vessel served the same purpose.

The wolf pack patrolled off the west coast of Luzon. *Bonefish* reported contact with a four-ship convoy the morning of October 1, and *Flasher* raced toward the convoy's expected position north of Subic Bay, but could not locate it. She tried unsuccessfully to reach *Bonefish* the afternoon of October 1. Frequent communication problems would plague *Bonefish's* last-minute wolf-pack assignment. *Bonefish* finally radioed during the night that she had been unable to close on the convoy due to enemy aircraft.

Flasher's main gyro compass broke the evening of October 1, and she relied on her auxiliary compass until repairs were completed the following morning.

On October 4 the subs were relocated to new coordinates closer to Luzon, with *Bonefish* northernmost off Cape Bolinao, *Lapon* off Point Caiman 20 miles south of *Bonefish*, and *Flasher* 30 miles south of *Lapon*. Separate sightings of hospital ships were made by *Flasher* (September 28) and *Bonefish* (October 2). It seemed the Japanese were using more and more hospital ships.

Lookouts sighted a vessel on the horizon before dawn the morning of October 4. Whitaker believed the vessel was probably the submarine *Hoe*. SJ radar also picked up the submarine, and Whitaker avoided. *Flasher* submerged ten miles off the coast of Luzon before daylight. Soon thereafter sound located a contact:

0532　Heard pinging bearing about 038° T.

0540　Sighted CHIDORI type torpedo boat bearing 040° T., range about 12,000 yards. (Ship Contact No. 17).

0600　Sighted smoke bearing 038° T. (Ship Contact No. 18). This appears to be a convoy coming out of Santa Cruz harbor.

0611　Sighted two planes bearing 022° T., distance about 12 miles (Plane Contact No. 31). They appeared to be searching above convoy.

0615　Convoy appears to be heading north. Guess we are out of luck.

0645　More ships are standing out of Santa Cruz Harbor.

0701　This convoy is headed our way. (Ship Contact No. 19). Battle stations.

0713　Convoy appears to be composed of about 8-10 ships in two columns of 4-5 ships each. There are many escorts and they have two planes above them. The sea is absolutely smooth. Not even a ripple on it. This will probably be fun. Commenced going to 80 feet between looks.

0730　Range now about 8,000 yards. We appear to be about on base course. Made ready all tubes. Range now 4500 yards. It appears that we may be able to fire three torpedoes each at two leading ships in starboard column. Angle on bow of leading ship in this column

now about 40° starboard.

0748   Range now 3600 yards, angle on bow about 45° starboard. Three escorts are on starboard beam of convoy. We are dead ahead of them. Planes close aboard above convoy.

0750   Track now about 60° starboard, torpedo run 2200 yards. Commenced firing forward as I was afraid we would be sighted if we waited any longer. Fired three torpedoes at ship with 2° divergent spread, and then fired three at second ship. Started deep immediately after firing as both planes were fairly close and our position should be well marked in this water. Heard one torpedo hit on first target one minute and thirty-five seconds after firing followed by two hits on second target at correct intervals.

0758   Escorts started dropping depth charges, some fairly close and some far away. From now until 0815 about 35 depth charges were dropped. The ocean appears full of escorts and they are all pinging. Believe they are getting in each other's way.

0815   Sound reported definite sinking noises in the direction of target. These were also heard by the commanding officer and are believed to have been from the second target.

0830   Escorts now appear to be interested in something in the general direction of the attack. There is much pinging but none very close. Started up for look.

0848   Made periscope observation. Saw damaged ship with his bow well up in the air bearing

123° T., range about 8,000 yards. One other unidentified ship and a CHIDORI are standing by him.

0849 Damaged ship sank with a loud explosion and with a cloud of white smoke above him. This is believed to have been the first target. Two float planes are searching the Area.

0852 The unidentified ship appears to be lying to and looks as if he may be down by the stern. He may be damaged. Commenced closing him at 2/3 speed to polish him off.

0940 Two power boats flying the Japanese Merchant flag are in the vicinity of the sinking ship.

1000 As we get closer there seems to be some doubt as to whether this so called damaged ship is even a merchant ship. He has a gun forward and looks now like a hybrid escort. He also appears to be pinging.

1009 All doubt was cleared up when our damaged ship suddenly whirled around to port and dropped four depth charges. Commenced clearing area to seaward as only two escort vessels and two planes remained in this vicinity.

1053 Watched two more CHIDORI torpedo boats join the search group. These seem to smoke very heavily.

1145 Escorts and planes still in sight searching, but they seem to think we went north. At least they haven't searched in our direction yet.

1305 Lost sight of escorts and plane. Still hear

pinging.

1341   Sighted plane again, but he is far away. No longer hear pinging.

1822   Surfaced. Will remain out from coast tonight and head in tomorrow morning to be in close for daylight patrol.

Bonefish and *Lapon* to the north were unable to close on the convoy attacked by *Flasher*. Whitaker claimed the sinking of one cargo vessel and the probable sinking of a second, both in the 5,000-ton to 6,000-ton range. Each ship was described as having a split superstructure and a mast-funnel-mast (MFM) layout, "similar in outline to the VIYO MARU, ONI 208 J (Rev), page 220." *Flasher* had fired all six forward torpedo tubes loaded with Mark 23 steam torpedoes, obtaining three hits out of the six fired. JANAC credited *Flasher* with sinking the 6,886-ton cargo vessel *Taibin Maru* in the October 4 attack. Alden lists a second name for the vessel as *Otoshi Maru*, giving the same tonnage. No credit was given for a second cargo vessel *Flasher* claimed to have sunk October 4, and it may have survived.

During a submerged periscope watch southwest of Hermana Mayor the morning of October 5, *Flasher* observed a convoy leaving Santa Cruz. It turned northward out of *Flasher's* range, toward *Lapon* and *Bonefish*. The rest of the day provided a few small coastal freighters and 14 separate aircraft sightings. Attempts that evening to contact *Bonefish* by voice failed. *Lapon* reported an unsuccessful attack on October 5 on a large southbound convoy escorted with seven planes.

On the morning of October 6, *Flasher* was submerged eight miles west of Palauig Point, Luzon, when:

0538   Sighted smoke bearing 006° T. (Ship Contact No. 23). Commenced approach. The water is absolutely smooth as glass. Not even a ripple.

0557   Sighted bomber in direction of convoy. (Plane Contact No. 47). This was the first of seven planes covering this convoy. There were five medium bombers and two float planes. The float planes seemed to fly fairly high while the bombers usually were within 100-200 feet of the water. As it was very smooth, this forces us to be very careful and go deep between observations.

0630   Range now 12,000 yards, angle on bow 20° starboard. We seem to be pretty well ahead of convoy now. Numerous planes are making it difficult though, and on this observation large bubbles were noted coming up from forward. There is no time to check for origin of these bubbles. Decided they were probably from bow buoyancy so closed bow buoyancy vent. We have only stern tubes so will attempt to get directly ahead and keep stern pointed at convoy during latter stages of approach.

0703   With planes all around made observation and found that convoy had given us a 25° port angle on bow. As stern as pointed toward them and as torpedo run is only about 1700 yards felt this was a favorable opportunity. This was further indicated as several of targets were overlapping. We hadn't been sighted now and it seemed probable that we would be at any time, so decided to fire.

0704 Commenced firing stern tubes with 30° port track, torpedo run about 1700 yards. Used one degree divergent spread. Started deep after firing as planes were all around. Expected to get at least one hit but were disappointed as all torpedoes missed. Believe they saw tracks and avoided.

0710 Screws and pinging from escorts all around but not a single bomb or depth charge. Don't understand it, but guess they decided to let us alone as we hadn't damaged them.

0808 Periscope observation showed convoy well past in the distance and many planes still searching our vicinity.

1117 Have sighted planes on every periscope observation.

1400 Planes no longer in sight. Feel that undue concern over planes caused us to miss this convoy. Had we held fire for a few minutes we could probably have gotten into firing position from which we could hardly have missed. The commanding officer had felt from the beginning of the approach that we would probably be sighted, and he was so relieved to get in to what he considered to be an acceptable firing position that he went ahead and fired.

1823 Surfaced.

Since dawn, *Flasher* had made 15 separate plane sightings of a total of 23 fighters and patrol bombers. There were 14 plane sightings the day before. It is not surprising that Whitaker felt pressured by enemy antisubmarine aircraft. His worries were not the "undue concern" he confessed, but were well justified.

After dark the sub surfaced and attempted to contact *Bonefish*, without success. Whitaker finally radioed Fremantle again to have them get *Bonefish* contact *Flasher*. *Bonefish* radioed in about midnight that she had failed in her attack and had chased another hospital ship. *Lapon* wisely suggested the wolf pack "let the area cool off."

Therefore, the pack patrolled farther off the coast of Luzon the following two days, before closing on the coast the evening of October 8. *Flasher* headed in for her station off Palauig Point, submerged there the morning of October 9, but sighted only planes and small coastal freighters.

Smoke was sighted on the afternoon of the 10th, but the subs were unable to catch the convoy before it put into Santa Cruz for the night. *Flasher* surfaced after sundown for Whitaker to order the three submarines to move in closer to the shore at ten-mile intervals south of Santa Cruz Harbor, so they could intercept the convoy when it continued its trip south. The convoy got up first the next morning, though, and got completely past *Bonefish* and *Lapon* without being spotted.

Flasher detected the convoy to the northeast on SJ radar, but it was too far from her to close on the surface before daylight. *Flasher* ran on the surface at high speed for a half hour, then made a running dive before a brightening sky. Travelling at high speed sub-

merged 80 feet below the calm sea, *Flasher* ran out of water:

0600   We are getting very close to shallow water. Navigator says we have about two miles before we are due to run aground.

(While *Flasher* raced toward the shallow water and possible grounding, Motor Machinist Frank DeBois passed through the crews' mess. Standing by the mess-hall ladder and watching the hatch above was off-duty Signalman Floyd Doty. DeBois saw that in one hand Doty held a loaf of bread, and in the other a large salami. At the start of the war, Doty had been stranded in the Philippines to face the invading Japanese, but managed to escape aboard *Trout*, along with the gold from the Philippine Treasury. Doty announced that, if *Flasher* ran aground and he became stranded again, he was going to do it with food in hand.)

0618   Range now 6,000 yards. Angle on bow about 90° starboard. Three of the ships are overlapping. If we had Mark XIV fish, believe I would fire low power shot. As it is, we have three Mk. 23 and one MK. XIV. Sighted two float planes over convoy. (Plane Contact No. 52).

0622   Convoy zigged away. Continued to close hoping they would zig back.

0635   We have travelled more than our two miles and should have already run aground on a five fathom bank. Reversed course to 280° and decided to give up. They are already in

shallow water. We don't even have a chance
of making an end around due to the water.
1205　Surfaced and headed for southern end of
area.

After surfacing, lookouts sighted a possible periscope, and *Flasher* evaded with left full rudder at high
speed. She left the area at sundown, headed home.
Both *Lapon* and *Bonefish* remained on patrol after
Flasher's departure. *Bonefish* sank another cargo vessel
on October 14. (The two submarines compiled significant records during the war, *Bonefish* with seven successful patrols and *Lapon* with six. *Bonefish* was sunk
with all hands the following June in the Sea of Japan.
Lapon survived the war. Both subs were to receive coveted Navy Unit Commendations.)

Late the evening of October 11, *Flasher* passed a
friendly submarine at five miles, before she transited
Apo East Passage, passed Ambulong Island to port in
the early morning hours, and then picked up another
convoy of three ships headed into shallow water north
of the Cuyo Islands. Whitaker concluded:

> We cannot make end around without
> running through much shallow water
> with many banks of from three-ten fath-
> oms. Do not consider it worth the risk.
> Will continue down to eastward of the
> Cuyo Islands and see if we can't recon-
> tact convoy there.

No contact was made, and *Flasher* continued on her
way south, avoiding many enemy plane contacts.

With dawn on the 12th, *Flasher* closed on another possible periscope that turned out to be a stick. *Flasher* cleared Sibutu Passage October 13 and Makassar Strait on the 14th, passing an enemy minesweeper at ten miles and exchanging calls with *USS Raton* (SS 270) while proceeding down the strait.

On October 15, another friendly submarine was passed, whose identity was not registered in the logs, and *Flasher* began late-night passage of Lombok Strait, avoiding a small patrol boat in the process. Early the morning of the 16th, she passed another American sub, *Becuna* (SS 319). (*Becuna* survived the war to become an exhibit in Philadelphia.) The Lombok Strait-Makassar Strait artery for Fremantle submarines was becoming congested. Once past Lombok Strait the enemy threat lessened for *Flasher*, and it was possible to relax more during off-duty hours.

Whitaker had a highly developed sense of humor, which was not always apparent to his officers and crew. Using reference books in his cabin, Whitaker would privately research obscure details about a subject in which one or more of his officers had expressed an interest, such as professional baseball—one of Glennon's hobbies. Later he would direct the wardroom conversation around to the 1932 season, for instance, and he'd get Glennon to say who played right field for one of the prominent teams. Whitaker's patsy would venture something wrong, so then Whitaker would hazard his own previously researched answer: "Wasn't that the year Smith was injured and then Jones finished the season?" He could PROVE he was right, of course. It took the wardroom several war patrols before they caught on.

Sometimes the officers got the best of their skipper. Once Lt. McCants observed privately to Whitaker, "You know, Captain, you're the most even-tempered man I've ever known." Whitaker quietly savored this compliment and swelled a little inwardly. Then McCants added, "You're always mad." Years afterward Whitaker would tell this story on himself.

In his first patrol as executive officer, Glennon had proved to be as aggressive as his predecessor, Ray DuBois. Whitaker later said,

> Phil Glennon was one of these nice gentlemen, you know, just would NEVER let a lady come into the room without jumping up and grabbing her coat — Hell! That guy was the God-damndest tiger at sea I ever saw! I don't think he knew he could get killed.

During one of *Flasher's* severest depth chargings, Whitaker had made a crack and turned to see Glennon chuckling. Whitaker was forever impressed with Glennon's coolness in *Flasher's* most dangerous moments.

The remainder of the trip down the west coast of Australia to Fremantle was uneventful. The morning of October 20, *Flasher* moored next to the noted veteran *USS Growler* in the nest of submarines alongside the tender *USS Euryale*.

Rear Admiral Christie came aboard, and left with his entourage less than an hour later. The officers and crew were not formally relieved until the following morning, when Lt. H.J. Messick and the relief crew took over.

Shortly before Christie came aboard, one of the major events of the war was unfolding with the American landings at Leyte Gulf in the southeast Philippines. The retaking of the Philippines would directly affect *Flasher*, as a forward base for submarines would soon be opened, and the Perth/Fremantle base would be left in the background, far removed from the action.

Whitaker noted in his war patrol report the ever-increasing Japanese antisubmarine activity through the enemy's use of greater aircraft coverage and more numerous escorts, making submerged approaches all the more difficult. He emphasized *Flasher* had encountered a single ship (*Saigon Maru*) that had been provided with four destroyers and plane coverage, and that *Flasher* had been heavily depth charged for her attack. Whitaker also complained in his report about failures in the important hydrogen detector and auxiliary gyro compass.

Other equipment failures listed in the report included the main engine failures and exhaust leaks, and the loss of the two RCA waterproof bridge speakers, that failed repeatedly during the fourth patrol although they had previously operated well. Whitaker also complained that because of the increased number of messages being received, two sets of decoding strips should be provided each sub, as they became worn and difficult to read, and the messages could be deciphered by two individuals in half the time if they each had decoders.

As a fresh note, Whitaker noted:

> The overhaul of the Pitometer log was
> accomplished by SPENCER, MARKOM
> G., Jr., EM1c, U.S.N., with the coopera-
> tion of the Submarine Repair Unit, Navy
> #137, Gyro Shop. Its performance has
> been entirely satisfactory this patrol for
> the first time since this vessel has been in
> commission. From this it is believed that
> if sufficient care is given its overhaul by
> skilled personnel this log can be made to
> give satisfactory performance.

Electrician's Mate First Class Spencer had made
Flasher's first, second and fourth patrols. He missed the
third patrol as the appendicitis case evacuated at
Exmouth Gulf. Things seemed to happen to Spencer.
He would be transferred from *Flasher* before her fifth
patrol.

Whitaker also congratulated the sub's cooks and
sub's baker for doing "a splendid job," in spite of
"mediocre" meats supplied for the fourth patrol. Still,
the meat was better than furnished on prior patrols out
of Fremantle.

Whitaker took pains to commend torpedo performance:

> During the past two patrols torpedo per-
> formance has been excellent. This is be-
> lieved due partially to the great pains
> taken by the ship's force in routine up-
> keep and partially to the careful overhaul
> of torpedoes by S.R.U. Torpedo Depot,
> Navy #137.

Ship's Party Following Fourth Patrol (Courtesy of Joseph Ferrell)

Flasher had again arrived at Fremantle with her fuel tanks almost dry (only 4,374 gallons), after having consumed more than 120,000 gallons on patrol. She still had five torpedoes aboard, however. Whitaker listed the "limiting factor" causing the termination of the patrol as the "provisions of operations order." *Flasher* had returned because of orders.

On the fourth war patrol, *Flasher's* crew had witnessed new Japanese tactics to avoid American submarines. Because of the Americans' radar, Japanese ships hugged the coastline as much as possible during the day, and put into ports each night. This hurt the effectiveness of wolf-pack tactics, and while *Flasher*,

Lapon and *Bonefish* had made successful patrols, they had done so operating independently, rather than as a coordinated wolf pack. *Bonefish* had also been part of the wolf pack for only half of the patrol. For these reasons Whitaker did not prepare a single, "coordinated attack report" for the wolf pack. Christie and his Chief of Staff disagreed, and told him there MUST be a joint report. Having lost the point but not his spunk, Whitaker turned to Glennon in front of the two men and said, "Take care of that." Glennon and McCants did the report.

Flasher received her usual glowing endorsement from Captain Bryant of Subron 18, who commended the patrol performance as follows:

> On this fourth patrol the commanding officer displayed the same sound judgment, aggressiveness and careful planning which have characterized his previous patrols. He, his officers and crew are to be congratulated on another fine patrol. The high state of training and morale are reflected in the heavy damage inflicted on the enemy.

Bryant agreed with most of the repairs and changes recommended by Whitaker, but rejected criticism of the auxiliary gyro compass, stating "the present auxiliary compass is not designed for continuous operation and if it is to stand up it must be used only when necessary." Bryant made it sound like the compass was aboard just for appearances. It would not seem that the submariners could put much trust in their auxiliary compasses if the compasses were so delicate that they could only be used infrequently.

The admiral's endorsement was also favorable:

> The Force Commander takes pleasure in congratulating FLASHER's Commanding Officer, Officers, and Crew on another fine patrol, and notes with pride that in four consecutive successful patrols this outstanding submarine has sunk seventeen cargo ships and one Light Cruiser for 109,900 tons, and damaged two cargo ships for 11,500 tons. FLASHER is credited with inflicting the following heavy damage on the enemy in a well planned and splendidly executed patrol:

	SUNK		
1-AK	(Large-EU)	7,500 Tons	(Attack No. 1)
1-AP	(Medium-EU)	7,500 Tons	(Attack No. 2)
1-AK	(Medium-EU)	4,000 Tons	(Attack No. 3)
1-AK	(Medium-EU)	4,000 Tons	(Attack No. 3)
Total Sunk		23,000 Tons	
	DAMAGED		
1-UN		4,000 Tons	(Attack No. 2)
Grand Total		27,000 Tons	

> R.W. Christie

On October 28, the relief crew took *Flasher* into the dry dock where her hull was scraped. Just before midnight after the dock had been pumped dry, relief crewman G.A. Mallams was knocked unconscious when a jack shifted, striking him on the bridge of the nose. He was turned over to the *USS Euryale* sick bay. *Flasher* was moved back alongside the tender on October 30, under the supervision of Lt. Frank Kristl, formerly of the *Flasher* and now assigned to Submarine Division 182.

In formal ceremonies on October 31, 1944, Commander Reuben T. Whitaker was relieved of command of *Flasher* by Commander George W. Grider. The crew presented Whitaker with a watch inscribed "What Devastation!" The quote was from his exclamation after *Taishin Maru* had been torpedoed on the first patrol. They had collected money and sent it to Ray DuBois to buy the watch and have it engraved. Whitaker had completed ten war patrols, four as *Flasher's* captain. He was lucky to be still alive. Whitaker was also one of America's leading submarine skippers, ranking high in the top ten, regardless of whose statistics are used and whether the test was tonnage sunk or number of ships sunk. He held an impressive three Navy Crosses and four Silver Stars. His skills were to be used at the New London Submarine School, where he would instruct past war's end. After the change-of-command ceremony, *Flasher* was officially returned to the relief crew, who resumed repairs and refit as before.

George William Grider was assuming his first command in *Flasher*, but, like Whitaker, was a seasoned veteran, having participated in seven previous patrols. Grider had patrolled in the famous *Wahoo* (SS 238) with two of the war's most aggressive skippers, Mush Morton and Dick O'Kane, the aged *Pollack* (SS 180), and the new *Hawkbill* (SS 366). By pure coincidence, he was also from Whitaker's home town of Memphis, Tennessee.

George Grider (with Pipe) and Reuben Whitaker (with Tom McCants
Departing at Left) Alongside *USS Euryale* (Author's Collection)

The morning of November 4, *Flasher's* crew returned and held muster, disclosing 14 new crew members. Over the next several days, the sub conducted repeated sound tests and practice approaches with her new commanding officer, returning to moor alongside *Dace* and *Cavalla* (SS 244). (These two distinguished subs had recently earned permanent places in history. *Dace* had combined with *USS Darter* to sink two heavy Japanese cruisers and seriously damage a third two weeks before. She had also warned the American fleet of the Japanese approach toward Leyte Gulf, and had rescued *Darter's* crew when that sub grounded chasing the fleeing, badly shaken Japanese force. *Cavalla*—now a museum submarine in Galveston, Texas—provided the same kind of vital information on a Japanese force prior to the Battle of the Philippine Sea and the Marianas Turkey Shoot, then sank the 30,000-ton aircraft carrier *Shokaku*.)

Flasher departed again for gun drills, maneuvering exercises and practice approaches on *USS Isabel*. She entered Gage Roads the morning of November 10, and took aboard ComSubDiv 182 as training officer for continued exercises. Radar trials were conducted with *HMAS Launceten* and *HMAS Bunbury*, a fleet minesweeper. *Flasher* returned to go directly onto the keel blocks for inspections of the hull, hull fittings, rudder, propellers and shafts. Both propellers were removed and new ones installed. *Flasher* was hard on propellers.

On November 13, while *Flasher* was still in the dry dock, recently promoted Chief Electrician Spencer fell from an iron railing, hitting his head on the concrete bottom of the dry dock 15 feet below. He was carried by ambulance to the tender for observation.

Flasher's Officers at Change of Command (L to R: Glennon, Burke, McCants, Harrison, Hamlin, Atkinson, Grider and Whitaker. Author's Collection)

Spencer would miss the fifth patrol. The deck log indicates he was neither intoxicated nor guilty of any misconduct; he had just slipped on the slick metal surfaces.

Prior to the fifth patrol, Electrician Robert Briggs, veteran of *Flasher's* four patrols and three patrols on *S-37* at the beginning of the war, was transferred. He went first to New London and then to *S-18* in San Diego. For his distinguished service in submarine warfare he was awarded the Silver Star, together with a citation signed by Secretary of Defense James Forrestal. Strangely, Briggs received the medal and citation three days after Forrestal had leapt to his death, and years after the war ended. Motor Machinist Bill Beaman received his well-deserved Bronze Star award from Forrestal at the same time. Also leaving *Flasher* after four patrols were "Stoway" Joe Holmes and "Gunner" Schwartz, the strong sailor who reminded his shipmates of actor Victor Mature. Holmes would marry an Australian girl and eventually settle near New London, Connecticut.

The dry dock was flooded the morning of the 13th, and *Flasher* went alongside the tender to begin taking on fuel, lubricating oil, stores and torpedoes. Ensign Eddie Atkinson inspected the quantity of stores taken aboard, and Pharmacist Mate John Paul Buss checked their quality. *Flasher* then went out briefly to conduct sound tests with the new propellers.

Muster the morning of November 15 showed two absences, who were later brought aboard in the custody of Lt.(jg) Jim Hamlin. The two men and an earlier AWOL sailor were transferred to *USS Bashaw* (SS 241), a submarine acting as Admiral Christie's nominal flagship in Fremantle.

CHAPTER 8

THE "FLAMING ACTION" PATROL - *FLASHER'S* FIFTH WAR PATROL

Flasher departed November 15, 1944, on her fifth patrol with two of her main engines over-hauled, the two new propellers to eliminate noise, and new electronic equipment including IFF ("Identification—Friend or Foe" for contacting Allied planes), VHF (for additional radio coverage), APR (for detecting radar), and Loran (Long Range Navigation, for navigational fixes based on radio beacons). Unfortunately, there was only one Loran station (Darwin) that could reach *Flasher* at her patrol station in the South China Sea. Still, the new Loran set would give her one good navigational line of position.

Grider also had an electric buzzer system installed on the bridge. If a plane were spotted on radar inside five miles, the radar operator pushed the button, and the buzzer sounded on the bridge. The OOD was to dive the boat, no questions asked. With Bill Beaman on the SD radar watch one time, Grider questioned Beaman about the system, then pushed the button and, of course, the boat dived instantly. It was like a new toy to Grider. None of this electronic equipment had been on *Flasher* prior to her fifth patrol.

Grider was the only officer making his first patrol on *Flasher*. Glennon, as before, served as Executive

Chart of Fifth Patrol (Nov. 15, 1944 to Jan. 2, 1945) (by Author)

Officer. *Flasher* left Fremantle for her fifth war patrol shortly after noon, accompanied by submarines *USS Becuna* commanded by Lt. Cmdr. Hank Sturr, and *USS Hawkbill* under Lt. Cmdr. Worth Scanland, Jr., as a coordinated search-and-attack group. Unlike *Flasher's* prior wolf packs, this group was under the overall command of the submarine squadron's leader, Captain Bryant. He sailed in Scanland's *Hawkbill*, which probably relieved both Grider and Sturr.

    Hawkbill and *Becuna* were thicker-hulled *Balao*-class submarines that could dive deeper and survive closer depth charges than *Flasher*. Grider was familiar with *Hawkbill* since he was her executive officer before coming to *Flasher*. In their last patrols, both *Hawkbill* and *Becuna* participated in a wolf pack led by Cmdr. Ike Holtz in *Baya* (SS 318), forming part of a scouting line to intercept any Japanese fleet response to the Allied invasion of the Palaus. The subs had seen no Japanese response, but *Hawkbill* and *Becuna* chased a carrier, sank some shipping, and survived intense depth chargings on their trip from the scouting line to their new home at Fremantle.

    During *Flasher's* transit to Darwin (instead of her usual destination of Exmouth Gulf), she conducted additional drills and approaches with her two wolf-pack companions, and used the trip to check out some of her new electronic equipment. On November 19, Grider ordered battle surface drills, with the crew firing 135 rounds from the 20mm guns and 225 rounds of 30-caliber ammunition. The log indicated "no casualties"—meaning no jams or weapons malfunctions.

    As *Flasher* headed east November 21, she sighted and exchanged signals with fleet minesweeper

HMAS Castlemain. The next morning, the three subs met an escort vessel for the entry into Port Darwin, where they moored alongside the submarine rescue vessel *USS Chanticleer. Flasher* topped up with 33,000 gallons of diesel fuel, 600 gallons of lubricating oil, and 4,200 gallons of fresh water. Grider noted, "Effected repairs to SJ radar training gear, retuned the VHF, touched up the paint, beered the crew."

Flasher's crew was able to make the most of a very short liberty at Darwin. Radioman Filippone, Quartermaster Twiss, and Fire Controlman Webb went to visit Twiss' brother, who was in the Army Air Corps at an airfield nearby. They were told the brother was due back "in a few minutes," and an Army officer treated them to drinks at the Army Officer's Club while they waited. Time passed but the brother did not show. Neither did the bus they thought would take them back to the sub.

The three sailors finally got back to the boat to find themselves in very hot water. They had returned almost an hour and a half late, delaying *Flasher's* departure until five minutes after their return. She was scheduled to be the first boat out, so her delays were witnessed by her pack mates, Grider's former shipmates, and his immediate boss, much to Grider's chagrin. Three hurriedly picked replacements for the missing sailors were released back to shore duty. The three AWOL men were supposed to forfeit all leave following the patrol as punishment, but Grider ultimately relented, and they got their liberty back.

Flasher proceeded northwesterly from Port Darwin to pass east of Timor, before turning west across the Banda and Flores Seas toward the now-familiar

Makassar Strait. On the 23rd *Flasher* made a pre-dawn radar contact with a flight of Allied bombers headed out from Darwin. Another sighting occurred later in the morning, as Grider described in the war patrol report:

> At 1043 lookout reported plane close aboard. Dived. Surfaced fifteen minutes later directly under the guns of a large frigate bird. (Bird Contact Number 1).

Clearly, the war patrol report narratives would be less formal under Grider.

Flasher's dive to avoid the frigate bird disclosed a problem with the bow buoyancy vent, which refused to close prior to surfacing. Whitaker had experienced problems with bubbles from the same vent on the last patrol. The crew tried both the hydraulic controls and hand controls unsuccessfully. Physical inspection showed no worn or broken parts, no foreign materials jamming the mechanism and no binding. Auxiliary repairman Bill Beaman had a hairy experience working on the vent from INSIDE the bow buoyancy tank. Although *Flasher* was already well into enemy-controlled waters, he had to remove the manhole cover at the top of the tank, then lower himself inside to make the linkage adjustments. Then he had to remain inside while they tested the linkage to see if the valve fully closed, all the time worrying if *Flasher* would have to dive with him in the tank. It turned out all the vent mechanism needed was a slight adjustment, and by tightening the linkage one turn the problem was solved, but not before an all-night effort.

That afternoon *Flasher* also received recognition signals on her new IFF receiver from a contact 35 miles away. The contact "closed in to five miles before we sighted him in a cloudless sky; a silver Liberator, very hard to see. Drove him off with recognition signals and emergency flares." Another four Liberators were sighted the next morning and one of those closed within four miles before opening, but Grider could never get them to respond to IFF transmissions from *Flasher's* new equipment, and he found this exasperating.

Grider's personality and manner differed greatly from Whitaker's. Grider never got as mad as Whitaker, was more restless on the boat, and had some difficulty sleeping. Whitaker tended to be well rested, leaving much of the worrying to his exec. With Whitaker, the officers and crew were supposed to KNOW what the captain wanted, by checking the night-order book, by talking to the navigator, etc. Grider was more accessible, less demanding, and more forgiving. When Grider had trouble getting his new procedure for aircraft sightings across to the crew, Glennon told him, "Look, tell me what you want done and I'll write it down as a procedure to be approved by you." Whitaker would never have allowed his execs to talk to him that way, and they never tried to. Grider, however, took the advice, approved the procedure, and the crew complied.

Contrasted with Whitaker's terse night orders, Grider's became detailed and informational, as in the night orders for November 24-25, 1944:

Underway at three engine speed. Course 303° (T). Zig zagging. We are passing north of Tiger Islands and south of Saleier Island tonight.

Change course as advised by the navigator, either verbally or in writing.

After we are clear of the pass between Saleier and Tana Djampea, slow to standard speed.

SJ and APR are manned. There is a radar station somewhere near the SW tip of the Celebes, frequency 193-195 megacycles.

Man the SD at daybreak. Dive on all plane contacts that do not show a friendly IFF at a range of 8 miles. If they show IFF <u>and</u> if you recognize the plane as friendly by sight, do not dive unless he turns directly toward you. If they show friendly IFF but you do not sight the plane, dive at six miles and pull the flare.

We are now in a submarine patrol zone and may attack suitable targets.

Respy

G.W. Grider.

Signalman Corneau climbed topside to read the night orders to the Officer of the Deck, and to add color to this dull duty, read them with an important, dramatic flair, highlighting the exotic names of the islands. As he ended with, "Ree-SPECT-ful-ee, Gee-orge, ah Double-you, Gur-I-der!" he turned to find the Captain had been silently standing close behind him the whole time. Grider quipped, "We're going to have to send YOU to Hollywood!"

The fifth patrol would be a testing ground for whether Grider conformed to the methods already established aboard *Flasher*, or whether *Flasher* changed to adapt to her new skipper's ways. Grider did make Burke get *Hawkbill's* torpedo-spread formulas, but the *Flasher* fire-control team ignored the *Hawkbill* data. As the patrol progressed, Grider told them, "I don't know what you're doing, but whatever it is, it's working, so keep it up." Grider was willing to listen to advice, and he was wise not to change successful practices on a successful boat. Overall, Grider conformed more to *Flasher* than the other way around. Practices begun under Whitaker, such as shorter watches for lookouts to keep them sharp, were left in place. Grider, experienced in procedures from at least three other subs, could have easily imposed changes, but he refrained.

Very early on the morning of November 25, *Flasher* got an SJ radar contact just two miles off the starboard beam. The contact was headed on a southerly course at 20 knots and came within one mile, so *Flasher* "finally slowed down and let pass ahead." Grider commented: "The executive officer believes it was an ionized sea gull." *Flasher* got another contact three hours later, but the small vessel passed through Saleier (Salajar) Pass between Celebes and Salajar Island before *Flasher* could complete her end around. She had tried unsuccessfully for an hour to close at flank speed.

Later the same morning, *Flasher* closed on a native sailboat, coming to a stop and then BACKING at two-third's speed to maneuver alongside. The sailboat

was identified as a "friendly native boat," and was given a carton of American Chesterfield cigarettes.

The sailboat was also given a loaf of fresh bread baked by one of *Flasher's* cooks, Charles "Ski" Ezerosky. Ezerosky personally brought the bread to the bridge, and proudly watched as it was handed to a sailor on deck and tossed with the cigarettes to the sailboat. One of the Indonesian natives suddenly ran from the boat's stern and picked up the bread with both arms extended full length, as if he were carrying a bomb, and heaved it into the sea. Ezerosky's jaw "dropped about a foot"—he was justly proud of his freshly baked bread. If that weren't bad enough, the entire crew soon learned of the incident and kidded Ski for the rest of the patrol.

The sub continued around the southwestern tip of Celebes (now "Sulawesi") headed into Makassar Strait. She passed DeBril lighthouse to the west and Cape Mandar on November 25, and passed Cape William and *USS Besugo* (SS 321) on the 26th.

Flasher's Torpedo Data Computer (TDC) failed to pass the numerous daily routine checks made on November 26 by Fire Controlman Joe Webb, one of the tardy tourists at Darwin. Webb was irreplaceable to the fire-control team. The TDC was essential to accurate shots, but *Flasher's* TDC was now useless and she had yet to fire her first torpedo. The TDC had broken once before, while *Flasher* was still in New London. That time Webb and Glennon had worked long and hard to isolate the problem to a bad follow-up motor. Webb and Chief Cypherd isolated the TDC problem to the same motor, but it was beyond repair.

Grider, after the fruitless repair attempts and

with visions that his first war patrol was already a failure, radioed the 27th requesting a spare TDC motor from any southbound submarine. Amazingly, the *USS Hardhead* (SS 365) delivered the ordered spare about four hours later. Grider commented in the patrol report: "That's better service than one gets alongside the tender."

(*Hardhead* was just finishing her second war patrol. On her first patrol, she sank the Japanese Light Cruiser *Natori*, and on her second she sank a tanker and a frigate. *Hardhead* performed lifeguard duty on both patrols, and on her second stumbled on a Navy fighter pilot from the *USS Enterprise*, Cmdr. Fred Bakutis, on his seventh day in a life raft in the Sulu Sea. He had been shot down during the Leyte Gulf air battles. By coincidence, Bakutis, Annapolis class of 1935, was a friend of *Hardhead's* skipper, Frank Greenup, class of 1936. *Hardhead's* valuable contributions to the war effort were to continue with the donated follow-up motor, for *Flasher's* fifth war patrol would become one of the war's greatest.)

Hardhead departed the area after the exchange, but *Flasher* remained to patrol the northern mouth of the channel between Doc Can Island and Pearl Bank, searching for two cruisers reported to have left Balikpapan, Borneo, the previous morning. Nothing was sighted, and *Flasher* left the afternoon of November 28.

The problem with enemy and "friendly" plane contacts continued the following day:

Proceeding north in the Sulu Sea.
At 0937 made SD contact with friendly

aircraft at 32 miles. He did not close. At 1019 made another SD contact at 50 miles, friendly. At 1136 made SD contact on friendly plane at 38 miles. Sighted him at 20 miles. He moved in slowly to 3 miles and circled us. It was a PB2Y. We gave him recognition signals and flares and he pulled away to the westward. Established VHF communications and asked him if there were any targets in the area. He said "Negative"; we then asked him politely not to come so close next time. He said, "Roger Wilco," and shoved off.

At 1335 OOD and lookout sighted two engine bomber flying low and headed at us. Dived. Surfaced at 1423. At 1613 made SD contact and later sighted three planes; They passed 21 miles ahead, flying high.

On the 29th *Flasher* passed through the Sulu Sea, exchanging signals with *USS Gunnel* (SS 253) while transiting Apo East Pass prior to entering Mindoro Strait and then the South China Sea. Two days later *Gunnel* would rescue 11 lucky Navy airmen from nearby Palawan Island. Other captured Americans on Palawan would be executed by Japanese captors irate at Allied air raids.

Flasher arrived at the wolf pack's rendezvous point 120 miles west of the Philippines the evening of November 30 and began circling, awaiting *Hawkbill's* arrival. As *Hawkbill* had not arrived at the rendezvous point an hour later, an impatient Grider decided to head back east to intercept a convoy reported by friendly aircraft to be in Palawan Passage. He figured he might catch the convoy if it headed north out of the narrow passage between Palawan and Dangerous Ground.

No convoy appeared by 10 a.m., so Grider changed course to the northwest to search for *Hawkbill*, sighting her around 4 p.m. that afternoon. *Flasher* patrolled her assigned station December 2 uneventfully, and met with her pack mates *Hawkbill* and *Becuna* after dawn on December 3 to receive supplementary patrol instructions. The new orders placed *Flasher* at the northern end of a patrol line 200 miles west of Luzon. She arrived at the new station that afternoon.

The next day was an important date for Signalman Corneau. December 4 was his 21st birthday, and he had promised himself it should be a special occasion. It would be a memorable day for all as events developed in the new assigned area, or what *Flasher's* crew thought was her new area. Because of a break in the persistent cloud cover, Glennon was only then able to take his first navigational bearing in 36 hours, and found *Flasher* "about 15 miles west of assigned station." She started east to her correct station, but soon received a message that altered matters.

The wolf-pack subs had code names, with *Becuna* as "Tiger," *Hawkbill* as "Wolf," and *Flasher* as "Teacup." (The *Flasher* crew figured the less-experienced *Hawkbill* and *Becuna* had chosen the names to poke fun at *Flasher*.) Wolf sent a message to Teacup of a convoy sighting, stating the convoy was approaching the northwest corner of area "Zebra," and added: "You

take the escorts; we'll take the tanker." Because of her navigational error, however, Teacup was at the best attack location, not Wolf or Tiger:

> <u>Ship Contact No. 3</u> At 0745, received contact report from HAWKBILL on westbound convoy. A plot showed us directly in its path. At 0749 sighted convoy bearing 080° (T). Could see three or four sets of masts and one large ship through the rainsqualls. Began tracking from ahead.
>
> Sent message to HAWKBILL and at 0844 dived thirteen miles ahead of convoy. Large swells made depth control very difficult. Visibility conditions were poor with many heavy rainsqualls in the area. A mast could be seen occasionally, but nothing more. When the generated range closed to 8000 yards the whole area was blotted out in a heavy downpour. Much pinging and screw noises on sound; periscope up almost continuously.

Signalman Corneau was then at the end of his watch and due to be relieved, but the convoy report changed normal procedures. At battle stations Corneau became assistant to the Plotting Officer. *Flasher's* Plotting Officer since the third patrol was Lt.(jg) Kiko Harrison, who, in Corneau's words, was "brilliant with the pad and pencil." When Harrison first reported aboard *Flasher*, Whitaker asked him where he attended college.

Harrison replied, "Princeton."

"Oh?" said an amused Whitaker, "I suppose you're a Phi Beta Kappa too, then?"

Harrison admitted he was. (Harrison would be a professor at Princeton after the war. The well-mannered, good-looking and recently-married Harrison was the son of a pre-war American representative to the Philippines, and was partially raised in England. He was well liked by the crew, who told ribald tales of their activities ashore to see if they could make him blush.)

During *Flasher's* approach and attack, the assistant to the Plotting Officer (in this case Corneau) was required to record the data announced from the captain's periscope observations. Corneau wrote on his pad the target's announced bearing, range, estimated speed and angle on the bow, as well as the precise time of the observation.

As Plotting Officer, Harrison worked from Corneau's notations instead of the frequent reports from the conning tower, that might come as often as every 30 to 40 seconds. Harrison would compare his data with the TDC operated by Gunnery Officer Tom McCants. Harrison and McCants worked together, with Harrison's penciled calculations sometimes correcting the TDC-generated data.

Flasher's crew first sighted the convoy when it was still 13 miles away. Because of the priority accorded tankers, and perhaps because his old boat (*Hawkbill*) had already jokingly claimed the tanker for herself, Grider focused on it and ignored its many escorts. He repeatedly called out range and bearing of the tanker. Glennon, the exec, kept asking Grider about

the numerous escorts, thought to be destroyers, patrol boats, and a net tender. But Grider cared only about the tanker. The Japanese obviously valued the tanker enough to accord it so many scarce escorts. With no reports coming from Grider on the other vessels, and Sound reporting the presence of other, fast screws close by, Glennon finally began firmly rotating the periscope (with Grider still glued to the eyepiece). Suddenly Grider barked new bearings and range for a destroyer:

> <u>Attack No. 1</u> Finally at a range of 2000 yards an ASASHIO class destroyer popped out of the mist; relative bearing 14, angle on the bow 30 starboard. Started swinging right but the gyros were swinging faster. At 0915 with gyros ranging from 28 to 51 and runs from 1650 to 1100 yards, track angles from 80 to 103 starboard, fired four torpedoes spread by periscope. Estimated target speed 15 knots. Down scope.
>
> Heard first hit as scope was going back up. Heard second and saw the spray rising around his engine room. He began to smoke heavily; his screws stopped, and he fell off to his left, settling aft and listing.
>
> Sometime before firing, a sweep around showed that the rain had lifted and there were three or four escorts, one a net tender, and a large tanker on the starboard quarter of the destroyer.
>
> After hitting the destroyer, took a

TORPEDO ATTACK REPORT FORM:

U.S.S. FLASHER Torpedo Attack No. *1* Patrol No. *5*

Time: *0915* H Date: *4 December, 1944* Lat. *13°12.5'N* Long. *116°37.0E*

TARGET DATA – DAMAGE INFLICTED:

Description: *Insert from attached sheet.*

Ship's Sunk: —

Ship's ~~damaged or~~ probably sunk: *One DD (EC).*

Damage determined by: *Insert from attached sheet.*

Target Draft: *9* Course: *316°* Speed: *15* Range: *1650*

OWN SHIP DATA:

Speed: *3.3* Course: *188°* Depth: *64'* Angle: *½°D.*

FIRE CONTROL AND TORPEDO DATA:

Type Attack: *Insert from attached sheet.*

	:	:	:	:	:
Tubes Fired	: 3	: 4	: 5	: 6	:
Track Angle	: 80 S.	: 92 S.	: 91 S.	: 103 S.	:
Gyro Angle	: 028°	: 040°20'	: 038°45'	: 051°30'	:
Depth Set	: 6	: 6	: 6	: 6	:
Power	: —	: —	: —	: —	:
Hit or Miss	: Hit	: Hit	: Miss	: Miss	:
Erratic	: No.	: No.	: No.	: No.	:
Mark Torpedo	: 23	: 23	: 23	: 23	:
Serial No.	: 65769	: 65384	: 65668	: 50485	:
Mark Exploder	: 6-5	: 6-5	: 6-5	: 6-5	:
Serial No.	: 26764	: 25828	: 25357	: 11467	:
Actuation Set	: Contact	: Contact	: Contact	: Contact	:
Actuation Actual	: Contact	: Contact	: —	: —	:
Mark Warhead	: 16-1	: 16-1	: 16-1	: 16-1	:
Serial No.	: 14692	: 19397	: 19408	: 5632	:
Explosive	: TPx	: TPx	: TPx	: TPx	:
Firing Interval	: —	: 7	: 12	: 13	:
Type Spread	:	Divergent			:
Sea Condition	:	Condition Four:			:
Overhaul Activity	:	U.S.S. Euryale (AS-22)			:

Remarks:-

Torpedo Attack Report Form, Attack No. 1, Fifth Patrol,
Handwritten Initial Version (Author's Collection)

set up on the tanker and started firing
our stern tubes at him.

Attack No. 2 At 0918 fired first stern
tube. Gyro angle 233, torpedo run 1900,
track angle 60 port, estimated speed 10
knots. After firing first one the scope
went under and wouldn't come back out.

The assistant TDC operator was instructed to fire three more, spreading by offset. Consequently, the second torpedo was fired seventeen seconds after the first without a spread.

The scope then came back out. The target was turning toward; angle on the bow 30 port and growing smaller. Checked fire.

Turned attention to destroyer for killer shot. He was dead in the water with his stern almost under and very close; he had drifted around to about a 130° port track now. Took sweep around and saw another destroyer or patrol boat boiling down on us at about 500 - 1000 yards. Went deep.

As we were going deep, heard two timed hits on tanker. Apparently he was making more than ten knots and his maneuver slowed him down just enough to let him catch them both in the tail. Verily, we smell of the rose.

At 0925 the depth charges started; about sixteen in all, mostly close. At 0931 heard screws through the hull. Executive officer: "If he drops now, they're gonna be close." At 0932 four depth charges. They were.

We were under a good negative gradient which started at 250 feet. We retired to the south and west, gradually pulling away from the searchers.

It became clear *Flasher* had lost the escorts. With ships still "up there," Glennon recommended to Grider that they go back up for a second series of attacks.

> At 1053 we were back at periscope depth. To the north we saw: a. The tanker on fire in his engine room aft and settling by the stern. b. An ASASHIO class destroyer standing by, about 500 yards nearer and a little off to the left of the tanker. c. Two escort vessels and the net tender making sweeps around the tanker. Range to the destroyer was 7500 yards.
>
> Started a reload. At 1136 turned around and headed in to attack the destroyer and finish off the tanker. The plan is to fire three at each, depth set six feet. At 1205 reload completed. When the range to the destroyer was 4400 yards, another rain squall closed in and visibility was reduced to zero.
>
> This may have been the same destroyer we attacked in the morning. It doesn't seem natural that a healthy, intelligent destroyer would lie to for so long. On the other hand, this destroyer was on a perfectly even keel with his boot topping a little above the surface and parallel; his starboard side showed no signs of damage; his searchlight and echo ranging gear were in excellent operating condition; and the escorts were not protecting him while they were circling the tanker.

It is the commanding officer's opinion that it was another ship.

Continued to close taking almost continuous looks at the rain. At 1239 saw an outline that looked like our target. She was under way beyond, and off to the left of where she should have been. We started to swing left.

At 1249 the rain squall lifted somewhat and we saw that we were chasing an escort. Destroyer was still lying to, range 1400 yards, angle on the bow about 110 starboard. Tanker not in sight. An escort was crossing the bow of the destroyer and coming in our general direction, so decided to go ahead and fire four at the destroyer.

Attack No. 3 At 1251 commenced firing four torpedoes at the destroyer, spread by periscope, coverage one and one half target length. While firing, saw bow of tanker projecting beyond stern of destroyer by about an eighth of his length, so tried to lob five and six close under destroyer stern to hit the tanker.

Heard two hits on destroyer followed by two more. We almost broached so periscope was put down and negative flooded. By time periscope was up we were too deep. The last look at the escort showed him close and coming in so went down to deep submergence, speeded up and got off the track.

At 1256 the depth charges started. This turned out to be a very thorough working over with many king sized explosions very close aboard. However, the worst of it was over in four minutes and the remaining ones were comfortably distant. A total of 46 were dropped, the attack lasting for 29 minutes.

We retired to the southwest, came to periscope depth at 1410 and sighted three escorts and the tanker, now burning fiercely along his whole length. No sign of the destroyer even with fifteen feet of periscope out and the escorts in sight down to their water lines.

A post firing analysis of explosion times indicates that all four hits on this attack were in the destroyer. The two targets were not in line until the last look and consequently all torpedoes were set on six feet. The two fired at the tanker hard under the destroyer's stern must have hit the destroyer. The breaking up noise heard in the direction of the destroyer lasted a very short time.

We continued to retire to the southwest, assuming that the tanker would sink; reloaded and checked all torpedoes that had been in flooded tubes.

It appears that this convoy consisted only of the tanker, the two destroyers and the three escorts. If there had been more ships, it does not seem reasonable that a destroyer and three escorts would remain with the damaged one. A thorough sweep all around was never obtained before the first attack this morning because of rain squalls.

At 1700 sighted BECUNA coming up from the westward; surfaced and exchanged calls with her. Heavy black smoke was still coming from the tanker. We expected her to be on the bottom by now.

Sent message to ComWolfPack reporting results and telling him that we would finish off tanker after dark. Received instructions to return to assigned station when mission was completed.

As darkness fell, we started in. Obtained radar ranges at 19,000 yards. Eased in carefully and found the tanker burning briskly with deep oil fires in her wells and her bridge structure a skeleton of flames, completely abandoned and all escorts departed. She was back on an even keel, however, with her well decks still about a foot above water. She appeared to be salvageable.

We came in parallel and to windward at 300 yards to check identification. Swung away and stopped at 600 yards.

Attack No. 4 The movie camera and two after tubes were made ready. At 1921 fired one torpedo at her after well and started the camera. One of the great shots of the war was lost to posterity when the torpedo hit, practically put out the fires, and sank her in an almost complete darkness.

This target appeared loaded when first seen in the morning. The odor suggested bunker oil and was very strong when she sank. She was the TEIYO MARU, 9850 tons.

Proceeded to assigned station, arriving at 2300. Reported results to ComWolfPack.

Admiral James Fife, who had replaced Christie in Fremantle, gave *Flasher* credit for sinking one *Asashio*-class destroyer (1,700 tons) and one tanker (10,000 tons). After the war, JANAC, with unusual generosity, gave *Flasher* credit for two 2,100-ton destroyers of the *Takanami* or *Kagero* class, namely the *Kishinami* and the *Iwanami*, as well as the 10,022-ton tanker *Hakko Maru*, for a total of 14,222 tons. This was not a bad total for Grider's first patrol as a commanding officer. In fact, it was an excellent score for any war patrol, and this patrol was just beginning.

The *Kishinami* was launched in August, 1943, and was completed only a year and a day before she was sunk by *Flasher* in 2,300 fathoms of water 270 miles west-southwest of Manila. (In the famous attacks by the submarines *Darter* and *Dace* less than six weeks earlier, the Japanese heavy cruisers *Atago* and *Maya* were sunk, and the heavy cruiser *Takao* was severely

Imperial Japanese Destroyer *Kishinami* (by Author)

damaged. It was this same destroyer *Kishinami*, already a veteran of the Battle of the Marianas, that rescued Admiral Kurita from the water following *Atago's* sinking, and continued on to participate in the engagement off Samar Island in the Battle for Leyte Gulf.)

Naval Intelligence Captain W. Jasper Holmes called the *Kishinami* one of Japan's best destroyers. She had been one of three attacking destroyers that sank the submarine *USS Trout* on February 29, 1944.[20] The other two Japanese destroyers, *Okinami* and *Asashimo*, were in turn sunk by Navy carrier aircraft on November 13, 1944, and April 7, 1945 (along with the battleship *Yamato*), respectively.

Just as *Kishinami* had rescued survivors following *Atago's* sinking, the Japanese minelayer/escort *Yurijima* rescued survivors after *Flasher's* attacks, according to Alden's research of Ultra intercepts. And just as *Kishinami* was sunk within six weeks of her res-

---

[20] *Undersea Victory II*, New York: Kensington Publishing Co., 1979, p. 44.

cue actions, *Yurijima* would be sunk within six weeks by the *USS Cobia* (SS 245), now preserved as a memorial/museum in Manitowoc, Wisconsin.

Iwanami, the second destroyer identified by JANAC, is not listed in *Warships of the Imperial Japanese Navy, 1869-1945*,[21] and Alden has questioned its attribution as possibly a duplication of *Kishinami*. *Iwanami* is not listed in *Warships*, but the book may not be exhaustive. The authors do refer to "phantom" ships created by problems in transcribing Japanese characters. The names "Kishinami" and "Iwanami" are also similarly drawn in the Japanese pictorial characters that serve as words, and it now seems likely only one destroyer (*Kishinami*) was sunk. It is unfortunate that the Japanese destroyed their records and that those considered by JANAC were returned. *Flasher's* crew believed they sank three vessels.

The submarine approached close to the abandoned tanker for the last torpedo attack of December 4, and in his war patrol narrative Grider stated, "She was the TEIYO MARU." That might give the impression he read her name prior to the sinking. As such vessels normally did not display their names during the war, and as *Flasher* had only closed to 300 yards at night, Grider was referring only to her vessel class. The real *Teiyo Maru* had been sunk August 18, 1944, by *USS Rasher* about 300 miles to the north of *Flasher's* sinking of a similar vessel, the *Hakko Maru*.

The *Hakko Maru* had an even shorter life than the *Kishinami*, since the tanker was built earlier in 1944,

---

[21] Hansgeorg Jentschura, Dieter Jung and Peter Mickel, Annapolis: Naval Institute Press, 1986.

and had not lasted out the year. She was of the 1TL tanker pattern developed by the Japanese during the war. Like *Kishinami*, *Hakko Maru* had sortied with the Japanese forces to contest the Leyte landings in October, as part of the First Diversionary Attack Force.

In his war patrol comments, Grider criticized the Japanese counterattacks:

> The anti-submarine measures during the attacks of December 4, 1944 were very heavy. The tactics of the escort vessels were to run down the torpedo track, drop a pattern of charges and then to commence searching with echo-ranging equipment. This type of searching was ineffective, since they never did appear to have sound contact. On both attacks there was a negative temperature gradient at 250 feet.
>
> Normal evasive tactics were to go deep, keep the stern toward the escort, and make 70 RPM.

Seventy shaft rotations per minute must have been a relatively silent running speed, as disclosed by *Flasher's* sound tests at Fremantle.

By the fifth patrol, *Flasher* had a brief on-board newspaper called *War Shot News*, initiated by Torpedoman Bill Newton. After the December 4 attacks, the paper included a satirical poem about the attack, possibly written by Grider, in what may best be described as "Pig German." The work needs to be read aloud to understand it. Although no translation was

included in the newspaper, one is provided here for
those needing some help. The paper gave the following
preamble:

Patience is a virtue, stick with this poem, we know you
will enjoy it.

> Truder middle hufder hoshun
> Wendt der Flasher hupan down
> Lukking halvays forder Jeppos
> Hupan down han rounan roun.
>
> Hall hat vance der Yoman hullers
> Vat his did hi lukansee
> Hon der horison han hubject
> Kummink kwik han rite hatme
>
> Mander essdee mander essjay
> Truder perrizkope hizee
> Mests hanzhips all kummink queekly
> Zturter hup der teedeecee
>
> Kullder kepten telim huffit
> Hulso telder hohodee
> Bettle stayshuns izzit giffing
> Pessit honder wanemcee
>
> Tekker downder keptens sayink
> Runner hupder perrizkope
> Kummink disway hisder kunvoy
> Horhat lees daswutihope

Markder berrin markder deestence
Markit hulso hinder buk
Hangle honder bowhis tirty
Podden wilhi takhalook

Kudhit beehay gep deestroyer
Sohitis handat hainthall
Honder quadder hisha tenker
Kummink kwik tewtak derfall.

Geddem reddy hallder peekels
Mechder hangles four hand haft
Firem deesway firem datway
Firem tilder haintnun laft

Bangdey goesen tewder tenken
Bangdey goesen tenker tew
Hupder perrizkope highs lookink
Ferto seejes wutwe dew

Hinder tenken hizza beeghol
Hand his harse his mytelow
Duntluknow bud komsder heskort
Hengle honder bow zeerow

Fludder naga tivwif wudder
Tekker downhun tishes deep
Wutkums nex his hulmos zerten
Tew wekkew hup hif yewzasleep

Bengshe gosder depchurg klosly
Bengshe goshan densommor
Sezder quoddermester meekly
Derdey gohoos keepenskor

Sezder kepten tewder hexo
Hinvestigate kundishuns pleez
Whershe kumfrum hallder prassure
Wut kawses hall der stinkin breez

Hulso gifts hit dempness tewmoch
Lemme no juswatyewtink
Startin vestigation queekly
Mosly forder mighty stink

Sezder hexo tewder kepten
Higotder hanser ridaway
Der dempness kumsin essjay pekken
Wutder depchurg nokaway

Prassure kumsfrum hall der hairleeks
Frumder hair hinside der flesk
Bout der steenk huf wich yer hesking
Homi kepten plis dunt hesk.

(Translation)

Through the middle of the ocean
Went the Flasher up and down
Looking always for the Jappos
Up and down and round and round.

All at once the Yeoman hollers
What is this he look and see?
On the horizon an object
Coming quick and right at me!

"Man the S.D. man the S.J.!"
Through the periscope he see
Masts and ships all coming quickly
"Starter up the T.D.C.!"

"Call the captain! Tell him hoof it!"
"Also tell the OOD"
Battle stations is it giving
"Pass it on the 1 M.C."

"Take her down!" the captain's saying
"Runner up the periscope"
Coming this way is the convoy
Or at least that's what I hope.

"Mark the bearing - Mark the distance"
"Mark it also in the book"
"Angle on the bow is thirty"
"Pardon while I take a look."

Could it be a Jap destroyer?
So it is and that ain't all
On the quarter is a tanker
Coming quick to take the fall.

"Get ready all the pickles!"
"Make the angles four and a half"
"Fire them this way! Fire them that way"
"Fire them till there ain't none left!"

Bang! they goes into the tin can!
Bang! they goes in tanker too!
Up the periscope I'se looking
For to see just what we do.

In the tin can is a big hole
And his arse is mighty low,
Don't look now but comes the escort
Angle on the bow zero!

"Flood her negative with water!"
"Take her down until she's deep!"
What comes next is almost certain
To wake you up if you'se asleep

Bang! she goes the depth charge closely
Bang! she goes and then some more
Says the quartermaster meekly
"There they go! Who's keeping score?"

Says the captain to the X.O.
"Investigate conditions please"
"Where she come from, all the pressure?"
"What causes all the stinking breeze?"

"Also gives it dampness too much"
"Let me know just what you think"
"Start investigation quickly"
"Mostly for the mighty stink"

Says the X.O. to the captain
He got the answer right away
"The dampness comes in SJ packing"
"What the depth charge knock away."

"Pressure comes from all the air leaks"
"From the air inside the flask"
"About the stink of which you're asking"
"Of me captain, please don't ask."

The ruptured flask was probably one of the compressed-oxygen tanks stored inside the pressure hull, and the stench came from sewage relased into the sub by a leak or popped valve in the sanitary tank. This damage was typical of depth-charge attacks. Motor Machinist DeBois remembered that one of the inboard exhaust valves in the forward engine room would spin open from close blasts, so fast that they couldn't see the 20-inch valve wheel spinning. The valve had to be manually spun shut after each concussion.

The sanitary tank was often blown clean of sewage to avoid accidental venting inside during an attack, but if enemy ships were in the vicinity, it was too late to empty the tank, as the discharge could alert the Japanese to *Flasher's* location. The crew had learned the hard way to empty the tanks frequently, because the boat's posted orders failed to include such a procedure.

That evening *Flasher* arrived back at her assigned station, where she patrolled uneventfully the next few days, except for repeated plane contacts. A misunderstood order from *Hawkbill* sent *Flasher* on an eight-hour cruise northward before instructions were rectified. Grider noted "an error in one character of the Wolf-Pack Code can cause serious misunderstandings." On December 8 *Hawkbill* ordered the scouting line moved eastward to 118° longitude, closer to the Philippine coast. *Flasher* closed on a vessel late the afternoon of December 9, but it displayed hospital markings. *Flasher* returned to her station while *Hawkbill* followed the hospital ship.

The scouting line for the wolf pack moved back to 117° longitude during the night of December 10, after sighting nothing but plane contacts and the hospi-

DO YOU *REALLY* NEED TO GO?

Here are the instructions:

"Before using a water closet, first inspect the installation. All valves should have been left shut. Operate the bowl flapper valve to ascertain that the expulsion chamber is empty.

"Shut the bowl flapper valve, flood the bowl with sea water through the sea and stop valves, and then shut both valves. After using the toilet, operate the flapper valve to empty the contents of the bowl into the expulsion chamber, then shut the flapper valve. Charge the volume tank until the pressure is 10 pounds higher than the sea pressure. Open the gate and plug valves on the discharge line and operate the rocker valve to discharge the contents of the expulsion chamber overboard. Shut the discharge line valves and leave the bowl flapper valve seated. For pump expulsion, proceed as previously stated except that the contents of the waste receiver are to be pumped out after the gate and plug valves on the discharge line have been opened.

"If, upon first inspection, the expulsion chamber is found flooded, discharge the contents over board before using the toilet. Improper operation of toilet valves should be corrected and leaky valves overhauled at the first opportunity."

Of course, if you're using one of the two <u>gravity flush</u> type heads aboard, there are different instructions...

Source: Navpers 16160, The Fleet Type Submarine

tal ship. At noon on December 13, *Hawkbill* again ordered the line shifted closer to Luzon, this time at flank speed. The wolf pack received radio orders from Fremantle the evening of December 13 "to patrol off Manila Bay north of Lubang Island to watch for combatant ships coming out." The Allies were planning to leapfrog from Leyte to invade Mindoro Island December 15, and then continue by launching the major invasion of Luzon in early January, 1945. The wolf pack's location was controlled by these unfolding events.

The war had progressed by December of 1944 to a point where Allied aircraft were becoming a fixture in the skies over the Japanese-held Philippines. The wolf pack had been moved to intercept departing ships, and possibly to serve lifeguard duty for downed aviators, as a massive air strike was begun by Allied aircraft against the Japanese base at Subic Bay near Manila. Grider noted the attacks from his front-row seat on December 14:

> Watched our planes make two strikes on Subic Bay. Lots of planes and flak over the islands; no one paying much attention to us. Could hear conversation of VHF: "Transport in Subic Bay, lets get him," etc. Plane Contact No. 25 At 1001, when at a point bearing 240 (T) 18 miles from Corregidor, we were chased under by a plane that came in from seaward. We were on station, so remained submerged and patrolled east and west in the bight of the 100 fathom curve.

That evening, *Flasher* surfaced and headed north to a point ten miles north of Cabra Island, and immediately enemy aircraft began to drive her down. The SD radar mast would be raised above water long enough for new contacts to develop and *Flasher* would go down again. Grider: "Decided to give them an hour to go away." *Flasher* surfaced just before midnight, but was forced to dive 40 minutes later as the enemy planes reappeared:

> At 0025, they came back and we went down when they closed to 3 miles. Their radar is 180 mgcs. Decided to give them another hour and to quit using the SD. The night is very dark.
>
> Surfaced at 0130. We have been getting interference on the SJ from Cabra Island and strong indications on the APR at 530 mgcs. Thought Cabra might be the stool pigeon and decided to open out to 20 miles. Made a couple of distant SJ contacts on planes while doing so.
>
> <u>Ship Contact No. 5</u> At 0320 while congratulating ourselves on having eluded the planes, made SJ contact on patrol boat standing out of Manila Bay, bearing 270, range 14,000 yards. Put our stern to him. He closed to 9500 yards and we progressively increased speed before he began to open range with us at flank speed. Single small pip. Decided not to investigate. He appeared to have a 150 mgcs radar.

We were working around him to the north when we received orders to take station on scouting line fifty miles west of Cape Bolinao. We cheerfully set course for that position. This night was worse than the training period.

The patrol boat gave no indication of having contacted us. The planes evidently could locate us with their radar, given time, and could come in like a homing pigeon on our SD. Effective reconnaissance of this area by a single submarine would be very difficult while the enemy was using night search planes on a large scale.

Continuing north past Manila Bay, *Flasher* encountered another five enemy planes, none of which sighted or attacked the submarine despite daylight and their closing to within a few miles. While patrolling on a new scouting line, *Flasher* offered to join *Hawkbill* and *Becuna* as they chased a convoy, but *Hawkbill* replied "Negative." *Hawkbill* succeeded in sinking the 1,262-ton destroyer *Momo* the same day (December 15).

On the 16th, *Flasher* tracked an enemy hospital ship, was chased under by six enemy fighters, and received orders to head west to patrol off Camranh Bay, French Indochina, with *Becuna* and *Hoe*. Headed to her new station, *Flasher* spotted and was chased by *Hawkbill*, until she radioed her identity and "greetings" to *Hawkbill*. *Becuna* and *Flasher* met after dawn the next day, so *Becuna's* captain (*Flasher's* new wolf-pack commander) could pass over *Flasher's* new operation orders. *Hawkbill* was left to patrol alone off Luzon.

On December 19, in increasingly rough seas, the new wolf pack of *Becuna*, *Hoe* and *Flasher* was joined by *Dace* and *Paddle* (SS 263). The deteriorating weather was due to a severe typhoon that had already sunk several Navy surface ships in the Pacific. Two of the submarines patrolled close in to Camranh Bay while the other three were stationed farther out to sea. One northbound convoy leaving the bay got by *Dace* and then *Flasher*. The two subs were unable to pursue given the four-knot southbound current and heavy seas. During the night *Flasher* took over *Dace's* northern, inshore position after *Dace* was damaged by the rough weather and a grounding close inshore. On the evening of December 20, *Flasher* obtained permission to move farther north to patrol off Hon Doi Island near Van Fong Bay, and just south of Cape Varella, arriving there at dawn the next morning.

Wishing to remain undetected, *Flasher* began a submerged patrol off Hon Doi. The boat stayed at 100 feet, rising to periscope depth only for short observations. Lt. Burke had just relieved Lt. Coffin on the morning conning tower watch, and ordered the boat up for his first periscope sweep. Sighting the mast of a patrol craft, Burke immediately retracted the scope, ordered higher speed to head out to sea, and sent word for the captain. Grider ordered the boat to slow to three knots, and made his own periscope observation:

> <u>Ship Contact No. 7</u> At 0905 sighted patrol boat bearing 177(T) coming up the coast. Maneuvered to seaward of him and he passed 3000 yards astern. At 0932 heard

more screws to the south; headed for them. At 0945 sighted a torpedo boat bearing 257. At 0955 sighted several large tankers on landward side of the CHIDORI. The visibility was very poor due to high seas and spray.

At 1008 sighted a destroyer on starboard beam of last ship. He passed about 2000 yards ahead. Did not fire because of doubtful depth performance of torpedoes in heavy sea and because of poor solution. Convoy passed and proceeded up the coast.

At 1031 headed east to open out from the beach.

Surfaced at 1204; sent contact report to pack; headed north in pursuit at three-engine speed. Heavy seas prohibited faster speed. We were making about 12 1/2 knots through the water and fighting a three-knot current. Estimated convoy speed at 8 1/2 knots through the water.

FLASHER stayed about twenty miles offshore until dark, then closed to seven miles. Received permission from BECUNA to chase; no other ships in pursuit. Expected to regain contact at about 2200.

At 2043 tracked four side lobes from the beach for a few minutes.

Grider noted "after 2200 our spirits began to

droop." As midnight passed, and it became December 22, the only good news was that the weather began to improve, and the seas abated. With midnight the watch changed, bringing Radioman Filippone and Signalman Corneau on duty. Signalman Doty, as he was relieved, told the two that something wasn't quite right with the land contacts, and to watch them closely. Sure enough, after a while one of the contacts seemed to have moved. Filippone and Corneau alerted the OOD, and suggested Glennon be summoned:

>   We had decided to reverse course at 0100. At that time the navigator noticed that Tortue Island was underway. This turned out to be our convoy. It developed into five large tankers, three smaller escorts and a destroyer. Speed eleven knots, not zig zagging.
>
>   Commenced tracking and working ahead on their starboard, seaward side. It took us until 0400 to get ahead of the convoy. All the time we were working ahead, the destroyer remained exactly between us and the nearest ship. Occasionally he would turn on his radar and create very heavy interference on our SJ. Disquieting.
>
>   The other three escorts were distributed along the seaward side of the convoy. The formation was very tight with less than 500 yards between tankers. They were not zigging, but appeared to shift from column to line of bearing from

time to time. Attack from the seaward side appeared impracticable.

Decided to try and attack from the land side. Convoy was twelve miles off the beach and about fifteen miles south of the pass between Cape Batangan and Kulao Rai Island. FLASHER was 10,000 yards, 30° on the port bow of the leading ship; ships in column. As we moved into this position, the destroyer stayed between us and convoy until he was dead ahead of leading ship. He then began to drop aft on the starboard side of convoy. A-h-h-h-h!

Possibly the destroyer's radar had difficulty detecting *Flasher* with the backdrop of land, but attacking from the land side of the convoy was extremely dangerous. Glennon states: "This required us to make our attack in water 100 feet in depth. By doing so, we lost the ability of evading an escort by the usual means of submerging and going deep." It also meant *Flasher* was trapped between the coast and the escorts. She was sacrificing her normal three-dimensional operating area for a narrow two-dimensional strip of shallow water. The patrol report continues:

There was one escort on port bow of leading ship; all others were on the starboard flank of the convoy; convoy in column. As we started in, a light appeared on the beach abeam and another on Cape Batangan. These apparently were navigational lights turned on by request. The horizon was hazy in the direction of the convoy. There was a black cloud behind FLASHER, but it was moving away fast.

Started in at 0415. Sighted targets at a range of 6000 yards. At 0446 began firing three bow tubes at leading tanker; torpedo run 2500 yards, track 115 port. Shifted to second tanker and fired three at him. Then swung right to bring stern tubes to bear on third tanker. While swinging observed two hits in each of first two tankers. A small fire started on the first one.

After firing all six bow tubes at the first two tankers, *Flasher* was rapidly swinging to bring the stern tubes to shoot at the last one, but the swing and setting the spindles in the rear torpedoes was taking too long. Also, it was time to clear the area. There were three antisubmarine escorts and one destroyer guarding the convoy, and the stern tubes might save *Flasher* in a getaway. Grider ordered "Check Fire!" from the bridge.

In the conning tower below, McCants was operating the TDC with Burke assisting on the spreads. Just after Grider's order to cease fire, excellent computer-generated solutions came up. Burke called over to Glennon: "Gyros matching aft Phil! Jesus Christ, let's shoot!" Burke also knew these were just about *Flasher's* last torpedoes and it was "all ahead Australia" once they were launched. Despite Grider's order, Glennon figured he had checked fire long enough, and without

Flasher's Torpedo Tubes (Courtesy Mobile Press — Register,
Copy Furnished By Eddie Atkinson)

hesitation, ordered the four stern torpedoes launched.
It should be remembered that, under both Whitaker
and Grider, the Exec. in a surface attack was the Attack
Officer–the skipper on the bridge being "Safety Officer." Nevertheless, there could be real problems with
ignoring Grider's orders if the torpedoes missed. The
patrol report does not reflect the fire-control team's in-
dependent initiative:

> Just prior to firing the stern tubes, the second tanker blew up and illuminated the area like a night football game.
>
> At 0448 fired four stern shots at the third tanker. Torpedo run 1900, track angle about 110 starboard. He exploded immediately when hit and made the visibility even better. The flames from the second and third targets flowed together and made a really impressive fire.

Grider never mentioned a word about the unauthorized stern-tube launches.

> Swung to course 180 and went ahead flank plus. This put the convoy abeam but we didn't want to get any nearer the shallow water. Took a fathometer reading; fifty six fathoms.
>
> When we fired, the destroyer had dropped back to the starboard quarter of the last ship. When we headed south, we sighted him two points forward of our port beam at a range of 4000 yards. He made one circle to the left and fell into position on FLASHER'S port beam; course 180, speed 19, range 3200 yards, FLASHER guide. Sent the lookouts below. We could see him in full detail with the unaided eye.

Unofficial word of the shadowing destroyer reached the maneuvering room, causing strained diesels and electric motors long before Grider officially called for increased speed. *Flasher* sped along as fast as her equipment could manage without melting the bearings.

This weird formation cruised south for about two miles before the destroyer slowed down and dropped aft. Apparently he never saw us. We breathed a prayer of thanks to the camouflage artists and slowed to flank speed.

Shortly after the destroyer dropped back, the first target blew up and added his light to the flames. The entire sea aft was covered with billowing red fire which burned for about forty minutes. All hands came up, two at a time, and had a look. It was something to see. When we passed to leeward of the mess, there was a strong odor of naphtha. The explosions suggested gasoline, but the fire gave off great clouds of heavy black smoke that resembled oil.

All three tankers disintegrated with the explosions; were swallowed in the flames and not seen again.

The destroyer went back to the formation for a moment, then proceeded southward along the coast in the direction from which he had come. No depth charges were dropped; no guns were fired. Apparently they believed they had struck a minefield.

FLASHER opened out to the south-east, sent a message to CTF 71 reporting results, then dived for a rest at 0630.

Surfaced at 1631 and headed for the barn.

Ensign Eddie Atkinson said later that there was a light fog or mist that morning, and this, coupled with *Flasher's* haze-gray camouflage paint, made the submarine virtually invisible to the destroyer, although the destroyer stood out distinctly to the men on *Flasher's* bridge. The sub was also against the land whereas the destroyer was silhouetted against the eastern horizon. Atkinson stated: "Even with binoculars I don't think the destroyer would have seen us."

Grider noted that the convoy of December 22 had produced SJ radar interference:

Interference from other than friendly forces was noted on the SJ radar screen. This occurred during a four-hour approach on an escorted convoy on the morning of 22 December, 1944 in position Latitude 14° 04' N, Longitude 109° 06' E. The interference was encountered four times during the four-hour approach for periods of about 2 minutes on each occasion. At these times the enemy convoy was 10,000 yards distant.

The enemy radar did not appear to be sweeping and on the occasions when interference was encountered, it

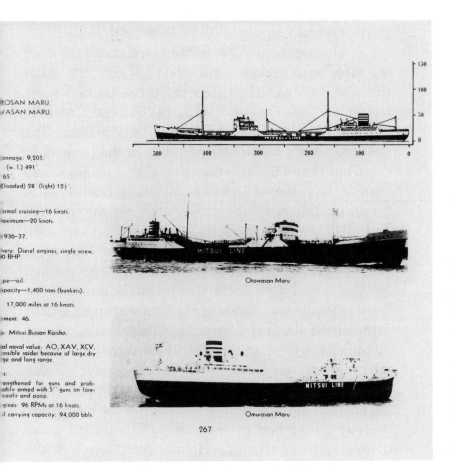

ROSAN MARU.
VASAN MARU.

onnage: 9,205.
 (w. l.) 491'
65'.
(loaded) 28' (light) 12½'.

ormal cruising—16 knots.
aximum—20 knots.

1936-37.

hery: Diesel engines, single screw,
0 BHP.

pe—oil.
pacity—1,400 tons (bunkers).

17,000 miles at 16 knots.

ment: 46.

: Mitsui Bussan Kaisho.

al naval value: AO, XAV, XCV.
ossible raider because of large dry
ge and long range.

s:
engthened for guns and probably armed with 5'' guns on fore-
castle and poop.
gines: 96 RPMs at 16 knots.
il carrying capacity: 94,000 bbls.

Otowasan Maru

Omurosan Maru

267

Omurosan Maru and *Otowasan Maru* (ONI 208-J)

seemed to be trained on us. The enemy
gave no indication of actually having
contact with us.

Whereas the destroyer had seemed to sense
Flasher's presence, it was never able to make positive
identification. It was a good thing for American subma-

rines that the war ended before the Japanese fully developed and equipped their ships with radar.

During the war *Flasher* received credit for sinking three large tankers for a total of 30,000 tons. After the war, JANAC identified the three tankers sunk December 22 as *Omurosan Maru* (9,204 tons), *Otowasan Maru* (9,204 tons), and *Arita Maru* (10,238 tons). The *Omurosan Maru* was a fuel oil tanker of the *Hoyo Maru* class, built in 1937. Her sister ship *Otowasan Maru* was similar, capable of 16 knots, and believed by U.S. Naval Intelligence to be armed with 5-inch guns fore and aft. These two modern, high-speed tankers each carried 94,000 gallons of oil for the Empire.[22] Japanese convoy "HI-82" (identified in Ultra intercepts studied by Alden) had been decimated by one submarine.

Despite the success of *Flasher's* war shots, Grider complained about two torpedoes that flooded due to missing gaskets when checked. These were repaired by the crew and appeared to run satisfactorily. He also complained that loosening gyro clamps slipped about the shaft of the side setting wheel on three torpedoes, thereby giving bad gyro settings. This would mean definite misses or possible circular runs. *Tang* (SS 306) and *Tullibee* (SS 284) were lost to circular torpedo runs, and other submarines had near misses. The three torpedoes with their repaired gyro clamps were later fired successfully, the first at the tanker on December 4, but hitting the destroyer, the second hitting the last tanker sunk December 22, and the third being a miss at the last tanker. Grider stated this clamp problem could easily be solved by "keying" the clamp to the shaft, but

---

[22] ONI 208-J, August 24, 1942, p. 267.

in the meantime he recommended all personnel be cautioned to carefully check the faulty gyro-setting mechanisms.

Now that *Flasher* was down to her last torpedo, targets became plentiful:

23 December
Ship Contact No. 8 At 0325, when 48 miles bearing 135° from Camranh Bay, made SJ contact on a northbound convoy of three ships and two escorts. Sent contact report at 0400 to BECUNA, DACE, HOE, and PADDLE on Wolf Pack frequency. Tracked them until 0500; course 355, speed 13. Could not see them at 6000 yards. Sent another contact report at 0500, then broke off and resumed course to southward.

At 2100, exchanged calls with U.S.S. GURNARD, northbound.

On December 24 OOD Eddie Atkinson made the following deck log entry:

0901 Sighted floating mine, commenced steering various courses at various speeds while shooting at mine with 20mm and 45 cal submachine gun. 0948 Ceased firing at mine, four hits but mine still afloat, having fired 240 rounds 20mm and 40 rounds of 45 cal., commenced constant helm zig on base course 211° pgc at 14.5 knots.

On Christmas Day, 1944, *Flasher* passed down the west coast of Borneo and through the shallow Karimata Strait, where she met another sub headed for Fremantle:

> Crossed equator at 0930. Picked up BARBERO'S SJ interference at 1930, she was overtaking us very slowly. Exchanged calls at 2145; she passed abeam about midnight.

(*Barbero* hastened by, but a run-in with an unidentified plane two days later would delay her trip. While proceeding through Lombok Strait on December 27 at periscope depth, she received a bomb close aboard her port shaft, shaking her severely and putting her port reduction gear (and her port shaft) out of commission. She limped home to Fremantle. Because of the damage *Barbero* returned stateside for extensive repairs, before ultimately returning to the Pacific to start a new patrol under a new skipper, *Flasher's* own Ray DuBois.)

Crossing the equator in enemy waters, *Flasher's* officers and crew celebrated Christmas Day with appropriate presents. Grider received a baseball cap with a greatly exaggerated bill, a reference to his prior service on the submarine *HawkBILL* and his preference for baseball caps over more formal Navy head gear. Glennon, a cigar smoker, received a huge, simulated cigar. Burke received enormous shoes crafted out of barrel staves, partly from the notoriety of his large shoe size as memorialized in the poem about "Four Fathoms Burke." Grider ORDERED Burke to wear them to the bridge when he assumed his OOD station that afternoon, despite Burke's protest of the danger they presented in an emergency. And a prematurely balding, 25-year-old McCants received a wig, made from stuffing out of an old seat glued to cardboard. Signalman Doty and Chief Torpedoman Newton received corsets made from canvas sea bags to wrap their respective stomachs. Motor Machinist Beaman, who had let his hair grow long (by Navy standards), was presented with a dress made from rags.

Copies of a Christmas Day edition of *Flasher's* typewritten newspaper *War Shot News* were circulated. For its first page, Grider had detailed the tanker attacks of the previous Thursday, and praised his crew's performance:

> Nothing I can say can express the excellence of the Flasher team half as well as the record itself. Six ships sunk for a total of forty three thousand tons. Two DD's and four tankers. We are now headed for Fremantle. Remember that the patrol isn't successful unless we get ourselves home. Don't let down your vigilance. The area is patrolled by Jap submarines and planes. We can relax when the order is received to "Double up and secure," and not before.
>
> Signed: G.W. Grider

Grider had a healthy respect for enemy submarines. He had been manning *Wahoo's* periscope a year earlier when he spotted the unsuspecting Japanese sub *I-2* on the surface. After *Wahoo* attacked and those aboard thought the enemy sub sank, Grider was never at ease in a surfaced submarine.

The remainder of the trip south did require vigilance, as it involved mines, subs, planes and patrol boats:

26 December

Exploded a drifting mine at 1418. Sank another at 1450.

Just after sinking second mine, at 1453 sighted through the periscope what appeared to be a submarine bearing 072 (T); submerged to avoid being sighted. Tried until 1556 to close range, but never saw more than a single tall stack with no masts. May have been a small trawler or the shears of an American submarine; there was considerable mirage effect on the horizon. Surfaced at 1556.

27 December

Set course to pass west of Kangean Islands, between Goa and Kangean Island. Sighted about twenty sailboats during day.

At 0537 exchanged recognition signals with U.S.S. BLUEGILL, northbound.

At 0830, gave carton of Chesterfields and loaf of bread to the first sailboat that passed close aboard. Crew of friendly natives.

At 1142, just after passing between

Goa and Karang Takat Reef made SD
contact on plane at nine miles, closing.
Dived.

    Surfaced at 1229.

<u>Plane Contact No. 43</u> At 1615 sighted a
RUFE at a range of about 15 miles coming from direction of Soerabaja en route
Lombok Strait. Submerged to periscope
depth and watched him pass. He made
several dips and circles in vicinity of the
northwest point of Bali and finally disappeared over the Strait at 1655. He was
painted black: a float plane.

    Surfaced at 1659. At 1729 sighted
him returning. Submerged and watched
him pass by headed for Soerabaja. We
were then thirty miles from the entrance
to Lombok Strait. Decided to remain submerged until sunset.

The Rufe avoided by *Flasher* may have been on
the very bombing run that almost sank *Barbero*. *Barbero*
was already miles ahead of *Flasher* in Lombok Strait.
Grider waited for darkness before he would attempt
transit of the dangerous strait.

    Surfaced at 1835 and set course for
the Strait.

<u>Ship Contact No. 9</u> At 1909 while some
twilight remained and with a full moon,
sighted a patrol boat against the back-

ground of Bali, bearing 203° (T), range 6 miles, angle on the bow zero. Picked him up on SJ at same time.

Went to flank speed and put him broad on the starboard quarter. Estimated his top speed to be about fifteen knots. He was about the size of a PC boat. Intended to work to the south of him and continue through the Strait. He cooperated by always giving us a zero angle on the bow. Had he attempted to head us off he could have succeeded.

By 1930, when the range had closed to 4860 yards he opened fire with two automatic guns of about 20mm caliber. His speed was 17 1/2 knots. Sent lookouts and OOD below. At this time we were on course 130 (T) and headed for Lombok Island.

Grider told Burke to go below with the lookouts, leaving Grider alone on the bridge. Burke resisted and Grider made it an order. Grider then sent word below for the steward to bring him his baseball cap and chewing gum. Corneau received the items and climbed with them to the bridge, requesting permission to stay up as a lookout. Permission was denied—Grider was going it alone.

Flasher's crew had prepared two gadgets to fool enemy gunboats in such chases. One was a helium balloon that trailed foil to fool radar, but the small gunboats probably lacked radar. The second device was a can full of oily rags and a fuse to decoy the attacker, but it was not used either on this occasion, as Grider figured igniting the fuse would just give the enemy gunners a better target.

He continued to shoot at us during the remainder of the chase. His shells landed astern, ahead, and on both sides, but never hit us. The shells did not seem large enough to cause serious materiel damage.

From time to time he would turn on his searchlight and send a short signal in the direction of Bali. It appeared to be "6T."

We continued to make small course changes to the right. Finally, by 1950, we were on 190 (T) headed for the middle of the Strait with the escort almost astern and the range opening. Minimum range was 4500 yards.

By 2020 the range was 7050 yards, most of his shots were falling astern and the situation was improving.

Ship Contact No. 10 At that time, sighted another patrol boat sharp on our starboard bow at a range of about five miles. Submerged.

When the boat submerged and shifted to battery power, the fresh-air ventilation system was shut off and the water pumped to cool the diesel engines was stopped. The enormous diesel engines, hot from the flank-speed, four-engine surface run, caused the heat in the engine rooms to skyrocket. *Flasher's* throttlemen collapsed at their stations and had to be carried from the engine rooms.

Went to 300 feet, got off our track to the westward, rigged for depth charge attack, and waited. We were almost in the center of the northern entrance to the Strait. There was a sharp negative gradient beginning at 250 feet.

We could hear shells hitting the water for about five minutes after the dive. He then slowed and commenced echo-ranging. We ran 1½ miles to the west and then resumed our course through the Strait. The other patrol boat was pinging to the south.

They never contacted us and did not drop depth charges. Apparently they thought we would try to escape to the northward. By 2100 both searchers were north of us. Came to periscope depth at 2150 and could barely see one patrol boat moving away slowly to the north.

Navigational fixes show a 1/2 knot current against us. We had about 25 miles to go to clear the Strait.

At 2320 surfaced with the patrol boats out of sight though still pinging. Proceeded through the Strait without further incident. We gave this southwest cape of Lombok a wide berth, passing 4

miles east of Nusa Besar and seven miles from Lombok.

28 December

We were clear of Lombok Strait at 0055 and very glad to feel the Indian Ocean swells under the keel. At 0430 sent our Serial Six to CTF 71 describing speed and gun range of patrol boats, current, and the method we used in clearing the SW cape.

Transit of Lombok Strait can be made very difficult by two patrol boats during bright moonlight. We were sighted against a clear background before we either sighted or radar-contacted the patrol boat, which was against a land background.

Flasher continued south from Lombok, under the navigation of Lt. Coffin. After the three tanker sinkings of December 22, navigational duties for *Flasher's* voyage home were transferred from Glennon to Coffin. Grider had navigated before becoming an executive officer, and decided to employ this training practice on *Flasher*. This gave Glennon a break and Coffin some valuable experience. Coffin was a "Mustang," serving as an enlisted man before becoming an officer, and he lacked the formal navigation schooling. Nevertheless, he had some prior exposure and was able to navigate successfully based on the charts and publications aboard. In his new duties, however, he encountered three difficulties.

His first problem was that *Flasher* was very short of fuel. Coffin knew only too well about the fuel problem since he still served as the sub's Engineering Officer, in charge of monitoring fuel consumption. This meant there was no room for error in plotting the shortest course to the nearest friendly fuel depot, Exmouth Gulf, also known to the submariners as "Potshot." This added considerable pressure to Coffin's new assignment.

His second difficulty concerned the navigation tables aboard. *Flasher's* American publications covered only the calendar year 1944, plus sun sightings for 1945. While star sight data for 1945 was aboard, it was in a British publication that defied all Coffin's attempts at interpretation. So, after December 31, he relied on sun sightings and dead reckoning to plot *Flasher's* location.

As *Flasher* surged into the swells of the Indian Ocean on her way to "Potshot," Coffin's plight was compounded by the third factor—his shipmates. *Flasher* was cruising south on the surface where there should be no shallows, when suddenly word came down that breakers were sighted dead ahead. As the officer on watch, the alarmed Coffin called for "All Stop!" and raced up to the conning tower.

He found the small conning tower space crammed with men, and Grider describing the breakers while looking through the periscope. Grider asked Glennon to take a look, and Glennon confirmed they sure looked like breakers to him. Coffin had not been able to get a navigational fix through the overcast skies for some time, but he could not imagine how *Flasher* could be anywhere near breakers. Between the skipper and exec trading looks through the periscope, Coffin was unable to get a peek. When he finally got the periscope, he saw the breakers dead ahead. He had no answers for the numerous pointed questions fired at him from Grider, Glennon and the others in the crowded conning tower.

The "breakers," it turned out, were an illusion produced by carefully positioning the periscope controls between high and low power. Coffin had been set up by his shipmates (led by Grider), who had created this navigational predicament.

Otherwise, the trip from Lombok to Exmouth Gulf was uneventful. *Flasher* exchanged calls with *USS Hardhead* and *USS Besugo* the morning of December 30, and reached Exmouth just before midnight to refuel. Under way again on the 1st, *Flasher* passed the submarine rescue vessel *USS Coucal* (ASR 8) around 9 a.m.

On the morning of New Year's Day, 1945, the OOD made the following unusual entry in the deck log:

0-2 Underway for C.T.G. Seventy one point one.
    Another patrol is nearly done.
Our Op Ord, Number 164 dash 44,
    Was issued to even a certain score.
The order is dated 12 November of '44
    But now tis '45, and '44 is no more.
By the gyro, 180 we steer -
    Perth and Fremantle must be near,
For at this speed of 17 point 5
    T'will be there that we will arrive.
Just one more thing that I must note,
    On the auxiliary we carry a float.
              J.E. Atkinson
                Ens., U.S.N.R.

The comment "even a certain score," referring to *Flasher's* Operation Order 164-44, may have included something about revenging the loss of yet another Fremantle boat, the veteran *USS Growler*, sunk on November 8, 1944. A "float" (or "zero float") meant that a hydrometer reading of the batteries showed they were fully charged, and the generator trickled in just enough amperes to keep them fully charged.

If the poetic log entry on New Year's Day was for good luck, it didn't work. That morning brought a complete failure of her No. 3 main engine. The engine's problems began three days earlier with excessive exhaust temperatures (975° Fahrenheit). Grider complained this engine had required new exhaust valves after only 300 engine hours, when the crew was replacing a cracked piston. He requested that "a more careful and thorough overhaul be given this engine during the coming refit."

Flasher made the rest of the trip home without incident. She arrived in Fremantle the morning of January 2, conducted sound tests in Gage Roads, and moored next to *USS Bashaw* (SS 241) outboard the tender *USS Euryale*. Admiral Fife, Christie's replacement and the new Commander, Task Force 71, officially called on what must have been a proud Commander George Grider and crew.

In his war patrol report comments, Grider condemned the continued inadequate air conditioning on *Flasher*, despite compliance with Bureau of Ships operational practices, ComSubPac Orders, and the directions of ComSubRon 4. *Flasher's* crewmen were not hot because of their uniforms. Dress aboard was very casual, with T-shirts and dungarees being the most a sailor

Officers of the Fifth Patrol (L to R, Kneeling: Hamlin, McCants and Harrison; L to R, Standing: Coffin, Glennon, Grider, Burke, and Atkinson) (Author's Collection)

would wear. Often they wore cut-off dungarees and no shirts. Leather sandals were popular, but shoes were required on the slippery deck topside.

Grider also complained that friendly planes needed to keep their ABK's on to identify themselves to submarines. The sub's new equipment was no help if aircraft ignored their own ABK equipment.

Grider commented on the crews' health and habitability:

> The health of the crew was excellent. One case of appendicitis was treated with sulfa and the application of ice packs on the abdomen. The patient responded very well to this treatment and gradually recovered from appendicitis. However, he developed a case of violent headaches shortly afterwards. These, it is believed, were caused by a combination of appendicitis, an old head injury, heavy seas, and depth charges.

And as to food:

> The quality of meats was extremely poor on this patrol and the variety limited. Since it is such an important part of the diet, better meats would be appreciated for the next run. Rest camp meats are noticeably better than those issued to submarines for patrol and it is believed that the reverse should be the case.

Flasher had spent 49 days on patrol, only one of them submerged, burned almost 160,000 gallons of diesel fuel, and travelled over 13,000 miles. She arrived back in Fremantle with only 7,485 gallons of fuel despite 22,800 gallons received at Exmouth, and she had only one torpedo left. The patrol was terminated for a

Ship's Party Following Fifth Patrol (Courtesy of Joseph Ferrell)

lack of torpedoes.

Cmdr. Creed Burlingame, Acting Commander, Submarine Squadron 18, who received an impressive three Navy Crosses and two Silver Stars as the aggressive skipper of the *USS Silversides*, gave *Flasher* a glowing endorsement for a truly exceptional patrol:

> Subject: U.S.S. FLASHER (SS249) - Report of Fifth War Patrol.
>
> 1. The fifth war patrol of the FLASHER was conducted in the SOUTH CHINA SEA, in areas west of LUZON and adjacent to the FRENCH INDO-CHINA Coast. FLASHER participated in

two wolf packs, one with HAWKBILL and BECUNA, the other composed of HOE, BECUNA, DACE and PADDLE.

2. This patrol was of 49 days duration, 34 of which were spent in the assigned areas. It is significant that only one full day was spent submerged. This resulted in excellent area coverage and presented the advantage of FLASHER being in the right place at the right time for the subsequent attacks which took place.

3. Attack No. 1. Acting on a contact report received from HAWKBILL on 4 December, the FLASHER was able to develop the first attack upon a DD which was part of a convoy composed of an AO, a net tender and several smaller escorts. Four torpedoes were fired at the DD from a range of 1650 yards on approximately 90° track angles to obtain two hits in the vicinity of the engine room spaces.

Attack No. 2. Immediately after disposing of the DD the FLASHER then brought the stern tubes to bear and two torpedoes were fired at the AO from 1900 yards on about 65° track angles both of which hit and caused it to catch fire. At this time the escorts took charge and FLASHER was subjected to a very thorough depth charging.

Attack No. 3. Upon regaining

periscope depth FLASHER again took the initiative and closed the convoy to attack what appeared to be another DD and the damaged AO which presented themselves as overlapping. A total of six torpedoes were fired from about 2000 yards on 120° track angles with four of them aimed at the DD and two aimed at the AO. Four hits were netted in the DD while the AO did not appear to be affected. Again FLASHER was given a very thorough working over which she successfully rode out and evaded.

Attack No. 4. Undaunted by counterattacks FLASHER surfaced in the late afternoon and observed the AO to be still burning and in an awash condition. At dark the submarine closed in for the kill and fired one torpedo from 600 yards on 90° track angle to dispose of this menace to navigation which had withstood the attacks previously described.

Attack No. 5. On the morning of 21 December FLASHER contacted a convoy of five AO's escorted by one DD and three patrol craft which she chased and tracked until the early morning of 22 December. Taking advantage of the lackadaisical tactics of the DD escort the FLASHER attacked from the surface the two leading AO's of the column with three torpedoes each from the bow tubes at a range of 2200 yards on 115° track

354 The War Patrols of the USS Flasher

angles. Two hits were obtained on each ship which set them afire and caused them to blow up.

Attack No. 6. This was the second phase of the preceding attack when FLASHER came about rapidly and fired four torpedoes from the stern tubes at the third AO of the column from 1900 yards range on 130° track angles to obtain two hits. After burning for some time it too blew up and disappeared. The engagement was broken off after a short period of evasion with the DD which apparently never sighted the submarine.

4. With the exception of number three main engine the material condition was very good. She will be given a normal refit by U.S.S. EURYALE and Submarine Division 182 relief crew.

5. Cleanliness of the ship upon return from patrol was exceptional. The morale of the crew is very high.

6. The Squadron Commander extends his heartiest congratulations to the Commanding Officer, officers and crew upon the results of this highly effective patrol and for adding to the already illustrious record of the FLASHER. Since there was so much incendiary activity on the part of the enemy, it might be called the "Flaming Action" patrol.

C.C. BURLINGAME,
Acting.

Admiral Fife also issued a glowing report, and awarded the Submarine Combat Insignia for *Flasher's* fifth patrol, her fifth such award. Fife's boss, Admiral Kinkaid, similarly endorsed the patrol as excellent.

On January 3, Commander G.H. Laird, Jr., and his refit crew relieved the officers and crew of *Flasher*. A week later they began the break-in routine for the troublesome, newly overhauled, No. 3 main engine. During her refit, *Flasher's* No. 4 main engine was also overhauled, stiffeners were welded in the safety tank, No. 2 auxiliary tank and No. 3 auxiliary tank, and three modifications were made to update the sub.

The first modification was the installation of lower pressure-proof hatches on the crew's mess hatch, the after engine-room hatch, and the after torpedo-room hatch. Depth charges could lift the upper hatches, causing the sub to flood and sink. *USS Salmon* (SS 182) was subjected to a severe depth charging in late 1944 and was saved only because of the added, lower pressure-proof hatches.

A second modification involved the installation of a dead-reckoning tracer (DRT) in the conning tower for plotting. The third modification was the replacement of *Flasher's* SJ-a solid antenna with the improved slotted version.

After dawn on January 15, *Flasher* maneuvered to the South Wharf marine railway and was "two-blocked" on the railway. While in the dry dock her hull was scraped and repainted. She left January 17 and moored alongside *USS Baya* (SS 318) in *Euryale's* nest containing *Becuna*, *Cavalla*, and *Blenny* (SS 320). The relief crew was discharged as Grider and the ship's force reported back aboard. *Flasher* began exercises and

Grider (L) and Creed Burlingame (Author's Collection)

sound tests that afternoon. A new officer, Ensign Robert A. Harnar, USNR, reported aboard January 18, prior to *Flasher's* departure for more exercises, fire drills, man-overboard drills and sound tests.

During Grider's first patrol on *Flasher*, he had received more than a little ribbing about his baseball cap and heard comments that "Grider's Little Helpers" needed baseball caps too. After the fifth patrol, a large supply of the non-regulation caps mysteriously appeared, and the crew soon sported the baseball caps regularly. The relaxed atmosphere aboard the sub, as usual, was not welcomed ashore.

Flasher was moored alongside the tender with other fleet subs after the refit. In loading supplies prior to exercises and departure, her sailors trailed to and from the tender. A Navy commander aboard the tender stood at the top of the tender's ladder, and he systematically confiscated each cap as the sailors came aboard, adding insult to injury with the comment, "You're out of uniform."

Word quickly came back to the boat that the baseball caps were being "stolen." Commander George W. Grider emerged from the submarine, and started for the tender, looking to his crewmen like a man headed for a showdown. Word of an expected confrontation spread like wildfire through the boat, work above and below decks stopped, and the periscopes were raised and manned for a blow-by-blow report. Comments passed through the boat like "That tender guy isn't even a submariner!" and "The Old Man ought to do like Moon Chapple and knock the guy on his butt!" Grider seemed to walk in slow motion, his hands on his hips, moving from sub to sub on his way to the tender. When he reached the offending tender officer, they exchanged a few words, before disappearing inside.

Before long, Grider emerged and made his way back to *Flasher*, carrying all the confiscated caps for all of the crews lining the decks of the subs and the tender to see. Once back aboard, he handed them to the Chief of the Boat with the comment "Here. The men can wear them and NOBODY will take them away from them."

Flasher left on the morning of January 19 for exercises, firing 11 rounds of the four-inch, high-capacity ammunition. She completed her exercises before noon and began the return to Fremantle. On her way into the harbor, a major fire began in the maneuvering room and the boat lost power. Lt. McCants, who had just come off watch, was in his bunk when he heard "FIRE!" He grabbed a fire extinguisher and ran aft to the maneuvering room. The fire was electrical, and generated intense heat in the cramped maneuvering room. It was repeatedly snuffed out with several extinguishers, only to reignite from the blistering heat as soon as the CO2 spray stopped. This process emitted an enormous amount of smoke, toxic fumes, and carbon dioxide. Twenty-six men on *USS Bass* (SS 164) died from the toxic smoke of burning phenolic insulation in a similar fire in 1942.

Grider decided the only way to stop the fire was to evacuate the compartment, seal it off, and pump all the air out so that the fire would be starved of oxygen. He gave the order. In the noise, smoke and confusion men evacuated the compartment, it was sealed off, and all of the air was pumped out.

Then someone decided to count heads to make sure everyone was evacuated from the blazing maneuvering room. The after engine room called the aft torpedo room on the 1MC intercom system. When the two compartments on either side of the sealed maneuvering room counted heads, they realized that McCants, Torpedoman Ray Snapp and Seaman Charles Gallagher must still be in the burning compartment. Gas masks were donned and the compartment entered to find the missing men inside and unconscious. They were dragged out through the ladders and hatches topside with some difficulty, and laid out on the deck in the warm Australian summer sunshine. McCants regained consciousness to see Grider's smiling face looking down. Grider said: "Oh, you're COMING TO? I was just going to lay a lily on your chest."

The fire lasted only 20 minutes. Ten minutes later *Flasher* was under way again, headed for the base. McCants, Snapp and Gallagher were sent to sick bay on *Euryale*, where they were examined for any adverse effects, pronounced in satisfactory condition, and returned to duty. McCants was sufficiently recovered to take the duty from 4 p.m. until 8 a.m. the next morning. The back of his head was a little tender—one sailor told him his balding head had hit every rung of the steel ladder as he was lifted unconscious, feet-first, to the deck above.

During the week of January 21, *Flasher* conducted a series of exercises with the Australian fleet minesweeper *HMAS Bunbury*, with the *HMAS Pirie*, and with the American submarine rescue vessel *USS Chanticleer*. Training officer for some of these exercises was Capt. Joe Willingham. Like *Flasher's* other training officers, Willingham had compiled impressive war patrols. He served as one of the skippers of *USS Tautog* (SS 199), which sank the highest number of Japanese ships during the war (26) and ranked 11th in enemy tonnage (72,606), and the *USS Bowfin* (SS 287), which sank 16 vessels and ranked 17th in tonnage (67,882).

The fire proved to be one of several very dangerous "operational" mishaps during a jinxed training period. While exercising off Fremantle with the Australian surface ships, Grider needed to time a full-speed dive. *Flasher* flooded her tanks and switched to battery power. As she plunged down, the IC electrical power completely shorted out. The bow planes had been switched by accident to a steep dive, but with the IC power gone the planes' indicator lights were out, so no one knew their position. The electrical motors powering the propellers were not affected, and they continued to drive *Flasher* at a steep down angle.

In the aft torpedo room, Torpedoman Ralph Heilstedt stared at the racing depth gauge while trying to keep his footing. In the engine rooms forward, one of the motor machinists fell from his seat in the aft engine room through the hatchway into the forward engine room. Heilstedt wondered how deep the bow must be if the uplifted stern was already so deep. The thin-hulled *Flasher* would not survive hitting the rocky ocean bottom at this speed and almost double her designed safety depth.

As with *Crevalle's* uncontrolled dive during *Flasher's* fourth patrol, Electrician John "Skinhead" Cook, acting without orders, switched the powerful motors to "all back emergency." After passing 400 feet, *Flasher* headed up to about 150 feet before starting back down toward the bottom, because of the planes' angle and the boat's rearward motion. Again, Cook reversed the props. With the ballast tanks now blown, *Flasher* finally ballooned to the surface only 800 yards from the Australian ship, and came to a stop.

As the shaken officers and lookouts clambered to the bridge, the Australian ship flashed the signal "What are your intentions?" Grider told the signalman to fire back "Go to hell," but the message wasn't sent.

There was still another mishap during training. Gun drills involved surfacing, moving men, guns and ammunition to the deck, mounting the machine guns, and readying the deck gun for firing. As the drill started, those assigned gunnery positions assembled near the deck-access hatches with guns and ammunition, ready to scramble through when the boat burst onto the surface. For battle surface action, Torpedoman Heilstedt was the "Hot Shell Man," wearing asbestos gloves to grab and heave overboard the searing-hot shell casings ejected from the deck gun. One of the men with Heilstedt carried a .50-caliber heavy machine gun, with the barrel's muzzle resting on the deck plating. When the man lifted the machine gun, he pulled the trigger of the supposedly unloaded weapon, causing a tremendous roar and blasting a half-inch bullet hole through the steel deck, with the bullet ricocheting around the forward battery below. Amazingly, the bullet caused no discernable damage other than the entry hole. The bullet's path through the batteries was never found.

The boat was fumigated the evening of January 25 and then ventilated, before all hands were allowed to proceed back to their stations. Maybe the fumigation would get rid of the bad luck.

That night Lt. Coffin, *Flasher's* third officer after Grider and Glennon, and her Diving Officer ever since commissioning, was detached to shore duty. For a man Admiral Nimitz's office had thought was too old to start in submarines, he had served in all five of *Flasher's* patrols, in addition to three Atlantic Ocean patrols on *Shad*. Tom Burke became First Lieutenant as next in seniority, Eddie Atkinson became *Flasher's* Engineering and Diving Officer, and Ensign Robert R. Harnar replaced Atkinson as Commissary Officer, a much-abused position because of continuous heckling about the quality of food supplies.

Bill Pearce, who had succeeded Felix Perkowsky as Chief of the Boat after the third war patrol, also left *Flasher* after the fifth patrol for medical treatment. Pearce had been a quiet, competent chief, serving on all five war patrols. A veteran of *Growler* before that, he survived the war only to die tragically shortly afterwards. Replacing Pearce as Chief of the Boat would be Chief Motor Machinist Spiva Lee Buck, Jr., who had served on all but *Flasher's* third war patrol. Buck would be a more fiery, more controversial COB than his predecessors. He did not hesitate to clash with some of the boat's officers.

The events preceding the sixth patrol were unsettling for many. Seasoned veterans like Heilstedt had always slept through past dives, but now they awoke whenever the diving alarm sounded, no longer comfortable that everything would be all right with the dive. Others in *Flasher's* crew, in need of tonic and facing still another dangerous patrol, decided to extend their stay, at least for one last, unauthorized fling.

Relaxing Sailors (Believed to Be, Standing, L to R: Francum, Wilkinson (or Metcalf), Bartl, and Ezerosky. Sitting, L to R: McLaren, Calloway, Heilstedt, McKay, Markham and McLaughlin. Courtesy of Joseph Ferrell)

The morning of departure for the sixth patrol found an unusual number of the crew who had last-minute excuses for a short trip ashore. After a while it became obvious that the flow of personnel was one way, and nobody was coming back. McCants, who stood only five feet, four inches tall (in shoes) was detailed to lead a foray ashore to bring back the "escapees." He arrived at one of the sailors' haunts, a nearby "gin mill." To encourage the return of those who might be reluctant, he brought a group of very large Marines sporting Thompson submachine guns. The sailors were herded into the Marines' weapons carrier and whisked back to the boat. They later joked that it was McCants' "commanding presence" and persuasive arguments, rather than the show of force, that convinced them to return.

Flasher was moored outermost in a nest of subs alongside the tender, since she was scheduled to leave for patrol next. As the repatriated sailors made their way from sub to sub along the gangplanks, a voice hailed from the tender, "Have a good patrol, George." George Markham, flushed from his trip to the bar ashore, stopped to wave thanks for the pleasant send-off, not knowing the voice was the Admiral's, or that the intended "George" was *Flasher's* skipper, George Grider, not Gunner's Mate Third Class George Markham.

CHAPTER 9

FLIGHT OF THE BATTLESHIPS - *FLASHER'S* SIXTH WAR PATROL

After noon on January 27, 1945, *Flasher* departed for her sixth war patrol. En route, she conducted still further training exercises with the Australian fleet minesweepers *HMAS Warrnambool, HMAS Dubbo* and *HMAS Inverell*.

The first night out was spent conducting convoy exercises along with *USS Mingo* (SS 261), before proceeding independently toward Exmouth Gulf. *Flasher* battle-surfaced January 28, expending four rounds of four-inch, 90 rounds of 20mm, and 370 rounds of the 30-caliber ammunition, all without jams. Gun drills were also held twice the following day.

Flasher entered Exmouth Gulf January 30, and took on 10,800 gallons of fuel from the fuel barge *YO 10* before departing. That afternoon the gun crew fired another ten rounds of four-inch ammunition at the wreck off Vlaming Head (probably a sad sight by now with many submarines using it routinely for gunnery practice.) Late that evening *Flasher* alerted to her first contact:

> At 2122, when 58 miles bearing 293° from Vlaming Head Light made SJ contact at a range of 45,000 yards on a single ship. Having received no notice of large ships in the area, we stationed the

Chart of Sixth Patrol (Jan. 27, 1945 to April 13, 1945) (by Author)

radar tracking party and investigated. (Shipcon No. 1).

The ship was tracked turning into the safety lane and heading for Exmouth Gulf, speed 12 knots. We worked into a down-moon position and observed him pass from a range of 4,000 yards. It was a submarine, apparently British.

At about 2246, in order to make certain of his friendly identity, FLASHER challenged from 4500 yards on his starboard beam. No reply, no reaction.

Fifteen minutes later FLASHER challenged again from the starboard quarter, using a bright aldis lamp; no response.

At 2300, FLASHER proceeded on her way, sending our Serial One reporting presence of unidentified submarine. (CTF 71 later informed us that this was the HMS SPIRIT).

There was a very heavy dust layer in the atmosphere that night which extended at least fifty miles to sea and which probably caused the phenomenal initial radar range. Even at 40,000 yards the pip appeared large and distinct.

Apparently the crew aboard the British submarine *Spirit* was anticipating leave in Australia and was not worried about attack. *HMS Spirit* was one of the older, smaller submarines used in gun actions against coastal vessels in the dangerous shallow waters around

Sumatra, Java, and the Bay of Bengal.

On the 31st, another gun drill expended four rounds from the four-inch deck gun and 120 rounds of the 20mm ammunition. The 20mm's were acting up again: "The 20mms could not be made to perform properly. Frequent prolonged stoppages whose cause could not be determined undermined Commanding Officer's confidence in these particular guns."

Additional problems were encountered with *Flasher's* pit log, which had only operated correctly on the fourth and fifth patrols. It began to read low at submerged speeds. The main gyro compass also broke, but was fixed within four hours. More gun training occurred on February 1 with repeated battle stations surface.

The dangerous passage through Lombok Strait faced *Flasher* on February 2:

> At 1727, dived 18 miles south of Lombok Strait to await darkness. Surfaced at 1927 and transited the Strait at four-engine speed without incident. The transit was completed at 2230 just as the moon rose.
>
> At 2305 sighted a patrol boat bearing 070° (Shipcon No. 2). She was lying to about eight miles north of the Strait. We passed her at 9,000 yards without disturbing her.
>
> FLASHER passed north of the Kangean Islands and set course for Karimata Strait.

3 February 1945

At 1010 sighted and exchanged recognition signals with U.S.S. BREAM.

At 1120 made SD contact on a Betty bomber (Aircon No. 1); sighted him at nineteen miles and dived at seven. Watched him proceed eastward and surfaced at 1140 when he was out of sight through the periscope.

That afternoon *Flasher* experienced a fire in the forward battery compartment that was controlled quickly with little or no damage, and she was able to resume standard speed after temporarily slowing. She then fired 60 rounds of 20mm ammunition at floating debris, and exchanged signals with *USS Bluegill* (SS 242). A veteran of three successful war patrols in which more than 40,000 tons had been sunk, *Bluegill* was returning from an unproductive fourth patrol. Enemy shipping was becoming scarce.

There was more practice the following day for the gunners, who sank two floating mines as the boat progressed westward, approaching the shallow Karimata Strait. (Even 50 years after World War II, charts of the Java Sea still report numerous areas of unexploded ordnance, depth charges, and mines.) Kentucky-native Mack Foxx was one of *Flasher's* best shots, often hitting the mines with a 20mm. Grider ordered speed increased to three engines that afternoon, so Karimata Strait could be passed during darkness. Transit was completed by dawn on February 5.

A large two-masted sailboat was soon sighted, but no attack was made "as we could not attack in the vicinity of Karimata Strait." It is unclear whether attack was too risky in the shallow strait, or whether U.S. subs were ordered not to attack there to prevent increased antisubmarine patrols, and possible loss of this valuable passage.

The evening of February 5, *Flasher* received orders to patrol an area in the northern part of the South China Sea between Hainan and Cape Tourane with the *USS Bashaw*. Grider would be in charge of the two-sub wolf pack. That night *Flasher* also exchanged contacts with *USS Boarfish* (SS 327). *Boarfish* was also experiencing difficulties locating enemy ships, but had sunk one vessel and damaged a second.

Over the next two days, *Flasher* dived twice to avoid enemy bombers and received a total of seven aerial bombs, none of which caused damage. On the 6th the SD radar was tested on North Natoena Island, and on the 7th the No. 4 fuel ballast tank was flushed out and converted to sea water operation. As before, Beaman and fellow crewmembers had to crawl into *Flasher's* superstructure to make the necessary mechanical alterations while the sub remained a sitting duck on the surface.

On February 8 she exchanged recognition signals with the veteran submarine *USS Hake*. A friendly aircraft was sighted generating IFF on February 9, but *Flasher's* new VHF radio and SJ radar were unable to raise the plane—a problem that would plague *Flasher* on this patrol. The same day she met with her wolf-pack partner *Bashaw*:

> At 2120 rendezvoused with U.S.S.
> BASHAW and passed over operation

> order for coordinated search and attack
> group. We will patrol the Hainan-Cape
> Tourane traffic lanes, midway between
> the two places. Distance between subs
> about thirty miles. As this area has been
> clear of subs for some time and because
> it is believed that most of the traffic will
> pass us at night, we are going to run sub-
> merged during daylight in order to keep
> our presence unsuspected.

Nothing was sighted the next several days, except for
two enemy planes that did not attack.

On the night of February 12, orders were issued
by CTF 71 for *Flasher* and *Bashaw* to move to intercept
a Japanese task force heading north. This force included the large, very strange Japanese battleships *Ise*
and *Hyuga*, converted after the Battle of Midway to
half-battleships, half-aircraft carriers, and displacing
almost 40,000 tons apiece fully loaded. With the focus
of the war shifting closer to Japan, the two hybrid
battleships were racing from Singapore to prevent being bottled up in the South China Sea.

A month earlier, Admirals Halsey and McCain
launched "Operation Gratitude," a raid by Task Force
38 into the South China Sea. A principal goal of TF 38
was to sink these two battleships, which Naval Intelligence knew were to depart Singapore for the Indochina
coast. The Task Force had to settle for destroying many
other targets, however, because the battleships were
delayed in Singapore after their refueling tankers were
lost to American submarines.[23] (Half of the Japanese

---

[23] Walter Karig, *Battle Report, Victory in the Pacific* (New York:
Rinehart & Co., 1949), p. 195.

tanker tonnage lost to subs during the preceding two months was attributable to *Flasher*, including *Hakko Maru*, which may have been one of the ships to have refueled the battleships off Saigon.) Now the two battleships were loaded with drums of fuel for the homeland and finally beginning their dash home in earnest.

In the path of the Japanese ships were many of both SoWesPac and SubPac submarines, alerted to the battleships by Ultra and the British submarine *Tantalus*. *Flasher* and *Bashaw* were the northernmost SoWesPac submarines in the scouting line, and as far as Grider knew, his "wolf pack" had the last chance to intercept the massive ships if they got by all the rest. The patrol report of February 13 provides the details:

> At 1400, cleared message to BASHAW instructing her to form scouting line at Lat. 16-45, course north, speed 10 at 1400, and to shift back to the wolf-pack frequency. Assumed BASHAW would catch up with scouting line before dark.
>
> At 1409 we were forced under by a plane for twenty minutes. (Aircon No. 8).
>
> At 1525, intercepted BLOWER message that she had attacked with one hit in BB and one in CA. She did not give task force position in this message.
>
> (At 1530 the task force came out of a rainsquall 12 miles from BASHAW. Sighting was mutual. Enemy opened fire

with main battery and launched a plane. BASHAW dived but was unable to close. She surfaced at 1715 with enemy still in sight and sent contact report. (This information is from an SJ message the BASHAW sent us later. It is not known whether or not she had contact prior to the mutual sighting.))

At 1600, received a contact report on the Baker schedule which placed the task force at 16 N at 1300. If true, we should sight them soon.

At 1622, sighted plane from bridge at six miles. Dived and watched him through periscope until he disappeared. Surfaced at 1638. (Aircon No. 9).

At 1720, received BASHAW's contact report giving enemy's 1715 position. Our position was almost abeam of task force. Went to flank speed and course 045 to intercept. We could make 15 knots into the sea, taking over much water.

At 1802, SD contact 10 miles. Did not close. (Aircon No. 10).

At 1825, began getting SJ interference bearing 124. Believed it was BASHAW and that she was in contact with enemy.

At 1837, SD contact 20 miles, friendly IFF. Retained contact until 1848. Called on VHF, no answer. Friendly snooper? (Aircon No. 11).

At 1938 exchanged recognition

signals with BASHAW. Still believed she had contact.

At 1958 BASHAW sent message by SJ reporting the events at 1530 and that she was now 40 miles behind task force.

At 2010, it being obvious that we were behind enemy and unable to overtake, we broke off the chase.

The enemy's ability to outrun us on the surface gave each line one chance at him. Our line might have made an attack except for the unfortunate lifting of the visibility on the BASHAW. The surface visibility where the FLASHER was never exceeded five miles.

Decided to spend tomorrow in northeast corner of sub patrol areas to be available for lifeguard duty tomorrow.

The racing *Ise* and *Hyuga* not only succeeded in making it past all SoWesPac subs, they continued their flight past another 11 SubPac submarines before arriving safely in Japan. The battleship/carriers were not just lucky. They were much faster than the submarines, had radar, and had air cover for some of their voyage. Communications among the many subs could also have been better. The inability of 25 forewarned submarines to stop the warships illustrates why American subs were better employed primarily against merchant shipping, than against Japanese warships in World War II.

Neither *Ise* nor *Hyuga* would help defend the

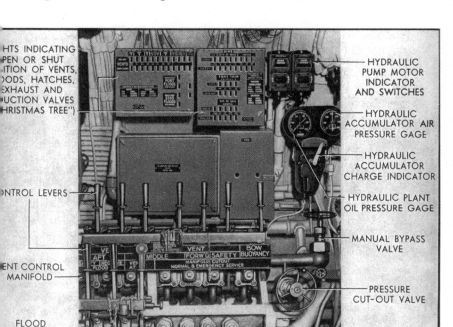

HTS INDICATING PEN OR SHUT ITION OF VENTS, OODS, HATCHES, EXHAUST AND UCTION VALVES HRISTMAS TREE")

HYDRAULIC PUMP MOTOR INDICATOR AND SWITCHES

HYDRAULIC ACCUMULATOR AIR PRESSURE GAGE

HYDRAULIC ACCUMULATOR CHARGE INDICATOR

HYDRAULIC PLANT OIL PRESSURE GAGE

ONTROL LEVERS

MANUAL BYPASS VALVE

ENT CONTROL MANIFOLD

PRESSURE CUT-OUT VALVE

FLOOD CONTROL MANIFOLD

MAIN CUT-OUT MANIFOLD

Main Hydraulic Control Station, and "Christmas Tree" to Show Open (Red) and Closed (Green) Hatches (Navpers 16160)

home islands, however, as they were both damaged the following March. They would be sunk in July, near the port of Kure, Japan, by forces they could not out-run: Navy carrier planes.

Lifeguard duty for downed aviators the next day was uneventful for *Flasher* and *Bashaw*. They were then ordered to patrol east of Hainan Island on the south coast of China, and off Sifa Point, where Grider worriedly observed, "[I]t looks like anybody's first choice for an antisubmarine minefield."

For the better part of the week the patrol droned on, with a solitary sound contact on a ship that was never sighted. A floating mine was dispatched by one of the 20mm guns and numerous enemy and friendly aircraft were seen. Grider's frustration at being unable to contact the friendlies was reflected in the war patrol report:

> At 1627, SD contact 30 miles; no IFF. (Aircon No. 20). Called him on VHF and by voice on 4475 kcs; turned on the ABK. No response. We have radiated with everything but cosmic rays in an effort to establish communications with these planes. If the visibility ever improves we may be able to communicate visually.

Patrol life continued as usual inside the sub's pressure hull. As always, the crew experienced inadequate air conditioning in the forward torpedo room and forward battery compartment. Although Whitaker and Grider had both complained of these conditions, repairs and supplemental blowers never solved the problem and the forward part of the boat was never adequately cooled. Grider recommended the installation of additional cooling coils and larger air conditioning compressors.

In such humid, cramped surroundings, any physical exertion produced rivers of perspiration. Each day *Flasher's* gunners had to disassemble and clean the two heavy 20mm machine guns to slow down the destructive effects of salt water. The sailors would be bathed in sweat by the time the guns were reassembled and installed topside.

Water for bathing was limited, but sizeable

freshwater tanks and the water condensers allowed enough water for *Flasher's* crew to take at least two freshwater baths, unlimited saltwater baths, and unlimited freshwater sponge baths during a patrol. Bags of potatoes were crammed in the shower stalls at the start of a patrol, however, so no showers were possible until after the potatoes were consumed in the first couple of weeks.

Despite this uncomfortable environment, one gunner's mate and some of his shipmates vowed to make it through an entire patrol without ever shaving, showering or shampooing. It did not take long before their bathing abstinence became a constant topic. Others may have caved in, but the gunner stuck to his vow.

The regular gathering place for off-duty sailors was the crew's mess, where they could sit, drink coffee, snack, talk, or play cards. With men concentrated in such a small area, it often became noisy. There was a stunned silence though, when the gunner's mate, suddenly clean-shaven, good-smelling and immaculately groomed, entered from the crew's sleeping quarters, passed through the mess without a word, and went into the adjacent control room. He then loudly called up to the conning tower: "Please report to the Captain and Navigator that I have shit, shaved, showered and shampooed, on advice of the Pharmacist's Mate!" Orders from above had ended his experiment.

Grider continued the "Sun Watch" practice aboard *Flasher*, so during surface daylight operations an additional lookout wearing polarized glasses looked straight into the sun for attacking airplanes. Members of *Flasher's* "Black Gang"—the motor machinists operating her diesels—often got the sun-watch duties to allow them some fresh air. Machinist Beaman had the sun watch one day when Grider was on the cigarette deck to jump rope, as he liked to do. Grider suddenly said, "It's a CLEAR day, isn't it?" Beaman was all the way to the conning tower hatch before he caught on to Grider's little joke.

The evening of February 20, *Flasher* chased an SJ surface-radar contact that turned out to be a plane. Grider decided the sub should try some other area:

> About 2300 sent message to BASHAW to form scouting line athwart the Hainan Strait-Hong Kong traffic route about fifty miles from the strait and to arrive by 1600 on 21st. Proceeded to new position.

> 21 February 1945
> At 1400 arrived on station and started patrolling. Visibility about four miles.
> At 1555, SJ contact bearing 040, range 9600 yards. Went ahead full and swung to put target astern. Sighted two craft through mist; looked like DEs. (Shipcon No. 5).
> Sent contact report to BASHAW. Tracked target on 220. Lost sight and radar contact at 10,700 yards.
> At 1628 SJ and sight contact with BASHAW ahead of us. Sent her message by SJ telling situation, that targets were "DEs or smaller" and that we were

diving to investigate and attack.

At 1636, headed on generated true bearing of targets and dived.

At 1739, long after the generated range had passed zero, made preparations to surface.

At 1743 sighted two sea trucks with zero angle on bow. Let them pass. Did not surface because we wanted to coordinate the gun attack with BASHAW. There would be enough moonlight for a gun attack.

At 1859 surfaced and headed after targets. Gave BASHAW the information by SJ. Picked up targets at 1918. It was now raining and visibility appeared too poor for a good gun attack.

Discussed it with BASHAW by SJ. She expressed a desire to shoot two torpedoes at them. Told them to go ahead.

Tracked BASHAW as she made her approach. At 2045 one sea truck disintegrated.

BASHAW reported missing one and suggested a gun attack. Told him to wait for us; we closed.

At about 2126 BASHAW opened fire with 20mm and 40mm. Her deck gun would not fire.

At 2128 FLASHER opened fire at about 1500 yard range. No return fire. Continued to fire spasmodically until 2154 at average ranges of 500 yards. Visibility prevented accurate shooting at greater ranges.

At 2154 after firing 26 rounds of 4" for about ten hits, plus many smaller caliber hits from both ships, the target capsized.

Maneuvered to pick up a prisoner. Many empty oil drums in water. There were about a dozen figures perched on the keel of the sea truck who would not come aboard. Finally picked up one man out of water who seemed quite willing. As we backed away, saw another figure crawling aboard. Didn't have the heart to push him back, so took him too.

The prisoners turned out to be Chinese who knew a small amount of English. They said the targets were bound from Hong Kong to Singapore and that each was carrying about fifteen Jap troops. The captain was a Jap and about half the crew were Chinese. They stated further that there were 100 empty oil drums aboard; probably to bring back oil. They had seen no other ships.

At 2229, after backing away about 500 yards from wreckage and as we went ahead we hit a heavy submerged object with propeller. No apparent damage. BASHAW reported sighting many survivors on rafts.

For the remainder of the patrol, we had a heavy pounding noise when-

ever the ship rolled. Could not locate it in superstructure.

Grider first tried interrogating his prisoners, who were teenagers, with a Japanese-language guide, but got nowhere as they were Chinese. Once that was discovered, they became favorites with the crew. The crew donated clean, dry clothes and shoes to the two young men. Since they were taken from a Japanese vessel, however, they had to sleep with one wrist handcuffed to their bunk. One became upset, and the sailors tried to explain they were just following orders. It turned out he wasn't upset about the handcuffs, but on being separated from the new leather shoes he had just received.

Sailors with small builds donated the shoes and clothes because of the prisoners' small sizes. One of the shoe donors was *Flasher's* generous baker, Charles "Ski" Ezerosky. The Chinese were billeted in the forward and aft torpedo rooms, to be supervised by the crewmen there. Gunner's Mate Markham took this opportunity to teach the prisoner in the forward room some English. After some effort, Markham taught his accommodating student to stick his head into the galley where Ski was baking, and say "Piss-poor chow" to a stunned Ezerosky.

Both of *Flasher's* prisoners wore religious medallions. It turned out they were from an orphanage in Queens Road West, No. 372/3, Hong Kong, called St. Antorly's or St. Anthony's, where they were impressed into service by the Japanese. The two teenagers had welts on their backs from their captors. They seemed glad to be on *Flasher* and fighting the Japanese. When they were given chores they would not stop until the brush or cleaning rag was taken from them. The Chinese became more a part of the crew as the war patrol progressed.

Flasher continued on patrol, as often the hunted as the hunter:

23 February 1945

At 0425 low order crankcase explosion in auxiliary engine. No serious damage. At 0600 started moving the scouting line to the Tonkon Point-Empire route.

At 0946 made SD contact at 4 miles. Dived. (Aircon No. 23). Surfaced at 1014. Visibility still poor. Arrived on new station at 1257.

24 February 1945

Chased down for ten minutes by SJ contacted plane at 0308. Dived at four miles (Aircon No. 24).

Visibility had improved during the day. Got first glimpses of the sun since entering the area.

Made six aircraft contacts during day. (Aircons No. 25-30). Chased under at 1058 by six twin-engined bombers. Apparently the clear weather has brought out all the Japs.

During evening received HOE's contact report of a convoy headed for

Yulinkan Bay. We could not intercept before they reached the coast. Decided to intercept the evening of the 25th off Hainan. Moved scouting line to a point that will cover both the Hainan Strait and Tonkon Point routes to the Empire.

(*Hoe* was successful in sinking *Coastal Defense Vessel No. 38*, a 900-ton frigate, on February 25.)

25 February 1945

Chased under three times by planes during day. (Aircons No. 31-33). The contact at 1133 was on seven twin engine bombers that we watched fly right over us; we were submerged. None of these planes showed any evidence of radar.

At 1700, heard two distant explosions through hull. Believed at the time that it was the BASHAW getting bombed.

At 1731 SD contact 22 miles. Did not close. (Aircon No. 34). This confirmed our belief.

At 1807 picked up BASHAW'S SJ interference.

At 1931 BASHAW reported by SJ that she was in contact with a small AK with CHIDORI escort, that she had missed the CHIDORI that afternoon with four torpedoes, and that her transmitter was temporarily out of commission.

Went to full speed to intercept.

Main Propulsion Control Cubicle (Navpers 16160)

BASHAW gave target course 180, speed nine. We should be on target's port bow.

At 2035 BASHAW reported by SJ that she was submerging for the attack. Full moon made surface attack impracticable although sky was overcast.

At 2045 established SJ contact with targets. Worked into position 8,000 yards ahead and awaited results of BASHAW's attack. Target took large zig to his right soon after BASHAW's SJ interference disappeared. (Shipcon No. 6).

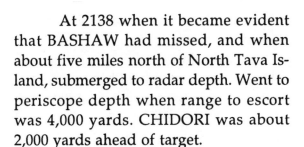

At 2138 when it became evident that BASHAW had missed, and when about five miles north of North Tava Island, submerged to radar depth. Went to periscope depth when range to escort was 4,000 yards. CHIDORI was about 2,000 yards ahead of target.

At 2148 heard two loud explosions. Must have been random depth charges dropped by escort as it seems a little late for BASHAW's end of run explosions.

In the forward torpedo room, Markham and the torpedomen tried to explain to their Chinese guest that *Flasher* was attacking a Japanese target. At the sound of the depth charges, the Chinese cheered, not knowing it was the Japanese attacking the subs, instead of the Americans attacking the Japanese.

Swung for stern shot when it appeared that we were dead ahead of target.

At 2200, with generated range of 700 yards, took a ping range: "Possible echo 900 yards." Set in 800 yards on TDC.

At 2201 with gyro angles very near 180 and with a generated range of 900 yards, fired three stern tubes at the AK, spread by periscope.

A minute and a half later when it was evident that we had missed, started preparing for a bow shot. Had already started the swing.

Two minutes and twenty seconds after firing stern tubes, heard one hit. Swung periscope on target, could see him enveloped in smoke. Observed second hit which caused a brisk explosion aboard. Observed third hit which left nothing but a puff of smoke where the target had been.

We had a range error of 1300 yards and witnessed the great advantage of small gyro angles for night shots. How they all happened to hit is unexplained.

The CHIDORI returned to the scene of his late convoy for a brief moment then began an ineffective search, finally disappearing to the south. We had him in sight for about an hour and could still hear distant pinging when we surfaced.

FLASHER reloaded and surfaced at 2335. Informed BASHAW of results and gave a scouting line for tomorrow, centered at Latitude 20-30, Longitude 1132-35. Did not deem it feasible to pursue the CHIDORI amongst the islands and shoals of the Hainan Coast. There was still a chance of intercepting the HOE'S contact.

The attack was a night submerged attack that had followed "about an hour of radar tracking." *Flasher*

had fired three Mark 18 electric torpedoes at an ideal 90° track angle and hit with all three torpedoes at a range far beyond Grider's estimates. This was an added benefit of 90° shots. Grider described the sunken cargo vessel as:

> ....one small AK with a CHIDORI escort. The target was of the double well-decked, composite superstructure MFM type. He was zigging about base course 210° T. at speed nine knots. The escort was stationed on the port (seaward) bow of the target at a range from target averaging 1500 yards. Visibility was fair, the target and escort being sighted from the bridge at approximately 13,000 yards.

The ship sunk on February 25 was the 850-ton *Koho Maru*. ONI 41-42 listed the *Koho Maru Numbers 1, 2* and *3* as "XAM's," i.e., auxiliary minesweepers. She was probably used as a cargo ship. This was the smallest vessel of over 500 tons (JANAC's minimum) sunk by *Flasher*. Nevertheless, added to her previously credited tonnage (and ignoring the 4,333 tons for the *Tosan Maru*), this last ship would officially raise *Flasher* over the 100,000-ton mark in JANAC's evaluation.

For this patrol, *Flasher* was equipped with two new, top-secret torpedoes nicknamed "cuties" or "doodlebugs." Their loading in Fremantle had been an event, with a squad of armed Marines present, and a ring of raised tarpaulins concealing all above-deck loading operations. Once launched, these short, acoustic torpedoes would home in on the noises of the enemy ship. Since the torpedo's depth setting would be shallow to hit the surface vessel, the sub was to dive immediately after firing so the cutie would not home in on the sub. These new devices were largely untried and were viewed with more than a little skepticism aboard *Flasher*. Grider and Glennon discussed whether they should be fired at the *Koho Maru*. The decision was made to use the proven Mark 18 electrics instead.

The next day provided more plane contacts, but still no successful communications with the friendly aircraft. Grider decided from "sightings to the south" that the convoys had apparently moved their routes farther away from the coast, so he moved the two submarines further offshore, into "*Pampanito's* hunting ground." Also, *Flasher* was running low on fuel:

> Proceeded to scene of last night's attack and sent message to CTF 71 reporting results and stating that FLASHER would have to leave area on the third unless we refueled in Subic.

What *Flasher's* crew obviously wanted was to terminate the patrol and head back to the States, where she was scheduled for a major overhaul and modernization. To the hard-working Admiral Fife, however, the idea of refueling to extend the patrol sounded great and that's what he ordered. *Flasher* had more contacts while waiting for Fife's reply:

> 27 February 1945
>   At 0701, while headed south about 20 miles off coast, sighted two ships on

hazy horizon. Sent contact report to BASHAW. (Shipcon No. 7).

After some time of dashing away because they looked close and then dashing in when we lost contact, BASHAW reported that they were two sea trucks. She must have had a better horizon than we did.

Went to battle stations and closed the range. They proved to be two luggers of about fifty tons each. One had a dummy gun on the deck house which he never manned.

At 0907, opened fire with 20mm and 4" at a range of about 2,000 yards. Closed range to 400 as action progressed and targets appeared unarmed. Targets stayed fairly close together and circled. BASHAW arrived on scene and joined in about 0930; her 4" was back in commission.

Fired 44 rounds of 4", 260 rounds of 20mm, 250 rounds of 30 caliber, and 3 hand grenades.

One lugger capsized, the other was left burning from end to end and listing with holes below the water line, but still afloat. Finally went alongside and threw three hand grenades into hull, but she was still afloat when last seen. We did not fire more 4" because we were down to 11 rounds and it was obvious that he was completely destroyed.

> During the action, sighted a sail on the horizon. Did not attack.
>
> Broke off at 1000. BASHAW opened fire again on remaining target at 1025 and may have sunk it.
>
> Two aircraft contacts during morning and early afternoon that did not close. (Aircons No. 38-39).

More aircraft were seen that afternoon, including a B-24 Liberator (a PB4Y to the Navy) that circled, but Grider was still unable to establish contact with friendlies on the new radio equipment. *Flasher* also received her new orders from Fife:

> At 2100, having received orders from CTF 71 to depart for Subic on the second, sent message to BASHAW to patrol independently in northern half of the area. We have not sighted a target worthy of a pack attack and it seems better to get the greater coverage afforded by splitting the area.

After receiving orders to proceed to Subic Bay, Grider decided to check the loud propeller noises very early on the morning of March 1:

> At 0030, after having cleared the area, laid to and sent a swimmer over the side to inspect the port screw. POOL, Sydney H. #615 32 65, QM2c, USNR volunteered for this job. He reported a small

nick on the tip of one blade.

Pool was the strong swimmer who had saved the lives of his captain and two others from the submarine *R-12* when it sank off Key West in 1942. Into the cold South China Sea with Pool went Lt. Tom Burke. Before they went in, Grider promised, "You have my word I will not start the screws under any circumstances." This made *Flasher* extremely vulnerable to any air, surface or submarine attack. Pool seemed to stay underwater forever. Some of the crew would not believe he actually found a nick in the propeller as he sketched it for Grider, but it was there for all to see when the boat was later drydocked. What the swimmers did not find and what generated much of the noise, was a piece of loose angle iron wrapped around the starboard prop. Grider offered the swimmers a shot of ship's whiskey when they climbed out of the cold water.

The trip to the recently liberated Philippines was uneventful, except for numerous contacts with Allied bombers (B-24/PB4Y Liberators). *Flasher* met with *USS Day* (DE 225) early on March 24, for escort into the bay, and in Subic moored alongside the tanker *Esso Portland* to refuel. She completed fueling in the early afternoon, and moved to nest alongside the tender *USS Griffin* (AS 13).

Subic Bay is on Bataan Peninsula near Manila, capital of the Philippines. Manila was only retaken from the Japanese in February, and fighting still continued nearby. The day *Flasher* arrived, U.S. forces prepared to attack the Japanese "Shimbus" line, a defensive perimeter east of Manila.

Syd Pool (Left), Vince Filippone (Standing) and Tom Burke (Right),
with *Flasher* Emblem, 1945 (Courtesy of Tom Burke)

Flasher unloaded her two Chinese passengers at Subic, turning them over to the Marines there. The crewmen were sorry to see them leave, and the young Chinese were somber for the first time as they met the no-nonsense Marines. They became prisoners again, after being an accepted part of *Flasher's* crew. The Chinese were dressed in Navy dungarees and had the submarine qualification "Dolphins" sewn on their shirt sleeves by the crew for their yeoman services aboard. Markham and some shipmates later visited them at the P.O.W. camp, taking supplies and chocolate.

Substantial repair work would be accomplished in the short stay at Subic:

4-7 March 1945
During this period the following items were accomplished:
Hull repainted.
Loose frames in superstructure were rewelded. This was the cause of the thumping noise we had experienced.
Removed negative tank flood valve, renewed gaskets and replaced flood valve.
Renewed VHF.
Flushed out one fresh water evaporator.
Filed down nick on port screw.
Removed angle iron that was bent around blade of starboard screw.
Conducted surface sound tests. Port shaft has a wiping noise that was just below the maximum permissible

limit. This could not be repaired.

There was an air raid alert every night.

The commanding officer made a trip to Mindoro to visit the Mindoro Search Group of Navy PB4Ys that is co-operating with our submarines off the coast of Indo China. The interest, enthusiasm, and knowledge of submarine problems shown by this group were highly gratifying.

Because of *Flasher's* problems communicating with aircraft, repairs at Subic Bay included a new VHF unit, a shortened antenna, and the replacement of steel bolts on the antenna insulator with brass bolts. Only after all of these repairs did *Flasher's* VHF finally work. While alongside the *USS Griffin*, the sub also took aboard three torpedoes aft.

Some of the crew were able to celebrate during the four days while *Flasher* was refueled and repaired at Subic Bay. One officer got back to the boat and quickly calculated the boat's trim with the new fuel and supplies, because the frequent air raids meant the boat might need to dive. The next morning, with a clearer head, he rechecked his calculations from the night before and found they would have sent *Flasher* directly to the bottom.

On March 8, 1945, the sub departed Subic Bay, escorted by the destroyer *USS Thatcher* (DD 514), to ward off attacks from Allied planes. The sixth patrol was to continue off Cape Varella, Indochina, with several submarines, among them *Blueback* (SS 326—pack leader), *Blackfin* (SS 322), *Bergall* (SS 320), and *Hawkbill*, all *Balao*-class submarines with thicker hulls and newer features than *Flasher*.

Patrolling off Indochina was largely uneventful for *Flasher*, although *Blueback* received and survived a depth charging from a small "hunter-killer" group that came out to sink her. *Flasher's* No. 1 engine blew an oil gasket, and was out of commission for over 24 hours. Submerged patrols were authorized by *Blueback* on March 14, because of Japanese submarines reported to the north. A repeat message as to submerged patrolling was issued on the next day after *USS Brill* (SS 330), 200 miles north of *Flasher*, reported sighting a torpedo. Submariners had a healthy respect for the danger from an enemy sub.

Bergall rescued an aviator on the 15th, the same day *Flasher* was passed by 200 sailboats. *Flasher's* look-outs witnessed numerous bombers (mostly B-24's and B-25's) on their way to air strikes, and communicated with them and their Lockheed P-38 "Lightning" fighter escorts, but saw no targets. Grider was also unable to get anyone to use *Flasher's* lifeguard services. The boat continued on patrol, with a constant lookout for enemy subs. Near midnight of the 22nd, Grider received word from a nearby sub:

> At 2330, BERGALL reported that an enemy submarine had just fired torpe-does at her in the position that FLASHER had occupied all day. Wonder how many approaches that sub had made on us.

Flasher was authorized on March 24 to terminate

her extended patrol, and head northeast for Saipan, Pearl Harbor, and ultimately, the States! At the same time *Hawkbill* received orders for Fremantle, so she departed to the south. On the 25th *Flasher* radioed her new command, ComSubPac, requesting routing instructions, and detonated a floating mine with rifle fire.

The evening of March 26 *Flasher* sighted her 72nd aircraft of the patrol:

> At 2238, SJ contact on plane at 24,000 yards. Friendly IFF. Turned on ABK. (Aircon No. 72). This plane was apparently suspicious of us; circling us many times and closing in as close as three miles. At 2320, plane dropped a flare about two miles abeam that might have been an illumination flare or a recco signal. By this time we were suspicious of him. Could not raise him on VHF.
>
> At 2339, when he had once more closed to 3 miles, we fired a recco grenade. This seemed to satisfy him and he went away.

Executive Officer Glennon was due to be relieved after this sixth patrol. Next in seniority was Lt. Burke. He took over Glennon's navigation duties for the long trip stateside, just as Snap Coffin did on the return from the fifth patrol. As with Coffin, Burke's first experience with navigating proved trying. Complicating his new duties, *Flasher* was required to remain on the surface, and travel in a moving "safety lane." She had to stay within the constantly moving square or

be subject to Allied attack. If *Flasher* did not navigate precisely and keep to her restricted timetable, she had to radio headquarters that she was straying from the safety zone. But she had to be able to plot exactly where she was to *know* if she was in or out of the lane. Due to continually overcast skies, however, Burke was unable to get star fixes, and he had to rely on occasional sun sights for several days.

Flasher transited Balintang Channel between Luzon and Formosa around midnight of the 27th, and entered the Pacific Ocean for the first time in over a year. The next day Burke's problems were compounded as *Flasher* experienced heavy traffic in the safety lane to Saipan:

> At 1015, sighted U.S.S. PIRANHA ahead. During the next twenty four hours overtook the PIRANHA, SEA OWL, and PUFFER; all headed through the safety lane to Saipan, as we were.
>
> At 1332, sighted a floating moored-type mine which we exploded with rifle fire at 1345. The PIRANHA saw the explosion and headed to our assistance. Told him on area frequency that we had sunk a mine. The SEA OWL reported sinking one at almost the same instant.
>
> At 1912, exchanged recco signals with the SEA OWL, bearing 115.
>
> At 2357, SJ contact on SEA OWL, bearing 110, range 9,700 yards.

29 March 1945

The following times are ITEM.

At 0100, received message from SEA OWL on frequency reporting her SJ contact on us and asking us to identify ourselves; we complied. Range was 7,000 yards at the time.

At 0615, exchanged recco signals with U.S.S. PUFFER. Closed range on her and exchanged info on the VHF; then pulled ahead.

At 0727 a Liberator flew over us headed south. (Aircon No. 79).

At 1815, began picking up APR contacts on 200, 225 and 425 mgcs. which generally grew stronger. Had characteristics of friendly radar.

At 1854, picked up interference on SJ bearing 152. Believed this was SG interference.

At 1859, SJ contact bearing 167, range 16,700 yards. Changed course to 045 to keep from closing. Ship was tracked on course 330 at 16 knots. (Shipcon No. 11).

At 1929 lost SJ contact to the westward. Noted new set of interference to south. We now had four APR contacts, all at saturation.

At 1956, SJ contact bearing 196, range 14,000 yards. Turned away and went to full speed. (Shipcon 12). This ship chased us for about 45 minutes, gradually closing the range. At 2016, when the range had closed to 11,000 yards, flashed the second identification signal at him. He answered the first challenge and we replied properly. He then asked for our call, which we gave. He responded with his call, which we could not read. He then departed to the northwest; we resumed course.

At 2034, another SJ contact to the south; two ships bearing 168, range 13,600 yards. They held their course and we passed clear without being challenged. (Shipcon No. 13).

After a year-long tour in enemy-controlled waters, where most surface contacts were Japanese, *Flasher* was finding travel in Allied-dominated seas dangerous. The high concentration of vessels was no accident. She had stumbled into massive Naval invasion forces headed for Okinawa. It was a challenging experience for *Flasher's* novice navigator.

At noon on March 30, *Flasher* exchanged signals with an outbound veteran, the very successful *USS Snook* (SS 279). She was headed for her ninth and final war patrol in the Luzon Strait and off Hainan, where *Flasher* had recently patrolled. She would be lost within a month to unknown causes, probably to the same Japanese submarines that patrolled the area and threatened *Flasher's* wolf pack. During this same period, five Japanese subs were sunk along the Nansei Shoto island chain, and the Navy believed one of them may have first sunk *Snook*. *Flasher's* crew was lucky to have survived more than a year in a perilous war zone, and to be headed home before their luck ran out.

Flasher, together with the submarines *Puffer, Sea Owl* (SS 405), *Piranha* (SS 389) and *Peto* (SS 265), entered ComSubPac's advanced submarine facility at Tanapag Harbor, Saipan, on April 2, where she received fuel in a nest alongside the sub tender *USS Fulton* (AS 11). The next morning the five subs departed together for the central Pacific:

> At 1614, under way in company with SEA OWL, PIRANHA, PETO, and PUFFER. Proceeded out of harbor and formed around YNS 374. Proceeded toward joint zone. The escort departed at dark.
>
> At 2035 saw and heard an explosion in the direction of the SEA OWL'S radar interference. At first we thought she had been torpedoed but it developed in ensuing radio conversation that she was alright and that the explosion had been something else. SEA OWL expressed the opinion that it was a jettisoned aircraft bomb. Saw two more flashes over the horizon at 2122.
>
> 4 April 1945
> Uneventful. Sighted other submarines of our group from time to time. Our formation never recovered from last night's scare.

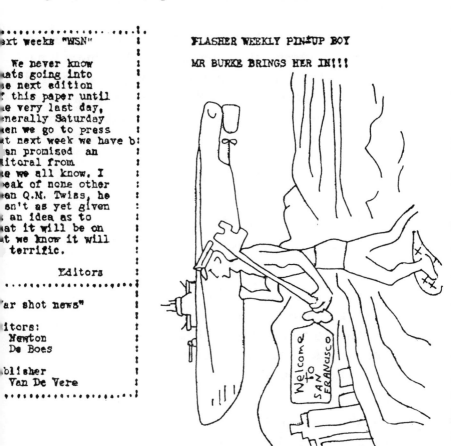

We never know
ats going into
e next edition
' this paper until
e very last day,
nerally Saturday
en we go to press
t next week we have b
an promised an
litoral from
e we all know. I
eak of none other
an Q.N. Twiss, he
sn't as yet given
an idea as to
at it will be on
t we know it will
terrific.

                    Editors

ar shot news"

itors:
  Newton
  De Boes

blisher
  Van De Vere

FLASHER WEEKLY PINSUP BOY

MR BURKE BRINGS HER IN!!!

Welcome to SAN FRANCISCO

War Shot News Page from the Sixth Patrol, with Cartoon of "Snowshoes" Burke Navigating *Flasher* on Trip to States

5 April 1945

Set course for Pearl Harbor at 2120. The other boats are heading for Midway.

Conducting daily dives and drills.

Several editions of *Flasher's* on-board newspaper *War Shot News* were printed during the sixth patrol, put together by crew members Newton, DeBois, Simmons and Van De Veere. Sometimes the paper contained official encouragement for the sailors to become submarine-qualified, but mostly it contained good-natured satire of submarine life, or the ribbing of someone on board, especially the officers. Grider, sporting a crew cut after the short stop at Subic, wrote the following:

Poem of the Week
"Hair Lines"

Oh the skipper's hair is barely there
    But what he's got is neat.
The First Lieutenant's grows quite long,
    But doesn't match his feet.

The Exec's mustache has a certain dash
    And doesn't wilt in the heat
And the lassies fair do oft declare,
    "It tickles but it's sweet."

And the gun boss' hair is black, not fair
    And certainly isn't thin;
But a bitter fate has stripped his pate,
    and put it on his chin.

For many weeks our engineer's cheeks
    show very little change.
But the paltry hair that groweth there
    is suffering from mange.

The communicator's rabid with a vicious habit
    that he must have got in Subic.
He fondles his chin where the hairs grow thin,
    as though he thought they were pubic.

And the tender young shoots lie dead
    in the roots, of the commissary's chin.
They were beginning to sprout when the ship
    came about, and the wind blew them in again.

"It's thin but it's cool," is the answer from Pool.
    And the point I'd like to impress
Is that scientists vow that the naked brow
    Shows concubinary success.

"Oh! rue the day," says Calloway,
    "I'll have to break the date,
And I looked just right to spend the night
    With Gargantua's mate."

"Now listen," says Sherman, "There
    ain't no vermin in this here beard, you boobs.
If you didn't know, that's were I stow,
    Them delicate radar tubes."

Oh, we're a hairy crew it's very true,
    and we go where duty calls,
But we live for that trip when we'll finally grip
    The hair on Tojo's -------- !!!!

(Executive Officer at the time was Glennon, First
Lieutenant was Burke, "gun boss" was McCants, and
engineer was Atkinson. The sub's paper also contained
ribbing of Glennon, who had suddenly awakened from
his berth and raced to his battle station, misunder-
standing an intercom announcement for a "sweep
down" of all compartments.)
        The rest of the trip was uneventful and on April

13, *Flasher* met with the subchaser *PC-782* for escort into Pearl Harbor. It must have been a somber atmosphere in Pearl, as President Franklin D. Roosevelt, who had led his nation for 12 years through economic depression and then the war, had died the day before, and the nation was in mourning.

From the report Grider turned in at Pearl Harbor, it was clear radar usage had changed on this sixth patrol. Since the enemy was "homing in" on the air-search radar of American submarines, *Flasher's* SD-4 radar was used very sparingly. The air-search radar was utilized only during daylight and only for three to six seconds out of each minute. During the night, the radar would be kept on "stand-by condition so that either the SD or BN could be used instantaneously." This was a far cry from just a few months earlier, when *Flasher* utilized her SD-4 radar almost continuously, and as much as her SJ-a.

Grider commented that the crew was healthy for this sixth patrol, as "only the usual minor ailments appeared and the Chief Pharmacist's Mate handled them with little difficulty." With regard to the perennial food deficiencies, there was a positive note as: "the food was well prepared and the quality was good. The meats showed a vast improvement of those issued on the last run." The complaints following the fifth patrol and the close inspection of meats taken aboard for the sixth patrol apparently paid off.

Weather for *Flasher's* sixth patrol coincided with the end of the "northeast monsoon season." Off Hainan, the sky had been overcast 95 percent of the time, and off Indochina it had varied from clear to completely overcast.

Grider was pleased with the performance of his crew and noted: "The aggressiveness, morale and performance of duty of both officers and crew were gratifying in spite of a long patrol with so few contacts." In fact, *Flasher's* sixth patrol was her most unproductive due to the dearth of enemy shipping.

The character of the submarine war against Japan had substantially changed in the year *Flasher* had been at war. Submarines and aircraft had almost eliminated Japan's merchant fleet. Because of this, *Flasher* arrived in Pearl Harbor with no fewer than 25 torpedoes still aboard. (Two of the short, homing torpedoes replaced one regular torpedo, raising *Flasher's* maximum torpedo capacity from 24 to 25.)

The sub had travelled over 9,000 miles in the first part of her patrol, and consumed more than 100,000 gallons of diesel fuel. On the second part of her patrol, from Subic Bay into the South China Sea and on to Saipan and then Pearl Harbor, she had travelled another 10,000 miles and consumed another 143,000 gallons. Her sixth patrol, from Fremantle to Pearl Harbor, had lasted a grueling 77 days, of which only ten were spent submerged.

Since *Flasher* ended her patrol at Pearl Harbor, endorsements originated from ComSubPac. On April 19, 1945, William V. O'Regan, Commander, Submarine Squadron 4, recommended *Flasher* be credited with 2,000 tons for the small freighter, 75 tons for the first gun attack on the sea truck, and 25 tons apiece (half credit) for the two luggers sunk in the second gun attack. Elton W. Grenfell, Commander, Submarine Division 44, congratulated *Flasher* for her "extremely well-conducted, long and arduous patrol, and for inflicting damage upon the enemy." Grenfell noted that "in spite of the thorough area coverage, however, only one target was contacted worthy of torpedo fire and this was sunk. Other smaller targets were attacked by gun fire." He also commented on *Flasher's* "extremely clean condition," but noted "the materiel condition of the FLASHER, however, is only fair and she will proceed to the San Francisco area for a modernization overhaul."

Commodore Merrill Comstock, Acting for ComSubPac (Admiral Lockwood), credited *Flasher* with excellent area coverage and the sinking of the small freighter and three smaller craft, but noted "it was unfortunate that the fast enemy task force was able to get by the scouting line of which FLASHER was a unit." He also noted:

> This is the sixth successful patrol for this valiant ship. During this time the FLASHER has sunk twenty-four ships for a total tonnage of 153,607 tons and damaged two ships for a total tonnage of 11,500 tons.

Comstock also credited *Flasher* with a total of 2,125 tons for her sixth war patrol and awarded the Submarine Combat Insignia for the patrol, her sixth award in a row. Total tonnage was to be reduced in the post-war JANAC study.

CHAPTER 10

STATESIDE OVERHAUL

On April 17, 1945, *Flasher* departed Pearl Harbor. Even though she was headed for overhaul in San Francisco, she continued training exercises. Maneuvering and gun drills were conducted on April 19, with the gun crews firing the four-inch as well as the unpredictable 20mm guns. On the 21st, collision and man-overboard drills were conducted, and gun drills focused on a glass fishing ball:

> 1535 Sank fishing ball having expended
> 300 rounds 20mm, 200 rounds 45 cal.,
> and 25 rounds 30 cal., no casualties.

That must have been one dead fishing ball.

Because of wartime secrecy, *Flasher's* movements were classified on a "need-to-know" basis, and as far as the Navy was concerned, wives and family had no need to know the sub was returning. Nevertheless, Grider was able to sneak a message stateside to his wife, Ann. She relayed the news to others.

Betty McCants, staying with her parents in South Carolina, made immediate plans for the cross-country trip. Such travel was not easy for the wives of servicemen in World War II America. Military priorities monopolized rail and air transportation. The trip was further complicated because she was taking her 1½-year-old son, Tommy, with her. Lt. Tom McCants had never seen Tom Jr., who was born while *Flasher* headed to the war zone.

After a difficult, delayed, and frustrating trip, Betty arrived in San Francisco to learn (1) her parents in South Carolina feared she was lost in a Texas air disaster; (2) her room reservation was only good for three days because all hotel space in San Francisco was promised for the international dignitaries convening to create the United Nations Organization; and (3) *Flasher's* arrival was going to be delayed. The United Nations Charter would be adopted in San Francisco on June 26, 1945, while the sub was there undergoing overhaul.

Facing eviction on the third day with no place to stay, she received a message from someone she had never met, former *Flasher* Officer Frank Kristl. He, his wife, and son would come by later to take Tommy and her to stay in their quonset hut at Hunter's Point, San Francisco. After leaving *Flasher*, Frank served in *USS Angler*, returning to the States before *Flasher*. He manufactured reasons to visit the office where daily ship arrivals were posted, and on April 24, he learned that the sub was expected that morning.

Before dawn, *Flasher* met with the destroyer *USS King* (DD 242) for escort into San Francisco Bay, passing under the Golden Gate Bridge at 8:46 a.m. Burke's wife, Anne, who had gone to greet *Flasher* from the bridge, could not see the sub arrive because of the thick fog. Meanwhile, Burke had to use the SJ radar to navigate into the harbor. The fog did not lift until the sub neared Alcatraz Island.

Betty and Tommy McCants were at Hunter's Point to meet the boat when it docked. Kristl took Betty to the foot of the dock and told her to walk down the pier with Tommy. No one challenged their presence, and, when *Flasher* docked stateside for the first time since November, 1943, there were Betty and Tommy McCants. With the crew lining the deck, Grider sent McCants down the gangplank to greet them. To cap the emotional high, the infant held out his arms and said, "Hello, Daddy." It was a greeting repeated for millions of returning servicemen later that year.

Flasher transferred her torpedoes to the Hunter's Point torpedo shop before departing for sound tests, and proceeded to Bethlehem Steel for overhaul and modernization. On May 2, she was moved to a floating dry dock where the overhaul would occur. Three days later a new officer, Lt. L.A. Walker, reported aboard.

On May 7, 1945, Germany unconditionally surrendered. America's massive war effort, which had been divided between Europe and the Pacific (with primary emphasis on Europe), would now be concentrated entirely against Japan.

While *Flasher* underwent modernization and overhaul, part of her crew began their well-deserved leave. Remaining personnel were moved to a berthing barge while major repairs were begun. They would have their turn at leave when the others returned. Most of *Flasher's* officers and crew were taking their first lengthy leave since their assignment to *Flasher*. The desire to extend precious leave time was universal. Lt. Eddie Atkinson, from his home in Pine Bluff, Arkansas, wired Grider:

Tom and Tommy McCants, During *Flasher's* Overhaul
at San Francisco (Courtesy Betty McCants)

BELIEVE THAT WITH TEN MORE
DAYS OF LEAVE I CAN COME
BACK AND WIN THE WAR SINGLE-
HANDEDLY.

Grider, without hesitation, wired back:

TAKE FOUR DAYS INSTEAD, COME
BACK, AND WE'LL HELP YOU.

On May 20, muster was held by recently promoted Lt. Cmdr. Glennon, after which a steward's mate was court-martialed for being absent over leave for a day, and for unauthorized possession of one of the boat's .45 automatic handguns. He was found guilty and sentenced to a drop in rating, along with a requirement that he perform "police duties" for six days.

Grider hosted a ship's party for the men of the *Flasher* at Trader Vic's the night of May 25. Special invitation booklets were printed which said, in part:

> Six war patrols have been marked up by the *U.S.S. Flasher* since her commissioning in September, 1943. Six times have the "Sons of Heaven" wished that that day had never come. And many times six are the ships that have felt the fatal sting of the *Flasher's* fighting punch.
>
> From the U.S.A. to His Majesty's Australia and back, the *Flasher* has blazed a brilliant path in her short but eventful lifetime. Her record is one of the best. The following officers and men are now attached to this, the "fightingest" ship in the fleet.

The invitation then listed the ship's company.

Not all of *Flasher's* crew attended, and those on watch aboard the barge baby-sat the McCants infant while his parents attended the party. Tommy got the royal treatment from the skeleton crew, but soon developed ominous skin spots. Instead of interrupting the party, the sailors called Kristl. He phoned the Navy Yard doctor and described symptoms similar to the measles Kristl's own son once had. That was enough for the doctor. He ordered the entire Bethlehem Steel facility quarantined, with no one allowed to enter or leave.

This was now a serious matter, and the ship's party was interrupted. Tom and Betty McCants raced back to Bethlehem Steel, but were told by the guard it was sealed and they could not enter. They explained that it was THEIR child who caused the quarantine and were urgently waived inside. Arriving at the barge, Betty discovered it was not measles but simply an allergic reaction to strawberries in the ice cream the sailors fed him. The rash subsided, and the Bethlehem Steel quarantine was lifted.

Glennon, veteran of all six of *Flasher's* war patrols and her executive officer for the last three, was transferred from *Flasher* in July, 1945, to a staff position at Mare Island. He received an impressive three Silver Star medals, the Combat Legion of Merit in lieu of a fourth Silver Star, and two Presidential Unit Citations for his wartime patrols on *USS Greenling* and *Flasher*.

Replacing Glennon as *Flasher's* executive officer was Burke, veteran of all but her third patrol (due to a broken foot). He had his hands full with *Flasher's* new equipment and many new crew members. McCants, the Gunnery and Torpedo Officer since the end of the third patrol, kept those assignments but replaced Burke as First Lieutenant.

Two items on *Flasher's* wish list while in overhaul were a ship's emblem and a professionally made battle flag. Many other subs had cartoon symbols reflecting the boats' namesake fish, that appeared on the ships' flags surrounded by small Japanese flags representing each vessel sunk.

The wife of Gunner's Mate Pealatere had Hollywood connections, it seemed, and an artist at the Walt Disney studios agreed to make a cartoon sketch for the boat. The story aboard *Flasher* was that the artist was in the midst of his project when Walt Disney came by his desk, and on learning of the project, Disney personally helped with the design. The sketch for *Flasher's* emblem bears the flasher fish, or tripletail, as the "flashy" driver of a sporty torpedo, wearing a derby, diamond stick pin, ascot, spats, and sports coat. With the drawing in hand, crew members got a commercial artist at the Navy shipyard to paint enlarged, colored versions on disks about three feet in diameter, to mount on the boat's conning tower.

Now that *Flasher* had her emblem, a battle flag was sought, and Signalman Doty was assigned the task of finding a flag maker. No novice at assignments, Doty requested, and got, a helper in junior Signalman Corneau. As Corneau remembers, they would leave the boat late each morning and go straight to a bar. Doty would then tell Corneau to "start walking" around San Francisco in search of someone to make the flag, while Doty awaited the results. This procedure worked for several days before there was some impatience from the *Flasher* officers at the lack of progress. A tailor was ultimately found to craft the large, gold flag, with the new *Flasher* emblem in the center, surrounded by the small flags representing each of the 31 warships, merchant ships, sampans, luggers, and sea trucks sunk or damaged.

Drawing of *Flasher* Emblem Obtained During Overhaul
(Author's Collection)

When *Flasher's* new Exec., Tom Burke, returned from his leave in New York, he often stayed nights aboard the shipyard barge. One night in early July, he was awakened by the shipyard shift manager and summoned aboard *Flasher*. A Bethlehem Steel employee had been seen removing a pair of the sub's binoculars. Burke advised the binoculars were "Title B" equipment costing about $150. That meant the theft was a matter for the Federal Bureau of Investigation. An FBI agent soon arrived, searched the employee's locker, discovered the binoculars, and arrested the employee. He told Burke the binoculars would be retained as evidence, and Burke had to go to the FBI office downtown if he wanted a receipt. The receipt was later used at Pearl Harbor to obtain a replacement pair.

During her overhaul, *Flasher's* equipment was repaired, repainted, replaced, checked and updated. Authorized modifications to the sub ran five single-spaced pages, with 93 separate changes. The Navy monitored problems reported from the battle zone, and sought to eliminate most equipment and design inadequacies. Corrections and improvements the Navy rejected as frivolous, too expensive, or too time-consuming when *Flasher* was conceived and built were now required changes in every major overhaul. Advances in all forms of equipment were to be incorporated into the older designs as boats like *Flasher* returned from the front.

Upgraded radars, an innovative periscope that incorporated a miniaturized radar unit surrounding the lens, an improved pit-log mounting, a depth-charge direction finder, and a TDC "speed-halving device" (to shorten the time required to compute a target solution) were a few of the modifications made. The forward diving planes were altered, so that in their stowed, surface condition they were slightly tilted forward. This allowed for speedier extension into the diving position and a quicker dive time. Other improvements provided for better sound isolation of *Flasher's* machinery to make the sub harder to detect.

The most technically innovative change was the addition of a QLA sonar device, designed by Westinghouse engineers and scientists at the University of Southern California. This would (ideally) allow *Flasher* to detect and penetrate Japanese minefields. Mine-cable clearing guards were also installed to prevent snagging the cables and pulling the mines against the sub.

Flasher's four-inch, forward-mounted deck gun was replaced by a more powerful and efficient five-inch gun on her after deck. Her two problematic 20mm machine guns forward and aft of the bridge were also replaced by a more effective 40mm Bofors gun forward, and a twin 20mm machine gun on the cigarette deck. A mounting for one of the displaced 20mm's was installed at the former deck gun location.

On Independence Day, July 4, 1945, *Flasher* celebrated by test firing her new 5"/25-caliber deck gun and the new 40mm Bofors gun. Both performed satisfactorily and there were no observed structural weaknesses. *Flasher* was almost ready to return to the war zone.

CHAPTER 11

JAPAN'S COLLAPSE
THE "SEVENTH PATROL"

Fresh from overhaul, sporting new equipment and many new crew members, *Flasher* departed for Pearl Harbor on July 14, training, as always, as she went. She was escorted into Pearl Harbor on July 24, and was photographed docking alongside the sub tender *USS Euryale* at the submarine base.

At Pearl was *Flasher's* former Executive Officer, Lt. Cmdr. Ray DuBois. Since leaving *Flasher* he had commanded the training submarine *USS Mackerel*. He preferred to get back into the "shooting war," so he advised his superiors in New London he would take the first available boat headed for the war zone. When an opening arose with a boat ordered to the Pacific, the *USS Barbero*, DuBois received command. *Barbero* was the sub that passed *Flasher* as both were returning to Fremantle, and was nearly sunk by an aerial bomb in Lombok Strait. She was now ready to return to action after extensive repairs. DuBois proved a genial host to his fellow *Flasher* officers when he met them again at Pearl. After one commented how tough and demanding DuBois had been as *Flasher's* Exec, Ray pointed out, "Sure, but I got you back alive."

The war had proceeded badly for Japan over the last six months. The addition of more submarines with

Flasher Arriving Pearl Harbor, July 24, 1945 (Author's Collection)

increased fuel capacity and closer forward bases allowed the subs to reach Japanese shipping lanes and ports quicker, in greater numbers, and to stay there longer, than ever before. Without shipping from abroad, a blockaded Japan lacked the fuel and raw materials for which she began the war against America, and could not build a replacement fleet, fuel the merchant and naval vessels in her ports, or train new pilots to replace her staggering losses.

With her remaining fleet bottled up in harbors by subs and by mines dropped from long-range bombers, Japanese ships were decimated by carrier raids and the increasing land-based bomber raids from Saipan, Tinian, and Iwo Jima. The role for Allied submarines was changing as a result of these developments. Targets in the South China, East China and Philippine Seas were almost nonexistent. To attack Japanese shipping, some submarines daringly entered mined harbors, or the dangerous Sea of Japan through its narrow, mined entrances.

Flasher's new equipment included the QLA (FM) sonar for the purpose of penetrating these areas. The device was a pet project of Grider's new boss, Admiral Charles A. Lockwood. When operating correctly, the new sonar produced an audible bell tone as the sub encountered mines.

For the next two weeks *Flasher's* crew trained on the sonar in practice minefields near Pearl. Training was scary, even though the mines were dummies. The mine cables would loudly grate along the hull, scraping the sub's beam from bow to stern. One dummy mine was pulled down right on top of the boat and hit with a loud "THUMP" and "BANG" as its cable was snagged. The minefields were difficult to negotiate, since turning from one mine often meant striking another. More than once *Flasher* snagged mine mooring cables in her props, planes or superstructure. There was distrust of the new equipment by some of the officers and crew, and concern about the upcoming patrol.

Submariners were aware that casualties were unusually high for their force, with the loss to enemy action of one out of every seven subs. Crew members on *Flasher* had lost friends on *Dorado, Robalo, Flier, Harder, Growler*, and other boats. They also knew the loss ratio was much higher for subs operating in the Sea of Japan where *Flasher* was apparently headed. It was clear that Japan was all alone and clearly losing, and it did not help that the submariners were going on a very dangerous patrol with the end of the war almost in sight.

The Sea of Japan was the last area the Japanese could sail with any reasonable hope of reaching port. It is almost land-locked, with access through only four heavily guarded and mined straits. Submarines had entered the Sea of Japan only a few times during the war. In July, 1943, three subs (*Permit, Plunger* and *Lapon*) had entered and exited through LaPerouse, sinking three ships for their daring.

In August, 1943, the now-famous *Wahoo* and *Plunger* went in and came out the same way, with three sinkings (all by *Plunger*), and miserable torpedo performance from *Wahoo*. (*Wahoo's* poor torpedo experiences on this patrol, coupled with strong evidence from Cmdr. Dan Daspit in *USS Tinosa* [SS 283], finally led Admiral Lockwood to test the contact exploders with his own personnel and cure that defect in late 1943.) Shortly thereafter, Grider's former skipper, Cmdr. Mush Morton, took *Wahoo* back with a fresh load of torpedoes, and the sub was later lost when it tried to leave the Sea of Japan. U.S. submarines avoided the Sea of Japan after *Wahoo's* loss until mid-1945.

By 1945, with targets hard to find and the new

QLA sonar to penetrate the mined straits, Admiral Lockwood once again proposed raids into the Sea of Japan. In the first week of June, nine subs penetrated the minefields of Tsushima Strait, with eight successfully exiting LaPerouse Strait on June 25, 1945. *Bonefish*, *Flasher's* wolf-pack companion from the fourth patrol, was the ninth submarine. She was sunk by depth charges off the Japanese west coast on June 18, 1945.

The loss of *Wahoo* and *Bonefish* fueled the inaccurate belief that Sea of Japan losses were one-in-three boats, versus one-in-seven boats in the rest of the war zone. While this impression was incorrect, it was true that two out of the 15 PATROLS in the Sea of Japan had resulted in the loss of submarines. Given that 52 American submarines were lost in over 1,600 war patrols (i.e., roughly one sub for every 32 war patrols), the loss ratio of one sub for every 7½ patrols in the Sea of Japan was over four times as hazardous.

The dangers associated with their new mission, the lack of faith in the QLA system to avoid mines and cables despite intensive training, the nearness of Japan's defeat, and the substantial rotation of *Flasher's* officers and crew, all made for a relatively worried crew.

Grider decided that his exec, Burke, was "too uptight," and that he and Burke could use a break from training, so he took Burke out partying one night to loosen him up. Because of the wartime curfew in Honolulu, they could not return to the boat until the following morning. Late that same night, Watch Officer Atkinson woke up McCants (the senior officer aboard with Grider and Burke absent), and told him he had better dress in full uniform and come up on deck.

When they arrived topside, McCants and Atkinson met a tense situation. What looked to them like most of *Flasher's* crew were assembled on the afterdeck. The crew told the two officers their misgivings with the boat and its anticipated mission. They also expressed their intention to present a petition not to go on patrol until their concerns were addressed. McCants reassured them that their situation was not as bleak as they imagined, and he convinced them that they couldn't do anything about it anyway. The possible perception of their actions as a "mutiny" by the no-nonsense Navy was also explained. In the end the crew dispersed. Not one person requested a transfer from *Flasher*. The incident was not officially written up, and few besides those present knew it even happened. One of *Flasher's* officers did not learn of the matter until years later.

Rumors of impending peace were continually in the press after the stunning news of the secret "atomic" bombs dropped on Hiroshima and Nagasaki on August 6 and 9, 1945, just two weeks after *Flasher's* arrival in Pearl Harbor. By August 11, the *Honolulu Star-Bulletin* was headlining that the Allied reply to Japan's "offer to surrender" allowed the Japanese to save face. Headlines proclaimed "SIRENS WILL SIGNAL V-J DAY; HERE'S PLAN!" A false alarm that the war was officially over caused premature celebration among the ships in Pearl Harbor with an awesome, unauthorized expenditure of military pyrotechnics. Every admiral in the harbor kept sending signals to cease the displays, but the messages were ignored. *Flasher's* crew made a substantial contribution to the illegal fireworks. Grider and Beaman teamed up to fire flares from the mortar-like signal gun on the cigarette deck.

Although Japan radioed verbal acceptance to the surrender terms on August 14, 1945, formal surrender was weeks away. After the news of Japan's concession, *Flasher's* crew was shocked and dismayed to learn they were STILL to conduct their seventh patrol, headed for Guam with other submarines, and ultimately the mined waters off Japan. Most of them were reservists, with no intention of serving in the military any longer than it took to defeat Japan. A nearby sub sharing *Flasher's* fate had a sign saying "Is this trip necessary?"

On August 21, 1945, a depressed and disheartened crew backed *Flasher* from her mooring, and headed toward Guam with a pack of submarines including Ray DuBois' *Barbero*. Many crewmembers were convinced there was no justice in the world, or at least not in the Navy. Proceeding in the pack on the high seas on August 24, OOD Atkinson received a message to reverse course for Pearl Harbor. Atkinson ordered the messenger to obtain confirmation for so dramatic a course change, and almost immediately Grider stuck his head through the hatch to personally confirm it. *Flasher* had received a priority coded message on the FOX schedule. Grider told Burke to have the message "broken" rapidly, hoping it was good news. It was: all hostilities were over and the subs were to return to Hawaii. Burke quickly took the news to Grider. *Flasher* immediately reversed course while her pack mates (and pack commander) still proceeded on towards Japan. The closest boat signaled *Flasher* to explain her strange behavior. *Flasher* signaled back: "BREAK YOUR MESSAGES" and continued off at flank speed, arriving at Pearl well ahead of her sister subs.

The trip to Pearl was a festive occasion with the war over and won, the need to penetrate enemy minefields abandoned, and the expectation *Flasher's* crew would soon be back among family and friends.

When *Flasher* had practiced minefield penetration exercises near Pearl, Grider commented how a brilliantly maneuvered sub might just be able to squeeze through two close pilings off to one side of the channel. He even boasted that after the war he would sail *Flasher* between the two pilings to prove it. No one took Grider's boasts seriously, of course. But now the war was over, *Flasher* had entered the channel, and Grider began a dramatic speech. Solemnly, and pursuant to official Navy procedures, he announced to the officers present that they were all witnesses, that he was formally relieving the Officer of the Deck, that all but Grider himself were fully absolved of any liability in the matter, and that he was taking complete responsibility for whatever might happen to seven million dollars' worth of official government property.

If *Flasher's* paint were even scratched in this escapade, Grider's career in the post-war Navy would be clouded. If *Flasher* hit the pilings, ran aground in the attempt, or, worst of all, became humiliatingly wedged between the two posts, Grider could be court-martialed. He was, after all, a career Naval officer, not a reservist serving only for the duration of the war with a civilian job waiting stateside. This was suddenly a peacetime Navy where aggressiveness and daring were frowned on, and damage to a vessel while violating Navy regulations was unforgivable.

Grider skillfully maneuvered *Flasher* to the pilings. The boat slid slowly through with minor clearance to each side and without grounding, to the relief of the worried officers topside, all obviously concerned except for the cool, confident Grider. Unknown to Grider's audience, he had earlier made Burke send two men in a small boat to record soundings and measure clearances between the pilings. McCants only learned of this later, after he assumed Burke's duties as navigator, and the two sailors told him of their secret surveying adventure.

Arriving at Pearl, Navy reservists with sufficient "points" from their wartime service were allowed discharges from the Navy. Veterans including Chief Radioman Sherman and Chief Quartermaster Twiss were discharged, only to then learn that as civilians they could not get transportation stateside any time in the near future.

It developed that *Flasher* would be the first of nine subs returning stateside, but could not transport the men already discharged. *Flasher* was to depart August 28, followed by *Sea Owl*, *Flying Fish*, *Finback* (SS 230), and *Bowfin* (SS 287) on the 29th, and *Atule* (SS 403), *Whale* (SS 239), *Cero* (SS 225), and *Gunnel* (SS 253) on the 30th. Grider wanted to stop for a couple of days to sightsee at Hilo on the large island of Hawaii, but the crew unanimously voted to head straight home. They therefore departed for the Panama Canal and the U.S. east coast.

Flasher's new Executive Officer, Burke, was among the reservists with sufficient points for discharge, but he stayed with the sub for the trip home. Still, Burke would soon be returning to civilian life, leaving the Navy to career officers like McCants, the boat's Gunnery Officer and First Lieutenant. McCants, who had made all of *Flasher's* patrols and was to be her next exec, took over some of the exec's duties just as Coffin and Burke had done, and served as navigator for the trip from Hawaii through the Panama Canal, and back to the United States.

On the trip to Panama the intensive training and exercises that characterized *Flasher's* operations since her construction finally stopped, and the crew enjoyed the most leisurely cruise they had ever experienced (and would ever encounter, if they stayed in the Navy). There was one notable exception: gun drills. Grider drilled the gun crews any time any target or flotsam appeared. Lt. Atkinson finally asked Grider if he realized the war was over, and learned Grider's reasoning. It seemed every cabinet, locker and storage area aboard was packed to overflowing, and Panama had some of the best liquor prices in the Western Hemisphere. For every five-inch shell fired, two or more fifths of duty-free liquor could be transported home.

There was another practice initiated to relieve the monotony of the trip home. Grider started a daily "swim call" where the boat came to a halt and "flooded down" with her decks awash so the crew could swim. Precautions included the "buddy system," and a manned gun in case of sharks. On the first day Grider had Burke swim to the far side of the submarine, and Grider swam all the way under *Flasher's* keel, no minor feat considering *Flasher* was at sea, flooded down, and about 30 feet in diameter.

The next day most of the swimmers had already returned aboard, but Grider, late into the water, was still swimming when an enormous "green and white" shark headed straight for him. Then the gun, which was never needed before, jammed. The shark reached Grider just as he reached *Flasher*. Grider dove under the shark, which had a longer turning circle, and was pulled aboard the extended bow plane before the shark made it around again. Grider, who had been on the Academy's water polo team, was an excellent swimmer and was exceptionally cool about the incident. He told the crew not to fire on the shark after the gun was cleared since "it hadn't hurt anyone." That ended the swim calls, however. Grider said, "I don't want to have to write some sailor's wife or mother that her boy had been killed by a shark."

After the ordeal of unloading and reloading torpedoes on both sides of the Panama Canal, *Flasher* exited the canal September 14, stocked with the new duty-free supplies and headed for New Orleans, where she arrived one evening a week later. Near the mouth of the Mississippi delta *Flasher* waited over an hour for a river pilot. Grider then decided he could go it alone, being in a hurry to dock back in the U.S. and obviously confident after years of combat in some of the world's most treacherous and poorly charted waters, that a veteran U.S. submarine could easily negotiate such a short distance up a major waterway marked with full navigational lights.

McCants, who navigated since Pearl Harbor, argued that proceeding without a pilot would be a mistake. It was a mistake. The river turned out to be packed with shipping, the moon was down, the night was pitch black, and the river lights were difficult to follow. The docks were not clearly marked and one of World War II's most distinguished submarines proceeded at a snail's pace up the river, narrowly missing complaining merchant vessels on several occasions, and yelling for directions from startled civilians on shore. After *Flasher* finally docked, it was time for a royal chewing out from the Base Commander and Cmdr. Paul Henry Grouleff of Submarine Squadron 28, a tough submariner who had been McCants' skipper on the *USS Marlin*.

Flasher remained for almost a month in New Orleans, before receiving orders for Philadelphia via Mobile, Key West and Norfolk. She was to be in Mobile to take part in the Navy Day (October 27) celebrations. Not only was Navy Day to honor the Navy veterans, it was a good opportunity for the Navy to toot its horn at a time of impending defense cutbacks and inter-service competition for future defense funding.

Grider sent Lt.(jg) Hank Drumwright ahead to Mobile to coordinate *Flasher's* arrival and public affairs. The Navy would also use the occasion for awards, including official presentation of the Presidential Unit Citation to *Flasher* for her very successful third, fourth and fifth patrols under Whitaker and Grider. To present the citation, Admiral Charles W. Styer sent none other than *Flasher's* previous skipper, Commander Reuben T. Whitaker, then attached to the New London Submarine School.

Amid substantial fanfare, and not a little publicity, *Flasher* made a hit in Mobile. One article credited her with 34 sinkings whereas she only claimed a total of 31 vessels damaged or sunk (2 damaged, 5 sampans or luggers sunk, 22 merchant ships sunk and 2 warships sunk). *Flasher's* crew was photographed marching in the Navy Day parade, perched on her conning tower

Flasher's Crew, Navy Day Parade, Mobile (Photo Courtesy of Eddie Atkinson - [*Either*] Official Navy Photograph or Mobile Press-Register Photo)

fairwater, and operating her torpedo tubes. A Navy photographer snapped photo after photo of Grider and Whitaker together (everyone thought that was great and wanted copies), and then dropped the film straight into Mobile Bay when he tripped on the submarine's gangplank. Luckily, the local newspaper photographer was there too, and at least one photo of the presentation survived.

The Presidential Citation awarded to the *Flasher* and her personnel reads as follows:

Flasher's Maneuvering Room Controls, Grider Beside 20mm Gun, and
Crew Displaying Ship's Flag, Mobile
(Courtesy of Ross Brown)

Ross Brown, *Flasher's* Guns, and Friends, Including Knop (Middle
Photo, Right) and Kazlauskas (Bottom Photo, Right), Mobile
(Courtesy of Ross Brown)

Crew with Emblem and Ship's Battle Record, Mobile (Mobile Press-Register Photo)

For extraordinary heroism in action during the Third, Fourth and Fifth War Patrols against enemy Japanese surface forces in restricted waters of the Pacific. Constantly forced down by fierce and repeated depth charging and threatened by strong hostile air coverage, the USS FLASHER persistently resurfaced to carry on a vigorous and determined offensive against the Japanese. She effected wide coverage of assigned areas far from home base and developed every contact; she boldly penetrated formidable screens to press home her attacks by day or night--in glassy seas or foul weather; she placed her hits with devastating accuracy, evaded fierce countermeasures of escort vessels and inflicted terrific damage on the enemy in vital ships sunk or severely damaged. Ceaseless in her vigilance and daring in combat tactics, the FLASHER has served with distinction in thwarting the war efforts of a fanatical enemy and her brilliant record of achievement is a reflection of the personal valor and superb seamanship of her officers and men.

Flasher, of course, only sank one vessel in the Pacific, but Washington probably considered everything west of California as the Pacific.

In October, a recently promoted Lt. Cmdr. Tom Burke left active Naval service, and Lt. Tom McCants became *Flasher's* fourth and last executive officer. One of his first duties was to prepare *Flasher's* history, as requested by Admiral Lockwood's staff.

After Mobile, *Flasher* stopped again at Key West, and then Norfolk. McCants' parents drove to Norfolk from South Carolina for a glimpse of their son and to visit their married daughter in Richmond, Virginia. McCants' brother-in-law, Paul W. Allman, Jr., and the family got the royal tour of *Flasher* by gracious host George Grider.

The skipper even invited civilian Paul Allman to ride the sub to Philadelphia. He warned him, however, that the only place they could let him off was at their

Whitaker Presenting *Flasher's* Presidential Unit Citation to Grider
(Mobile Press-Register Photo, Copy Furnished by Eddie Atkinson)

destination, the Philadelphia Naval Shipyard, and he had no idea how Allman could get off the base without a pass, or get back to Richmond. Allman said he could handle all that and jumped at the offer. As the sub backed away, the McCants family realized their only car keys were in Allman's pocket. Their yells were understood and the keys were tossed to the dock. Travelling up Chesapeake Bay to the Delaware-Chesapeake Canal and Philadelphia, Grider and Allman passed part of the time hunting ducks with the boat's submachine guns. In Philadelphia, Allman jumped ashore at the high-security shipyard and made it out and back to Richmond without incident. His trip on *Flasher* was an event he always treasured, but he could never get his friends to believe his strange stories of the unauthorized submarine ride.

Flasher arrived in Philadelphia for preservation, deactivation and "laying up." Work at the Navy Yard continued through the new year. From Philadelphia, with her engines now deactivated, the great submarine was ignominiously towed to the New London, Connecticut, Submarine Base. There crew members were transferred from the sub or discharged from active duty to return to civilian life.

Even though *Flasher* had recently been overhauled and modernized, and other, much older submarines were to stay in active naval service for years to come, BuShips personnel examined *Flasher* and determined her hull had been too weakened from depth chargings to justify her retention. So in March, 1946, *Flasher* was formally decommissioned. The decommissioning ceremony was a somber affair. The event was captured in the attached photograph, showing a sad

Flasher's Decommissioning Ceremony, March, 1946
(L to R: Coulbourne, Atkinson, McCants and Grider. Author's Collection)

George Grider (at right) and Tom McCants (behind Grider) saluting as *Flasher's* flag was lowered for the last time. Behind McCants are Lt. Eddie Atkinson and Ens. Thomas Coulbourne.

CHAPTER 12

WARRIORS AFTER THE WAR
POSTSCRIPT

The Navy retained most of its "mothballed" submarines until the late 1950's. Many of *Flasher's* sister subs stayed in active Navy service into the 1970's, and some of the diesel subs may still be in active service with foreign governments. *Flasher* sat, deteriorating, with other mothballed subs at New London for 16 years. In 1963, after a failed attempt by submarine veterans to save her, she was sold for scrap to the Intercontinental Engineering-Manufacturing Corporation, Kansas City, Missouri, for $41,000.

All of *Flasher* was not scrapped, however. The Navy salvaged her bridge/conning tower fairwater, and some of her equipment. Later, the Submarine Veterans of World War II voted to use *Flasher's* conning tower fairwater as a National Submarine Memorial to the crews of subs lost during the war. In 1990 the memorial received thorough repairs and a fine new paint job, thanks to the "Sub Vets" and some generous sponsors. The organization began a fund drive in 1993 to erect a "Wall of Honor" at the memorial costing $250,000, to commemorate those lost in World War II. It is currently receiving contributions in memory of those who died in the war as well as those who have

Flasher in New London (Courtesy Submarine Memorial Assoc. [USS Ling Memorial], Hackensack, N.J.)

recently departed.

Flasher's bridge, with fore and aft guns and periscopes, sits proudly between Electric Boat and the New London Submarine Base, Groton, Connecticut, just off Interstate 95 at the north end of Thames Street, overlooking the Thames River where she was launched a half-century ago. Around the conning tower superstructure are 52 granite markers for the more than 3,500 submariners who died in defense of their country during World War II—one marker for each submarine lost. Ceremonies commemorating the lost crews and submarine veterans who have recently died are regu-

Flasher Being Broken Up as Scrap (Courtesy Submarine Memorial Assoc. [USS Ling Memorial], Hackensack, N.J.)

larly held at the memorial. Special ceremonies were held there following the deaths of *Flasher* veterans in recent years.

One of the memorial's chief custodians is Joseph J. "Stowaway" Holmes, veteran of *Growler's* first three patrols (sunk in 1944), *Grayback's* seventh and eighth patrols (sunk in 1944), and *Flasher's* first four patrols under Whitaker. One flagpole at the monument was commissioned by *Flasher* veterans, and there is a plaque on the monument in honor of Admiral Reuben T. Whitaker, who died in 1985.

Flasher's battle flag with the cartoon emblem, and an earlier version (probably made in Australia) showing a ship sinking, were donated by McCants and LaPelosa, respectively, and are now at the Navy Submarine Museum outside the New London Sub Base. A few other mementos were salvaged. *Flasher's* special cooking utensils were "liberated" one night by Cook "Wop" LaPelosa and Torpedoman Joe Ferrell for use aboard the *USS Cubera* (SS 347), the sub on which they, Ralph Van Horn, and George Grider served after the war. Motor Machinist Bill Beaman was given a piece of *Flasher's* planking with his name on it, a present from Chief of the Boat Spiva Buck.

Until recently when the optics went bad, one of *Flasher's* periscopes was regularly displayed for visitors to peer through at the Navy Museum, Washington Navy Yard, on M and Ninth Streets in southeast Washington, D.C. It has been repaired and is now in storage, along with many of the other items saved from *Flasher* by order of the Chief of Naval Operations. The periscope will ultimately be used to replace one currently on display at the Navy Museum, when it, in turn, requires servicing. Other instruments, steering wheels, annunciators, the troublesome pit log, and *Flasher's* "Christmas Tree," etc., are stored by, or on temporary loan from, the Navy Museum. *Flasher's* five-inch gun was also removed, and was mounted at the New London Submarine Base.

Another memorial to *Flasher* can be found by the shore at Bayshore, Long Island. There, on a brick foundation, is a World War II-era torpedo. Mounted on the brick facade is a plaque from the *USS Flasher* Chapter and a bronze torpedo-tube door.

The memory of *Flasher* has also been honored with the launching of the nuclear-powered submarine *USS Flasher* (SSN 613) on June 22, 1963, almost 20 years to the day after the June 20, 1943, launching of the original sub. The new *Flasher's* commissioning ceremony was held in 1966, three years after launching. The first *Flasher* had been commissioned three MONTHS after her wartime launching. The first speaker at the 1966 commissioning was United States Congressman George W. Grider of Tennessee. He was joined at the ceremony by two of his executive officers, Phil Glennon and Tom Burke, and other *Flasher* veterans.

The new *Flasher* is an "attack" submarine, not a ballistic missile submarine. Home-ported in the Pacific most of her service life, the nuclear *Flasher* distinguished herself in Cold War service, receiving no fewer than five coveted "E's" for excellence, the Presidential Unit Commendation, the Navy Unit Commendation, and three Meritorious Unit Commendations. She also rescued 27 refugees from a sinking boat, receiving a Humanitarian Award. Aware of the first *Flasher's* leaking hull over Seaman Brokovich's bunk, crewmen of the nuclear-powered *Flasher* were issued raincoats. Some items from the old sub, such as some deck planking, and an "inclinometer," were sent to the new *Flasher* from the Navy Museum. After almost 30 years of service, the nuclear sub was recently decommissioned.

Some of the *Flasher's* officers stayed in the Navy after the war. Reuben Whitaker and Ray DuBois remained in, both rising to the rank of Rear Admiral before they both retired to Northern Virginia. Both received numerous staff assignments with ever-increasing responsibilities, overseas duties during the Cold War, and commands on surface vessels, including cruisers. DuBois was also commended for duties off Vietnam, in the same areas *Flasher* had patrolled 20 years earlier. Phil Glennon retired from the Navy in 1966 as a Captain, and worked as Chief of Planning and Deputy Program Manager with Electric Boat Division of General Dynamics Corporation, before retiring, ultimately to South Carolina.

Snap Coffin stayed in until retirement as a Navy Commander and then began a teaching career in California. Tom McCants, awarded one Silver Star and a Gold Star in lieu of a second for his service on *Flasher*, retired as a Captain after 30 years to the family farm in South Carolina. Bob Briggs, who also received a Silver Star, became a Chief, then an officer under Admiral Arleigh Burke's reign, and retired as a Lieutenant Commander to California.

Not long after the war, George Grider, awarded a Navy Cross, Silver Star, Bronze Star, and Navy Commendation Medal, had a heart attack that may have doomed a further career in the Navy, but not one in law. He attended law school, began a successful law practice in Memphis, Tennessee, and served a stint as a U.S. Congressman.

Frenchy Corneau stayed in the Navy for a while, then started a sewing machine business in Groton, Connecticut, near another *Flasher* veteran and local policeman, Joe "Stoway" Holmes, and close by Bill Beaman, who retired in Groton after almost two decades in diesel and nuclear submarines, followed by two decades with the City of Groton Utilities. Beaman received a Bronze Star at the same time Briggs got a Silver Star, years after war's end. Many men aboard received awards that are not reflected in this book, of course, but the delayed awards received by some *Flasher* veterans seemed to confirm the view that wartime awards and promotions were harder to get aboard her than on some other boats. Qualifying and advancement on *Flasher* tended to be tough and "by the book."

Frank Kristl went "back home" to Indiana where he spent 20 years with Uniroyal, a few years as a consulting engineer, and then went back to work as a plant manager. Torpedoman Ralph Heilstedt went to work with Union Carbide in nearby Illinois, and worked with that company and its successor in the lab.

George Markham, to the surprise of many of his fellow crewmen, became a history teacher in Peabody, Massachusetts, before retiring to Arizona, near another *Flasher* shipmate, former Torpedoman and later a successful building contractor, Joe Ferrell.

Naval Reserve Officers and engineers, both Tom Burke and Eddie Atkinson went to work for a company after the war that seemed promising, IBM. Burke had worked with IBM before the war. Eddie ultimately retired to his home state of Arkansas, while Tom winters in Florida and summers in his home state of New York. John "Skinhead" Cook also worked with IBM, before retiring to Texas. Atkinson recently commented on how the North/South rivalry aboard *Flasher* has been won by the Southerners, as so many of the devout Yankees seem to be gradually moving south.

To the veterans of *Flasher*, to their fellow submariners of World War II, and to those who follow in their footsteps, this country is truly indebted.

Caretaker Joe (Stoway) Holmes with *Flasher's* Bridge and Conning Tower Fairwater, National Submarine Memorial, Groton, Connecticut (Author's Photo)

VETERANS OF THE *USS FLASHER*

All crew members were awarded battle stars for each of the successful War Patrols 1 through 6 in which they participated. An entry for the "seventh war patrol," or "7," below, means that the individual was attached to *Flasher* at some time between July 14, 1945 when she left San Francisco, and March 16, 1946 when the boat was officially decommissioned. Abbreviations for ranks and ratings in the following roster refer to:

Bkr	Baker	Lt.Cmdr.	Lieutenant
BM	Boatswain's Mate		Commander
1c	First Class	MoMM	Motor Machinist Mate
2c	Second Class	MM	Machinist's Mate
3c	Third Class	PhM	Pharmacist's Mate
C	Chief	QM	Quartermaster
Cmdr.	Commander	RM	Radioman
Ck	Cook	RT	Radio Technician
Cox	Coxswain	S	Seaman
EM	Electrician's Mate	SC	Ship's Cook
Ens	Ensign	SM	Signalman
F	Fireman	ST	Steward
FCS	Fire Controlman,	StM	Steward's Mate
	Surface Weapons	TM	Torpedoman's Mate
GM	Gunner's Mate	WO	Warrant Officer
Lt.	Lieutenant	Y	Yeoman
Lt.(jg)	Lieutenant,		
	Junior Grade		

THE WAR PATROLS

1 = First Patrol	January 6, 1944 thru February 29, 1944
2 = Second Patrol	April 4, 1944 thru May 28, 1944
3 = Third Patrol	June 19, 1944 thru August 7, 1944
4 = Fourth Patrol	August 30, 1944 thru October 20, 1944
5 = Fifth Patrol	November 15, 1944 thru January 2, 1945
6 = Sixth Patrol	January 27, 1945 thru April 13, 1945
7 ="Seventh Patrol"	July 14, 1945 thru March 16, 1946

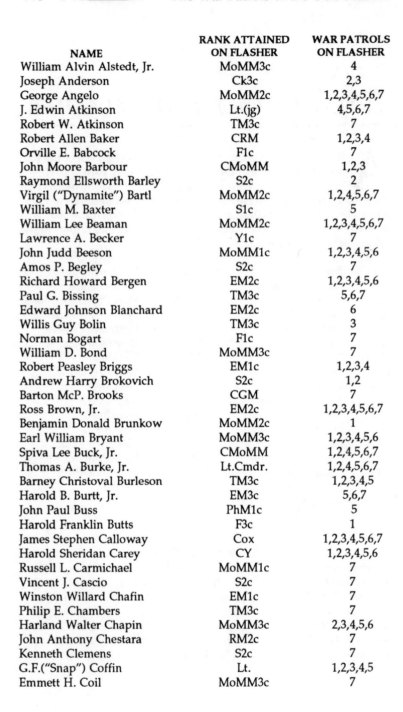

NAME	RANK ATTAINED ON FLASHER	WAR PATROLS ON FLASHER
William Alvin Alstedt, Jr.	MoMM3c	4
Joseph Anderson	Ck3c	2,3
George Angelo	MoMM2c	1,2,3,4,5,6,7
J. Edwin Atkinson	Lt.(jg)	4,5,6,7
Robert W. Atkinson	TM3c	7
Robert Allen Baker	CRM	1,2,3,4
Orville E. Babcock	F1c	7
John Moore Barbour	CMoMM	1,2,3
Raymond Ellsworth Barley	S2c	2
Virgil ("Dynamite") Bartl	MoMM2c	1,2,4,5,6,7
William M. Baxter	S1c	5
William Lee Beaman	MoMM2c	1,2,3,4,5,6,7
Lawrence A. Becker	Y1c	7
John Judd Beeson	MoMM1c	1,2,3,4,5,6
Amos P. Begley	S2c	7
Richard Howard Bergen	EM2c	1,2,3,4,5,6
Paul G. Bissing	TM3c	5,6,7
Edward Johnson Blanchard	EM2c	6
Willis Guy Bolin	TM3c	3
Norman Bogart	F1c	7
William D. Bond	MoMM3c	7
Robert Peasley Briggs	EM1c	1,2,3,4
Andrew Harry Brokovich	S2c	1,2
Barton McP. Brooks	CGM	7
Ross Brown, Jr.	EM2c	1,2,3,4,5,6,7
Benjamin Donald Brunkow	MoMM2c	1
Earl William Bryant	MoMM3c	1,2,3,4,5,6
Spiva Lee Buck, Jr.	CMoMM	1,2,4,5,6,7
Thomas A. Burke, Jr.	Lt.Cmdr.	1,2,4,5,6,7
Barney Christoval Burleson	TM3c	1,2,3,4,5
Harold B. Burtt, Jr.	EM3c	5,6,7
John Paul Buss	PhM1c	5
Harold Franklin Butts	F3c	1
James Stephen Calloway	Cox	1,2,3,4,5,6,7
Harold Sheridan Carey	CY	1,2,3,4,5,6
Russell L. Carmichael	MoMM1c	7
Vincent J. Cascio	S2c	7
Winston Willard Chafin	EM1c	7
Philip E. Chambers	TM3c	7
Harland Walter Chapin	MoMM3c	2,3,4,5,6
John Anthony Chestara	RM2c	7
Kenneth Clemens	S2c	7
G.F.("Snap") Coffin	Lt.	1,2,3,4,5
Emmett H. Coil	MoMM3c	7

Edward Albert Collins, Jr.	RT2c	7
John Franklin ("Skinhead") Cook	EM1c	5,6,7
Robert Allen Cook	MoMM3c	5,6,7
John C. Corder, Jr.	S2c	7
Robert Allen Corle	TM3c	6,7
Joseph D.C.("Frenchy") Corneau	SM3c	1,2,3,5,6,7
Emery Calvert Cosner	F1c	6
Thomas E. Coulbourne	Ens.	7
Charles Cox, Jr.	StM1c	1
Daniel Joseph Crilly	TM2c	1
Earl Eugene Crow	F1c	7
William B. Crown, Jr.	F1c	7
Richard P. Culver	S1c	5
Victor Murphy Cypherd	CEM	1,2,3,4,5,6
Frank Joseph DeBois	CMoMM	1,2,3,4,5,6
Carl Joseph DeCesare	S1c	3
John E. Desmond	RT2c	7
John Edward Dingledine	MoMM2c	1,2,3
Joseph Gilbert Dolese	GM3c	1,2,3,5,6
Floyd James Doty, Jr.	SM1c	1,2,3,4,5,6
Joseph Dozier	SC2c	4,6
Henry E. Drumwright	Lt.(jg)	7
Raymond F. DuBois	Lt. Cmdr.	1,2,3
Robert L. Eberling	S2c	7
John Alexander Edsberg	MoMM2c	3
James W. Ellis	S2c	7
Eugene Joseph Enders	RM3c	1
Richard L. Everitt	F1c	5,6,7
Charles Ezerosky	Bkr2c	1,2,3,4,5,6,7
Merle Michael Falvey	SC2c	1
Elmo McDowell Farmer	MoMM2c	1
Joseph Martin Ferrell	TM2c	2,3,4
Robert W. Fielding	Lt.(jg)	7
Vincent John Filippone	RM2c	1,2,3,4,5,6,7
Darrel Scott Fleck	EM3c	4,5,7
William Leroy Fletter	EM3c	6,7
Edmond Thomas Flynn	F2c	3,4,5
James Louis Fowler	StM2c	2
Mack Henry Foxx	TM1c	1,2,3,5,6,7
Herbert Calvin Francum	GM3c	2,3,4,5
Maurice A. Freightman	StM1c	1
Carold D. Furgeson	TM2c	1,2,4,5,6
Andy Henry Furman	S1c	3,4
Howard Joseph Gadbois	TM3c	1
Charles F. Gallagher	S1c	5,6,7
Philip Gioranino	S1c	6

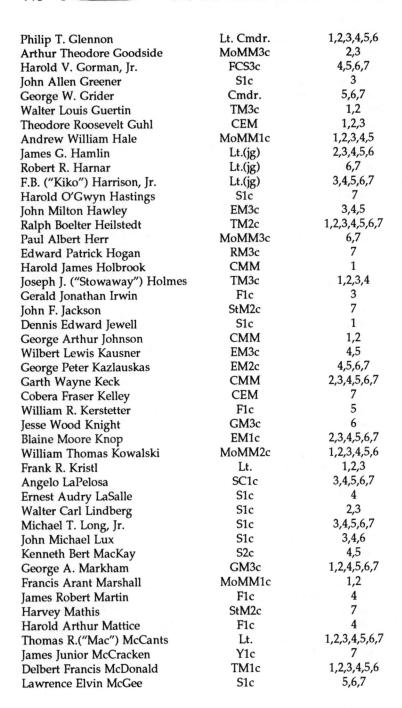

Philip T. Glennon	Lt. Cmdr.	1,2,3,4,5,6
Arthur Theodore Goodside	MoMM3c	2,3
Harold V. Gorman, Jr.	FCS3c	4,5,6,7
John Allen Greener	S1c	3
George W. Grider	Cmdr.	5,6,7
Walter Louis Guertin	TM3c	1,2
Theodore Roosevelt Guhl	CEM	1,2,3
Andrew William Hale	MoMM1c	1,2,3,4,5
James G. Hamlin	Lt.(jg)	2,3,4,5,6
Robert R. Harnar	Lt.(jg)	6,7
F.B. ("Kiko") Harrison, Jr.	Lt.(jg)	3,4,5,6,7
Harold O'Gwyn Hastings	S1c	7
John Milton Hawley	EM3c	3,4,5
Ralph Boelter Heilstedt	TM2c	1,2,3,4,5,6,7
Paul Albert Herr	MoMM3c	6,7
Edward Patrick Hogan	RM3c	7
Harold James Holbrook	CMM	1
Joseph J. ("Stowaway") Holmes	TM3c	1,2,3,4
Gerald Jonathan Irwin	F1c	3
John F. Jackson	StM2c	7
Dennis Edward Jewell	S1c	1
George Arthur Johnson	CMM	1,2
Wilbert Lewis Kausner	EM3c	4,5
George Peter Kazlauskas	EM2c	4,5,6,7
Garth Wayne Keck	CMM	2,3,4,5,6,7
Cobera Fraser Kelley	CEM	7
William R. Kerstetter	F1c	5
Jesse Wood Knight	GM3c	6
Blaine Moore Knop	EM1c	2,3,4,5,6,7
William Thomas Kowalski	MoMM2c	1,2,3,4,5,6
Frank R. Kristl	Lt.	1,2,3
Angelo LaPelosa	SC1c	3,4,5,6,7
Ernest Audry LaSalle	S1c	4
Walter Carl Lindberg	S1c	2,3
Michael T. Long, Jr.	S1c	3,4,5,6,7
John Michael Lux	S1c	3,4,6
Kenneth Bert MacKay	S2c	4,5
George A. Markham	GM3c	1,2,4,5,6,7
Francis Arant Marshall	MoMM1c	1,2
James Robert Martin	F1c	4
Harvey Mathis	StM2c	7
Harold Arthur Mattice	F1c	4
Thomas R.("Mac") McCants	Lt.	1,2,3,4,5,6,7
James Junior McCracken	Y1c	7
Delbert Francis McDonald	TM1c	1,2,3,4,5,6
Lawrence Elvin McGee	S1c	5,6,7

Hugh Christopher McGreevy	MoMM1c	7
Robert M.("Skip") McLaren	RM2c	1,2,3,4,5,6
Clyde Leroy McLaughlin	MoMM3c	4,6,7
Howard Brocks Metcalf	S1c	4
Andrew Robert Millspaugh	EM3c	3
Charles Joseph Moore	SM2c	1,3,4
William Fletcher Morrow	MoMM2c	6,7
Virgil A. Murphy	MoMM1c	7
William Henry Newton	CTM	1,2,3,4,5,6
Stephen Nikifor	RT2c	5
Roland Emile Noel	MoMM1c	1,2,3,4,5
Edward Robert Nugent	S2c	1
Alfred Gerhard Olson	S1c	1,2,4,5
Stanley Joseph Paczkowski, Jr	SC3c	1,2,3,5
Clarence Henry Page	StM1c	3,4,5,6,7
Robert F. Paul	S1c	5,6,7
Francis Stark Pealatere	GM2c	7
William Jeffrey Pearce	CTM	1,2,3,4,5
Felix Perkowsky	CTM	1,2,3
Howard Elmer Pike	S1c	4
Sydney Herbert Pool	QM2c	1,2,3,4,5,6,7
John Precup, Jr.	S1c	1,2,3,4,5,6
Victor Albert Prevost	PhM1c	1,2,3,4
Thomas Jackson Price, Jr.	EM3c	7
Kaarlo Randa	S1c	5,6,7
Louis Pious Reichert	BM1c	1,2,3,4,5,6
Durward Dean Ritter	F1c	6,7
Randall Angus Ross	F1c	7
Basil B. Rowe	EM1c	1,2
Joseph Saccone	EM3c	2
George Robert Sampson	MoMM1c	3,4,5,6,7
George Melvin Sartin	Ck2c	4,5,6,7
George Schlee, Jr.	TM1c	1,2,3,4,5,6
Ernest E. ("Gunner") Schwartz	GM1c	1,2,3,4
Frank J. Scire	EM3c	5,6,7
Francis Vincent Sheridan	GM3c	7
Francis Owen Sherman	CRT	1,2,3,4,5,6,7
Curtis Milton Simmons	EM3c	6
Ray Spencer Snapp	TM3c	1,2,3,4,5,6,7
Willie Ray Snow	RT1c	6,7
Markom George Spencer, Jr.	EM1c	1,2,4
Walter F. Stein	S1c	6
Raymond David Steinkamp	MoMM2c	1,2
Kenneth S. Storm	F1c	7
Edward Alex Sutton	S1c	3,4,7
Paul John Terandy	QM3c	2

Walter Thomas Tillman	SC1c	1,2
Edgar A. Tracy	EM2c	1
Edwin Turcotte	CEM	1,2,3,4,5,6
James J. Tvelia	MoMM3c	5,6,7
Francis J. Twiss, Jr.	QM1c	1,2,3,4,5,6,7
Paul Leon Van De Veere	RM1c	1,2,3,4,5,6
Robert W. Van Hooser	MoMM1c	3,4,5,6
Ralph J. Van Horn	MoMM1c	1,2,3,4
Herald Denny Venable	F1c	6
L.A. Walker	Lt.	7
William L. Washburn	S1c	7
James M. Watson	RM3c	6,7
Joseph W. Webb	FCS2c	1,2,3,4,5,6
Reuben T. Whitaker	Cmdr.	1,2,3,4
Teddy P. Wilkison	MoMM3c	5,6
David Theodore Williams	CPhM	6,7
Stanley P. Williams	EM3c	1,3,4
Barry C. Woodall	RM1c	2,3
Clyde Robert Wright	TM3c	6,7
Richard Merle Zachry	S1c	2,3,4,5,6
Edward Bird Zeller, Jr.	F2c	1,2
Edward Felix Zielinski	TM1c	7

Approximately 81 to 85 individuals manned *Flasher* for her war patrols. Because of Navy policy, many of the crew were "rotated" to other assignments after one or more patrols. One purpose for rotating experienced crew members was to spread their skills to the many new boats largely manned by inexperienced crews. Also, crew members would be transferred for promotion, for disciplinary reasons, or for a break from the hazardous duty if they had had prior extensive service in the war zone.

BIBLIOGRAPHY

OFFICIAL RECORDS AND PUBLICATIONS

Bureau of Naval Personnel, Department of the Navy. *The Fleet Type Submarine*, Navpers 16160. 1946.

Commander Submarine Force, U.S. Pacific Fleet, Department of the Navy. *U.S. Submarine Losses, World War II*, Navpers 15,784. Washington: U.S. Government Printing Office, 1949.

Defense Mapping Agency. *Catalog of Maps, Charts and Related Products, Part 2–Hydrographic Products, Vols. VII and IX* (and various charts). Washington: Defense Mapping Agency Combat Support Center, 1949, 1988.

Department of the Navy. *Facts About the Submarine Service*, Navpers-NRB-44205-12 Sept. 1944.

Joint Army-Navy Assessment Committee (JANAC). *Japanese Naval and Merchant Shipping Losses During World War II by All Causes*, Navexos P-468. Washington: U.S. Government Printing Office, 1947.

Office of Naval Intelligence, Department of the Navy. *ONI 41-42, Index to All Japanese Naval Vessels*. (Reprint by Naval Institute Press, Annapolis, 1987).

Office of Naval Intelligence, Department of the Navy. *ONI 208-J, Japanese Merchant Ship Recognition Manual, August 24, 1942*. Naval Historical Center, Washington Navy Yard, Washington, D.C.

Rowland, Buford and William B. Boyd. *U.S. Navy Bureau of Ordnance in World War II*. Washington: U.S. Government Printing Office, (No date).

Strategic Bombing Survey (Pacific), Naval Analysis Division. *The Campaigns of the Pacific War*. New York: Greenwood Press, (Reprint 1969).

USS Flasher (SS 249) Deck Log, September 25, 1943, through June 30, 1945. National Archives and Records Administration (NNRM), Washington, D.C.

USS Flasher (SS 249) General Correspondence File, Boxes 2084 and 2085, Department of the Navy, Bureau of Ships (Record Group 19).

Suitland Reference Branch (NNRR), National Archives and Records Administration, Suitland, Maryland.

USS Flasher (SS 249) Muster Rolls, September 25, 1943, through March 16, 1946. National Archives and Records Administration, (NNRM), Washington, D.C.

USS Flasher (SS 249) Night Order Book, November 9, 1944, through March 20, 1945. George Grider.

USS Flasher (SS 249) War Patrol Reports. Department of the Navy, Operational Archives Branch, Naval Historical Center, Washington Navy Yard, Washington, D.C.

War Damage Report #58, January 9, 1949, Appendix I, Briefs of War Damage Incurred by U.S. Submarines During World War II. Department of the Navy. (Reprint by The Floating Drydock, Kresgeville, Pennsylvania, 1976).

War Patrols of Coordinated Search and Attack Groups (a. *Flasher, Crevalle* and *Angler,* June 19, 1944, through August 23, 1944; b. *Flasher, Lapon* and *Bonefish,* August 30, 1944, through October 31, 1944; and c. *Becuna, Flasher, Hoe, Dace* and *Paddle,* December 16, 1944, through December 28, 1944). Department of the Navy, Operational Archives Branch, Navy Historical Center, Washington Navy Yard, Washington, D.C.

BOOKS AND OTHER SOURCES

Alden, John D. *The Fleet Submarine in the U.S. Navy.* Annapolis: Naval Institute Press, 1979. (A very well-illustrated, detailed, and well-documented analysis of the design and construction of all American fleet-type subs, that with the BuShips records, above, provided the details of *Flasher's* contracting and design.)

Alden, John D. *U.S. Submarine Attacks During World War II.* Annapolis: Naval Institute Press, 1989. (An exhaustive compilation of all torpedo attacks by American subs, with comparisons of JANAC and other data researched by Alden.)

Alden, John D. (Unpublished research on Ultra intercepts.)

Beach, Edward L. *Run Silent, Run Deep.* New York: Permabooks, 1956.

Blair, Jr., Clay. *Silent Victory: The U.S. Submarine War Against Japan.* Philadelphia: J.B. Lippincott Company, 1975. (The best, most thorough and most critical analysis of American submarine performance in WW II, with excellent appendices.)

Blair, Jr., Clay. (Unpublished interview of Adm. Reuben T. Whitaker, U.S.N., Ret.)

Cook, Haruko Taya, and Theodore F. Cook. *Japan at War: An Oral History.* New York: New Press, 1992.

Dull, Paul S. *A Battle History of the Imperial Japanese Navy (1941-1945).* Annapolis: Naval Institute Press, 1969.

Ewing, Steve. *Memories and Memorials.* Missoula, Montana: Pictorial Histories Publishing Co., 1986.

Evans, David C., Ed. *The Japanese Navy in World War II in the Words of Former Japanese Naval Officers.* Annapolis: Naval Institute Press, 1969.

Fitzsimons, Bernard, Ed. *The Illustrated Encyclopedia of 20th Century Weapons and Warfare* (Vol. 15). New York: Columbia House, 1969.

Goralski, Robert. *World War II Almanac, 1931-1945.* New York: Bonanza Books, 1981.

Grider, George, and Lydel Sims. *War Fish.* Boston: Little, Brown & Company, 1958.

Hashimoto, Mochitsura. *Sunk: The Story of the Japanese Submarine Fleet, 1941-1945.* New York: Henry Holt & Co., 1954.

Holmes, W.J. *Double-Edged Secrets.* Annapolis: Naval Institute Press, 1979.

Holmes, W.J. *Undersea Victory.* New York: Kensington Publishing Co., 1979.

Ito, Masanori. *The End of the Imperial Japanese Navy.* New York: W.W. Norton & Co., 1962.

Ienaga, Saburo. *The Pacific War - 1931-1945.* New York: Pantheon Books, 1978.

Jentschura, Hansgeorg, Dieter Jung and Peter Mickel. *Warships of the Imperial Japanese Navy, 1869-1945.* Annapolis: Naval Institute Press, 1977. (Probably the most extensive compilation of Japanese Naval vessels of the war, this provided more details of the ships and their losses than any other sources the author located.)

Karig, Walter, Russell L. Harris and Frank A. Manson. *Battle Report: Victory in the Pacific.* New York: Rinehart & Co., 1949.

Keegan, John. *The Price of Admiralty.* New York: Penguin Books, 1989.

Lengerer, Hans, Sumie Kobler-Edamatsu, and Tomoto Rehm-Takahara. "Kitakami." In *Warship* (Volume 10), pp. 33-43. Edited by Andrew Lambert. London: Conway Maritime Press, and Annapolis: Naval Institute Press, 1986.

Little Known Facts About the Submarine, Submarine Library, Electric Boat Division (Undated).

Lockwood, Charles A. *Sink 'Em All*. Toronto: Bantam Books, 1984. (Lockwood's overview of the submarine war and his role as ComSubPac.)

Lockwood, Charles A., and Hans C. Adamson. *Hellcats of the Sea*. New York: Greenberg: Publisher, 1955. (The penetrations into the Sea of Japan and the development of QLA sonar.)

Lowder, Hughston E. *The Silent Service: U. S. Submarines in World War II*. Baltimore: Silent Service Books, 1987. (Short Histories of most American World War II Submarines.)

The Maru Special, Japanese Naval Vessels No. 118 (Light Cruisers of the Imperial Japanese Navy) (Japanese Language publication) 1986.

McLean, Ridley. *The Bluejackets Manual*. Annapolis: Naval Institute Press, 1944.

Orita, Zenji and Joseph D. Harrington. *I-Boat Captain*. Canoga Park, California: Major Books, 1976.

Pacific War Research Society. *Japan's Longest Day*. New York: Ballantine Books, 1972.

Roscoe, Theodore. *United States Submarine Operations in World War II*. Annapolis: Naval Institute Press, 1949. (Still in print after almost a half century, this monumental, indispensable work covers the entire submarine war, and features the superb illustrations of Fred Freeman. A paperback version is occasionally published as *"Pigboats."*)

Ruhe, William J. *War in the Boats: My WWII Submarine Battles*. Washington: Brassey's, Inc., 1994.

Silverstone, Paul H. *U.S. Warships of World War 2*. Annapolis: Naval Institute Press, 1965.

Spector, Ronald H. *Eagle Against the Sun*. New York: Random House, 1985.

Stern, Robert C. *U.S. Subs in Action*. Carrollton, Texas: Squadron/Signal Publications, 1983.

Walkowiak, Thomas F. *Fleet Submarines of World War II*. Missoula, Montana: Pictorial Histories Publishing Company, 1988.

Walkowiak, Thomas F. *The Floating Drydock's Plan Book - Gato & Balao Class Submarines of World War Two*. Kresgeville, Pennsylvania: The Floating Drydock, 1990.

Watts, Anthony J. *Japanese Warships of World War II*. Garden City, New Jersey: Doubleday & Co., Inc., 1973.

Index